Contents

Introduction

Companies are one of the foundations of the economic system on which our society is built. In the last 100 years they have taken on unprecedented importance, rivalling that of the nation-state. Of the 100 largest economic entities in the world today, 51 are corporations and only 49 are countries. Moreover, although most of the governments of powerful nations are held to account by their electorate once every four or five years, no such direct system of accountability exists for those who manage corporations. It is obvious that the behaviour and language of corporations should be of interest to all of us, since we are all bound up with them in many different ways, and we are inevitably affected by their actions. From banks to retail businesses, from small manufacturing companies to huge multinational corporations, all of these entities play many different parts in our day-to-day lives, as we alternate our roles as employees and employers, borrowers and investors, clients and service providers.

These roles, and the complex network of relationships that holds them together, are built and perpetuated through discourse. Linguists and discourse analysts are therefore uniquely equipped to undertake the task of showing how language is being used to inform, persuade or manipulate in the ongoing creation, maintenance and reshaping of social roles and relations. They are able to identify discursive strategies, to document trends and developments and to shed light on the ongoing relationships that corporations construct with a multitude of different stakeholders in today's increasingly complex business scenario. The present book examines this area from a discourse perspective, looking in detail at the ways in which corporations around the world communicate with individuals and other collective entities.

Although this study of corporate discourse will inevitably offer a critical perspective on much of what takes place, the intention is not primarily to provide a radical critique of the underlying economic or sociopolitical structures. My aim is rather to provide a snapshot of corporate discourse in the early twenty-first century, centring mainly on Europe and the United States, and to investigate how language is being used to reflect and shape corporations' ongoing relationships with their employees, investors, clients and other stakeholders. In this, I draw extensively on previous work by other authors, but also explain my own quantitative findings from a corpora of Annual Reports and corporate social responsibility reports, qualitative analysis of a corpus of job interview simulations and various detailed in-depth studies of different corporate genres. This book will primarily be of interest to applied linguists, discourse analysts and communications theorists, but potentially also has relevance for practitioners in public relations, corporate communications and the business media. My own interpretation of the discursive phenomena described here is intended as a contribution to ongoing debates on corporate discourse, and I hope that this book will open the way to further research and discussion.

Finally, I would like to extend my warmest thanks to those people who have been important in helping me to pursue my interests in discourse studies. In particular, I wish to thank Professors Manuel Casado, Jaime Nubiola, Ignacio Vázquez and Helena Šajgalíková for their sound advice and generous support. I am grateful to Concha Martínez Pasamar, Carmen Llamas, Cristina Tabernero, Ramón González, Inés Olza and Dámaso Izquierdo, my fellow-researchers in the GradUN research group at the *Instituto Cultura y Sociedad,* for the intellectual stimulus I have received from them, and for their friendship and help. Naturally, I would like to express my thanks to my friends and colleagues at the Institute of Modern Languages, particularly Marian O'Reilly, Cóilín Ó hAodha, Paul Miller and Alessandra Agati. I must also acknowledge my gratitude to Maurice Johnson, Hugh Parnell and Graham Breeze for opening my eyes to different aspects of the corporate world. Finally, my special thanks to series editor Professor Ken Hyland for his invaluable help and guidance.

The Corporation and its Stakeholders: Identity, Action, Interaction

This chapter sets the scene for the book by addressing the basic question as to what corporate discourse is and why it is important. To do this, it begins with a brief history of how the corporation has developed, tracing its rise to prominence over the last 150 years. It then looks at the various ways in which a company can be said to have an 'identity', and asks whether companies can be said to 'speak' as entities, and who they may be said to speak to. After examining this, it sketches out some of the ways in which corporate discourse operates in society. Since this entails an analysis of the different ways in which companies interact with other social actors, and touches on the different discourses that they may employ to this end, the overview provided here will of necessity be brief. All of these points will be explored in more detail in the later chapters of this book. The purpose of the present chapter is simply to survey the landscape, providing an initial estimate of the importance of corporate discourse in our lives, and pointing to some aspects of its role in the ongoing reconfiguration of society.

1.1 What are corporations?

Businesses have always existed. People have always traded goods and services for other goods or services, and for money. But the industrial revolution and the expansion of empires in the late eighteenth and early nineteenth century led to the establishment of commercial enterprises on a scale never seen before. There was an unprecedented need for capital investment, accompanied by prospects of immense returns if the enterprise was successful. Yet the existing legal framework for establishing companies was restrictive, and the wealthy individuals who put up the capital stood to lose not only their initial contribution, but all their possessions and even their own freedom if their investments failed.

Companies as independent legal entities

The solution to this problem was a revolutionary idea that changed the nature of business and made it much more attractive for wealthy individuals to invest their capital in corporations. This idea developed gradually: it was first restricted to certain privileged groups, later to enterprises defined as being in the interests of the state, but in the end, by the mid-nineteenth century, this system was extended to a vast number of businesses. The idea that was so important came as the final stage in a process that had been unfolding over a long stretch of time.

In brief, the story is this. Over the years, a framework had been evolving that permitted business entities to have a legal personality of their own, distinct from the natural persons who invest in them. This is essential, because it means that a company can undertake actions, own property and do business in its own name. It can sue and be sued. It can pay its shareholders dividends in proportion to its profits and their investments. And it can go on existing long after the individuals who set it up have retired or moved on. These points are all extremely important, but they were not in themselves a radical departure from earlier practices. The concept that was to prove so important in the history of the Western economy was that of limited liability, which means that an investor's responsibility towards a company is limited in financial terms to the amount of capital that he or she initially puts into it. And most importantly of all, if things go badly, and the company goes bankrupt and ceases to exist, the investor will only lose the initial capital that he or she put into it. In other words, the investor has limited liability.

Although the concept of the limited liability company is almost universally accepted today, its history is slow and rather tortuous. In the eighteenth century and before, certain types of corporation could be formed by obtaining a 'charter' from the King or Parliament, which conferred legal personality on the corporation. But such charters tended only to be granted to projects that were perceived to be in the national interest. A few such chartered companies were even granted the privilege of limited liability for their shareholders during this period, but in the wake of the South Sea Bubble, this measure was understandably felt to be something exceptional which posed a grave risk to the economy and to individual investors. The economist Adam Smith (1723–90) expressed strong disapproval of such corporations on the grounds that the unrestrained exercise of corporate power by individuals whose personal livelihood was not at stake, and who would not be personally held responsible for their actions, could be damaging to society (Smith, 1776; Goodacre, 2010).

In fact, the eighteenth century was characterized by a general suspicion of trading charters, and the chartered companies that managed to survive in Britain, such as the famous East India Company, were those that obviously served British imperial interests on a geopolitical as well as an economic level. None the less, the pressures of industrial development meant that by the end of the eighteenth century, it had become difficult to keep pace with the need for huge capital investment in sectors such as mining and shipping. At the same time, there was an increase in the number of unchartered companies with shares that could be bought and sold, even though at this time the framework did not entail limited liability, and investors therefore put their personal fortunes at risk when they sank capital into new enterprises. Although such companies were strictly speaking not legal, they were allowed to flourish because they were in the public interest. In the end, the Companies Act of 1844 made it possible for companies to incorporate when their promoters wished to do so, but this legislation still left the investors unprotected in cases of loss or bankruptcy.

The real impetus for change in the legal status of the company came from the United States, where moves were afoot that would radically change the business world (Kempin, 1990). In the United States, to meet the demands of the rapidly developing economy, legislative measures were put into place in the early nineteenth century that made it much easier for people to invest in companies without risking their whole livelihood. The format that was devised, that of the 'limited liability company', was to prove hugely influential and has shaped the way the economy has developed across vast areas of the world ever since. For the first time, investors could put their capital into new enterprises without incurring risks above and beyond their capital outlay. This was an obvious incentive to investment. States such as Connecticut and Massachusetts were already issuing charters with limited liability as early as 1817, and the subsequent boost to industry and commerce in these areas made it difficult for neighbouring states not to follow suit (Hickson and Turner, 2005). Other countries observed the developments in the United States and noted – to their surprise – that far from collapsing, the economy seemed to benefit greatly from this system. Freedom to incorporate with limited liability was introduced in Britain in 1856, and most European countries had brought in similar legislation by the end of the nineteenth century.

The consequence of this change was that the economic landscape was now peopled with entities that had autonomy, which acted freely as independent actors on the economic stage, but which were not like people in other respects, and did not have the same obligation to pay their debts. The revolutionary nature and full potential of this new entity were just dawning on the world. Since then, other changes have altered the business landscape. Some areas of the world have seen the implantation of planned, controlled economies with scarcely any space for private enterprise, which were then swept away as the ideologies that sustained them evaporated. Other areas have seen cycles of nationalization, in which state-run corporations proliferated, followed by phases of privatization, in which these same corporations are uncoupled from the mechanisms of the state and released again into the free market. At the present time, the independent corporation is again the predominant structure for industrial and trading entities, and its status is firmly anchored in the legal systems of most countries across the world.

The corporation's rise to prominence

In the course of this development, other far-reaching changes have also been taking place. In the early twenty-first century, businesses have unprecedented importance and own immense wealth. Of the 100 largest economic entities in the world today, 49 are countries and 51 are corporations (Slapper, 2012). Today's businesses are not the geographically and sectorially defined manufacturing giants of the past. They tend to be highly specialized in their activities, and yet they may gather extremely diverse types of operation together under one company name. They may be concentrated in one region of the world, but are equally likely to operate across several continents. They are likely to control information, particularly if this is a way of maintaining power or keeping trade secrets safe, but they are also extremely concerned with communication both within the company and with the outside world. At the same time, they are subject to a considerable volume of rules and regulations imposed by the state, not to mention quality assurance criteria established and evaluated by external agencies, self-regulatory codes of practice in specific sectors and so on. They are constantly in the public eye, as the media are quick to pounce on any manifestation of corporate malpractice. Moreover, in an increasingly litigious culture, individuals are becoming more likely to take corporations to court over issues related to personal safety, employment law, consumer law and so on. Indeed, it has been argued that the company itself has become a porous entity, consisting of a partially open socio-technical system that interacts with different groups of stakeholders, as well as with social agents such as the media, government, pressure groups, NGOs, local communities and perhaps world organizations.

Against this background, discourse has assumed an enormous importance, since it is primarily through discourse that corporations construct their self-understanding and their relationships with other agents. In the age of globalization and instant, ubiquitous media coverage, it has become increasingly important for corporations to try to manage the ways in which they communicate with other parties. Today, it is harder than ever to 'hush up' a public relations disaster, or prevent a crisis from getting out of hand. Moreover, corporations are confronted with a media-wise audience that is critical of corporate communications, mistrustful of hype, and concerned with issues, such as social responsibility, financial accountability or environmental protection, which have not always been priorities for corporate entities. Other factors, such as the acceleration of product life cycles, deregulation and increased international competition have also added to the need for more effective communication with a range of different audiences. In short, the corporate panorama is more complex than ever, and the need for communication at all levels is perceived as never before. This book will explore the discourses used by corporations to interact with other entities, as they attempt to navigate the treacherous waters of the twenty-first-century economy.

1.2 The discursive construction of the corporation

As we have seen, one key fact in the history of the limited liability company is the establishment of a new entity, an entity which is not a natural person, and not a traditional social body or institution, but something entirely new. This new entity is the company, with legal personality in its own right, capable of owning, buying and selling, employing and firing, and above all, of conducting business activities in an independent way. Of course, the company has a board of directors, a group of shareholders, an executive director, managers and employees. But the company itself will go on long after those people have retired or moved on. So what is that company? Are companies all the same, as their legal frameworks would suggest, or are they different in the way that people are different? What can we say about the kind of personality they have? And what consequences does the existence of these legal persons known as corporations have for the societies in which they operate? Let us look first at the way that actors within the company itself seek to create and project a certain identity and image. After this, we shall look at some of the ways in which such projections are disputed.

Corporate identity

One area where these questions are constantly being posed is that of corporate communications, that is, the area of public relations that is most immediately concerned with constructing and communicating the company's self-understanding. An issue that has been hotly debated among specialists in corporate communications is whether a company can really be said to have an identity, and what this identity might consist of. Even more than in the case of other entities in public life, a company's identity might seem to be a fragile and disputed construct. A town or region, say, has a certain identity built on historical and geographical fact and the cultural affiliations of its inhabitants. Such identities may be debated, may be subject to constant updating and reworking, but at least there is some concrete basis, the participation of some definable and relatively permanent group of people who have a say in what this town's identity might be, who have a vote in its politics, the opportunity to contribute to its media, the chance to take part in its festivals or demonstrate on its streets. Such identities are constantly negotiated and renegotiated among those members who have a voice, but there is a relatively clear sense of who might be entitled to participate in this debate, and there are time-honoured patterns that show how such a debate can be conducted.

Corporate identity, on the other hand, is a more nebulous concept. How can something that can be established filling in a few forms, paying a fee, and submitting the evidence to Companies House, be said to have an identity in the way that towns and regions, time honoured institutions like schools and universities or religious organizations, have an identity? Is it justified to speak of a corporation as having an 'identity'?

One possible answer to this question is that we can assume corporations to have an identity, because people act as if this were so (Weber, 1978). Just as we assume that 'national identities' can be discussed and disputed, so 'corporate identities' are something that can be talked about and contested. Since identity is the representation (or re-presentation) of an individual or group, the group of people who form part of a company at a given time can choose to represent that company in the way they think fit. Moreover, the way that they do this will inevitably be mediated through discourse. According to communications experts Cheney and Vibbert (1987, p. 176), 'an identity is developed dialectically over time, by both the focal person or group and others. Moreover, much of what one calls an identity is composed of words'.

None the less, if we consider what this might mean in practice in the case of companies, we will soon see that the issue is not so clear. How exactly is such an identity created, and who can participate in its creation? Does corporate identity resemble, say, national identity, which is continually disputed and problematized by those who lay claim to it? Is it generated spontaneously by the 'members' of the company, or is it constructed deliberately by the more powerful echelons within the company in such a way as to serve the company's (or their own) strategic interests? Moreover, even if we take the simplest view, which is that the corporate identity is something defined by management in the corporate mission statement, and that all the members of the company acquiesce in that understanding, how does this fit with the divergent accounts and understandings that can emerge and be aired in any democratic society? In other words, how does a company's identity mesh with its outward image? And how does this fit with the internal image or 'organizational identity' that would be recognized by its employees?

Since the concept of corporate identity is widely used in the field of corporate communications, let us examine the broad idea of what it is generally thought to mean in this discipline, and then look at the competing definitions that have been put forward to fill in the conceptual gaps that this leaves. We shall then go on to examine these assertions from the 'outside', that is, from the perspective of discourse analysts who adopt a critical stance to corporate communications and their discourses.

In the so-called Strathclyde statement (van Riel and Balmer, 1997, p. 355) issued by the International Corporate Identity Group, the issue of corporate identity is phrased as follows:

Every organisation has an identity. It articulates the corporate ethos, aims and values, and presents a sense of individuality that can help to differentiate the organisation within its competitive environment. When well-managed, corporate identity can be a powerful means of integrating the many disciplines and activities essential to an organisation's success (. . .) Corporate identity differs from traditional brand marketing since it is concerned with all of an organisation's stakeholders and the multi-faceted way in which an organisation communicates.

The question as to what a company is must be answered in terms of activities and market position, but also in terms of ethos, values or company culture, history, tradition, concrete future plans, locations, sectors and a multitude of other factors, some of which are not entirely in the corporation's own hands. And of course, the answer to all of these questions should have some internal consistency. One thing is clear here, which is that those who are involved in corporate communication understand corporate identity as something that they need to control. If they can define and shape this identity, they will not only help the company to achieve inner consistency, but they will also help to ensure that the desired image is projected to the outside world. In other words, corporate identity and corporate image are intimately connected, to the extent that one might sometimes even seem to be a palimpsest of the other.

Corporate culture and values

Within the area of corporate communications, one of the core ideas that is often emphasized is the concept of corporate culture. Corporate culture includes 'myths, rituals and stories' which serve to integrate the various members and stakeholders in a single, shared reality (Christensen, 2002, p. 164). When we think of cultures, we usually think first of national cultures, which are paradigmatically situated within a specific community, which is held together by a shared history and way of life, or by a set of 'myths and memories' (Smith, 1991). This set may be something of an accident of history. Rather than a fixed way of understanding the world, it is an unstable concept as each generation reinvents itself, adapting the legacy handed down to it by the last one. Recent theorists have come around to the view that nations are 'imagined communities' (Anderson, 1991, p. 6), which cannot be examined in terms of what is genuine or false, but through 'the style in which they are imagined'. Along similar lines in the postcolonial context, Bhabha has emphasized that nations are narrative communities made coherent through shared stories (1990). Nations are 'symbolic communities' (Hall, 1996, p. 612), and their cultures are discourses that produce meanings with which people can identify. Such representations and the values inherent in them become embedded in the everyday discourses and actions of a nation, in such a way that national cultures come to be understood as part of the 'natural order' (Billig, 1995, p. 10).

If all this is true for national cultures, such processes are also enacted on a smaller scale in other communities or groups, including ethnic minorities, political parties, religious communities and so on. In all these cases, a sense of unity and commonality is built on a shared history, a common set of principles or beliefs, a specific way of living, of behaving, of being. In short, these groups are held together, not by material or historical facts, but by the discourses that they weave around these phenomena.

In a similar way, other entities within society can also be said to have a 'culture' or a way of saying, doing and being, which is characteristic of them and different from that of other entities. Those theorists who believe strongly in the existence of a corporate identity and culture, or those who, like public relations specialists, are professionally committed to such an idea, tend to argue that corporations have already attained this status. Large corporations today are wealthier than many states, and exert much more power in world affairs than the smaller nations do. Their cultures and identities are provisional, of course, and rooted in economic and political interests, but cultural theorists would argue that the same is true of many other cultures and identities that we tend to take for granted. The culture and identity of large corporations are increasingly being placed on the same level as other cultures and identities of a more familiar kind.

This process of identity creation is mediated through the 'values' which are revealed in the ongoing discourses of the individual or group (Rokeach, 1973; Cheney and Vibbert, 1987, p. 175). Many of the ways in which people, in general, participate in cultural activities involve the celebration of shared values (Melewar and Karaosmanoglu, 2006). In this sense, the word 'values' is simply used to mean something that people value, that they hold dear, wish to acquire or at least admire or respect in others. In the words of Rokeach (1973, p. 5), a value is 'an enduring belief that one mode of conduct or end-state of existence is preferable to an opposing mode of conduct or end-state of existence'. The underlying theory for an understanding of corporate value systems can be understood as being based on symbolic interactionism, according to which a person or organization engages in a process of self-definition in which he/she/it makes an object of some aspect, gives it meaning and then uses the meaning as a basis for directing its actions (Blumer, 1969). This meaning is projected outwards and encountered by others, who will react to it, and possibly have an effect on it in the long term. Such an object or meaning is enshrined in the system as a 'value'. In the corporate context, a management team can deliberately seek to define and inculcate a series of values that will underpin the activities of the corporation – and of its employees – and if this proves successful, the corporate culture will be reinforced, the employees will experience a greater sense of identification with the company and its activities, and the company will present a better, more consistent, more unified image to the outside world. Although corporate values may vary from sector to sector and company to company, most are underpinned by a neo-liberal understanding of the free-market economy, and by a utilitarian approach to ethics which seeks the overall good of the greatest number through a kind of moral profit and loss calculation.

Yet, at the same time, these cultures and identities are different from those of other social groups in a number of ways. First, the corporation is not a 'natural' community. People join it for a number of years, in order to earn a living, but their affiliation will end when their contract of employment terminates. In such circumstances, we would expect their integration into company culture to be at best provisional.

Secondly, the company and its culture are usually controlled in a top-down manner. There is little space for bottom-up definitions of what company culture might be about, or for spontaneous changes and developments in the way that things are done. More than most states, the company is organized hierarchically, with decisions made at the top, and little room for manoeuvre at the bottom. Although this might seem a sweeping statement, we should remember that national governments are obliged to call a general election every four or five years, whereas boards of directors are answerable only to the shareholders, not to the workers or customers.

Thirdly, because companies operate within the private sphere, they can undertake the kind of propaganda activities that would be decried as 'brainwashing' or 'manipulation' if anyone attempted them in the public sphere. What is more, since these actions are carried out mainly through discourse, and the channels of communication are in the hands of the management, there is little scope for oppositional discourses to attain any status of importance. When employees are dissatisfied, this may remain on the level of grumbling, or they can go to an external body such as a trade union or an employment tribunal to air their grievances. But it is rare for companies to offer employees the chance to participate on equal terms in the decision-making process, or to initiate processes of structural change. Corporate identity is understood as 'top down', as an aspect of leadership, and its discursive manifestations, such as the corporate value statement, are initiated and supervised by management. Although there are occasional exceptions to this (e.g. the IBM corporate values statement is the result of a grassroots movement in which employees participate), such instances are still very unusual. The paradigmatic expressions of corporate identity, such as the corporate mission statement or the company website, are generally maintained strictly under management control.

Defining the corporate image

Of course, what the corporate communications experts say is always shaped by their point of view: they write from a standpoint that is firmly located inside the company's boundaries. As discourse analysts, we know that it is not appropriate to take such statements at face value. The discourse of communications specialists is itself a situated discourse, which is subject to the constraints of their own position. The discourse analyst, on the other hand, enjoys greater independence, and has a commitment to observing and interpreting the discourses of others within a critical perspective. Let us step back for a moment in order to take in a broader perspective on ways in which companies are perceived, in order to gain greater insights into the type of issue that will form the subject of this book.

In reality, it is not just people within the entity who participate in the process of defining what a company is. Other people or entities that come into contact with it also have an active role in creating the understanding of the company as it is perceived by onlookers. The media, for example, will also talk about the company, evaluate its actions, praise its successes and criticize its failings. They will bring its hidden faults to light. If the owners of the company want the public vision of their company to be a positive one, they will have to acknowledge the participation of other, external actors in the way that the company is represented to the public. This outward projection of the company, or rather, the social consensus as to how that company is perceived, is sometimes known as the company's *image*, in order to distinguish it from *identity*, which is felt to be a matter of self-understanding.

Image is generally understood to refer to the impressions or beliefs that people in general have about a company (Balmer, 1998), and to the representation of the company, its actions and products, that is transmitted to internal and external audiences (Topalian, 2003). This image is related to the company's attributes in terms of actions and physical realities, such as its name, buildings, products and services, traditions and ideas, and the impressions made through interactions with employees, clients and other stakeholders. This is also bound up with the company's reputation, but the term 'reputation' is more generally used by specialists to refer to the degree of trust that the company inspires in its stakeholders, while 'image' refers to 'the firm's portrait in the mind of a consumer' (Nguyen and Leblanc, 2001, p. 229). Here we shall leave this thorny question aside, and discuss the question of corporate image, which runs parallel to the debate on corporate identity outlined above.

To address this point, let us go back for a moment to the issue of creating and fomenting company values, alluded to above. In any question of values, there is a process of action and reaction, or what might be termed a social feedback circuit. If a company takes 'customer service' as one of its central values, it will probably emphasize this in its advertising campaigns and on its information brochures. Since the media are likely to pick up on absurd or incongruous aspects of corporate behaviour, if the company's employees blatantly go against the principle of offering high-quality customer service, the media will be especially eager to take the company to task. Consumer groups are also likely to adopt a critical stance. If it has not already done so, the company will have to ensure that more effective quality management systems are put into place to improve customer service standards. As we shall see later, this process of value creation, propagation and maintenance is intrinsic to the process of selecting, training and maintaining staff. It also tends to recur in the discourses directed at investors and customers, and in the forms of communication intended for a wider public. However, the corporate 'value system' and the way it is implemented also plays a part in the way the corporation is judged from the outside, in other words, in the kind of public image that the corporation will acquire.

Constructing identity and image through discourse

Whatever the outcome of the complex debate on identity and image, in the worlds of Bhatia and Lung (2006, p. 266), it is clear that corporate identity is currently 'a multidimensional and dynamic construct that is realized in and through the discursive practices of members of business and disciplinary cultures'. In other words, the corporate identity is created, expressed and replicated through discourse, and it is also performed through the actions and practices of the corporate entity and its members. But not all of the members of the corporation seem to contribute in equal measure to the generation of the corporate identity. Identity, in short, is the firm's own understanding of itself, the 'self-representation that a firm wants to give of itself to the public it addresses' (Malavasi, 2010, p. 213). This has evolved beyond the original association of 'corporate identity' with logos and symbols, to a complex construct taking in the company's sense of who and what it is. This is distinct from its image, which is the way that it wants stakeholders to perceive it, which may or may not be entirely congruent with its self-perceptions.

This understanding is far from being a tacit acceptance of the way things are. More and more, companies are seeking to construct more positive identities, through strategic use of the increasingly powerful communicative resources that are at their disposal. This is not just an attempt to improve their image, that is, the face they present to the 'outside' world, although it is also intended to generate positive effects in this sense. It is part of an evolving social understanding of how work, industry, trade and the economy can be organized. It is a reflection of a pattern underlying much of contemporary life in which the means of persuasion and social control are maintained in a way that is more subtle and less explicit than was the case in the past (Giddens, 1984). For example, the discourse of employee socialization operates through suggestion, through a rhetoric that exalts hard work and commitment to the firm and through the offer of 'rewards'. Employees who do not live up to expectations can still be fired, and they know it – but this fact is not spelt out explicitly in the positively framed discourse of twenty-first-century employer–employee communications. Similarly, in corporate communications intended for other stakeholders, there is a pattern of implicit control, an increasingly allusive and careful discourse which avoids difficulties and negotiates tricky issues adeptly – sometimes so adeptly that few readers will pick up the fact that there was a problem at all. According to Dowling (2001, p. 33), stakeholders in a company can usefully be understood to fall into four categories: customers, who buy from the company; persons and entities linked to the company through some legal or normative relationship, such as shareholders or regulatory agencies; people or entities who habitually work in or with the company, such as employees, unions or suppliers; and the wider public, such as special interest groups, the media or the community. In what follows, I shall briefly point to four of the major areas of corporate communications, defined by representative addressees from those different areas.

Constructing employees

Corporate identities are a conglomerate of different aspects or facets that exist in relation to different groups of people. Companies devote a great deal of resources to communicating their identity to their employees, and to trying to persuade employees to adapt their way of working – and thinking – to what the company regards as appropriate. This communicative action is thus part of a training or 'employee development' initiative. On the other hand, a company may also make an effort to show employees how the company embodies certain values that the employees may already hold dear.

In fact, this is not a contradiction. In the theory developed by Burke (1969), identity and identification are a reciprocal process: one thing is not identical to another, but it may be identified with it because of shared interests; such identifications are generated through a process of persuasion. Identity is bound up with the concept of identification, and identification is related to comparison and linking entities and ideas together. Certain types of employees are likely to feel happier working for a company that ascribes to family values, for example. When they see their own value system reinforced, they will feel more inclined to accept other claims that the company makes on them. In other cases, employees who are not particularly safety-minded may have to be persuaded to observe safety measures. In this case, the company has to make plausible arguments in order to show that keeping to the rules is in everyone's best interest, particularly the employee's. This apparently two-way process is subsumed in the use of the pronoun 'we' that is so prominent in corporate communication at all levels. As we shall see in Chapter 3, a considerable volume of corporate communication is devoted to attempts to engage employees in the corporate mission, inspire their loyalty and encourage them to subscribe to specific values that are held to be central in the corporate enterprise. The object is to bring them into the corporate body, make them identify with its aims and value system and ultimately to ensure that they come to embody these in their own work. If this happens, the process of 'identification' will be complete. Of course, it is more likely that employees will distribute themselves along a continuum from fairly general identification with the company to total disaffection, moving up and down a little in response to different events or relationships. None the less, as companies increasingly endeavour to instil particular ways of working and thinking among their employees, their attempts at discursive construction are in themselves worthy of analysis.

Constructing investors

The type of communicative action that targets shareholders might be supposed to be mainly factual, or at least, to convey messages that are of prime importance to the investor who has put money into the company and presumably hopes for substantial returns on this investment. However, as we shall see, the literature aimed at shareholders tends to fall into two distinct categories. By examining the Annual Reports that are made available to all the investors each year, we will explore the important distinction between the sober presentation of information emanating from the annual audit of the company's accounts, on the one hand, and the kind of unrestricted discussion of the company's past performance and future prospects, often in a warmly optimistic light, found in documents like the letter to shareholders, on the other. The nature of such hybrid communications will be discussed, and the implications of this dual message will be analysed. In addition to this, we shall also explore the ways that companies seek to legitimize their own activities in the eyes of their shareholders, particularly in situations where they have received negative media attention. In general, it will be shown that company-investor communications are becoming more complex, as the shareholder base widens and the media take a greater interest in the affairs of large corporations. However, we shall also see that greater complexity does not necessarily mean greater transparency, and that seemingly plain, informative texts can be analysed to reveal a strong persuasive intent.

Constructing consumers

Traditionally, we all understand advertising as being a means of selling, that is, encouraging consumers to buy a particular product or service. The means of persuasion used are notoriously far ranging, from straightforward information, to suggestion, allusion, creation of positive or negative affect, invoking people's social aspirations, exploiting their insecurities and so on. Since these are familiar to all of us, advertisers have to go to increasing lengths to produce a persuasive message, not only by using the customary means, but by branching out into new technologies and new types of message. In all of this, we can trace a development that is not new, but which has gained enormous momentum over recent years, which is the rise of the brand.

Brands are increasingly understood as a network of associations in the mind of the consumer, a set of positive or negative associations or a symbolic language. Theorists believe that the people who come to share these associations end up having a common way of understanding some aspects of the world. As traditional communities are waning or being dispersed, communities based around consumption appear to be on the rise: many people gain a sense of identity and social belonging through buying a specific make of car or brand of clothing. Thus corporate communications appear to be bringing about radical changes in the ways that human beings relate to each other and to themselves. This trend is one of the most disputed developments in corporate communication, and has been the object of considerable criticism. Critics such as Baudrillard have decried the 'synthetic' nature of communities of consumption in which human relations ultimately dissolve into objects of consumption (1998, p. 172), and transcendent values give way to values determined by the system of symbolic exchange that structures the consumer society.

Communicating with a wider audience

In the era of instant communication and intense media coverage, corporations are increasingly aware of the need to present a good public image, not just to their immediate stakeholders, but to the world at large. When things are going well, this may entail promotional activities such as sponsoring a sports event or cooperating with an NGO. Such actions are felt to generate 'good will', enhancing the company's image by putting it in the public eye in a way that has good associations for the general public. Another very important medium for communicating with the world at large is the corporate website, which can be accessed by everyone, and which is often the 'shop front' that most people encounter first. One interesting facet of the website, which is also relevant in many other contexts, is the section that explains the company's understanding of itself. This may simply be an 'about us' section on the website. However, it may also link in with, or echo, or encapsulate, the company's 'corporate mission statement', which is a more formal declaration of the company's purpose. Since these declarations are not made to any group of people in particular, but to the world as a whole, it seems that they, too, are a way in which the company communicates with a wider audience. Finally, another area of corporate communications is to be found in the relationship with the world's media, and with critics of all kinds. Such communication is particularly important in times of crisis, or when a particular sector has been in the public eye for malfeasance of one kind or another. In the short term, if a disaster occurs, companies' communications departments undertake various forms of 'crisis management', in which they attempt to limit the damage. In the longer term, companies increasingly feel the need to produce environmental reports or corporate social responsibility reports, in which they document the actions that are being taken to ensure that the company is taking care of the environment and respecting human rights.

Disputed identities, tarnished images

Although this book focuses mainly on companies' attempts to construct an identity and image through discourse, it should be remembered that this is only one side of the coin. The 'official', company-sponsored identity and image are disputed in many ways, by many different entities. From the disgruntled employee or disappointed investor to the investigative journalist, people of all kinds give voice to negative perceptions about the company that run counter to its self-proclaimed identity and carefully fashioned image. Even more seriously, companies may sometimes be sued or prosecuted, or investigated by government inquiries. The outcomes of such affairs will be made known to the world in general, and if the company is found to have acted wrongly, no public relations campaign will entirely remove the stain on its reputation, and the consequent blemish on its image. For this reason, even though we are looking principally at the discourses that the corporation directs at different audiences, we will see that the examples we analyse are often what Fairclough would call 'sites of struggle' (1989): the text bears witness to major conflicts that are going on behind the scenes, often without addressing them directly. An insistence on quality may be particularly emphatic in a company whose observance of quality standards has been questioned; reference to 'appropriate management rewards' may be especially frequent when the generosity of management bonuses has caused a public outcry; and a stress on sustainability and environmentally friendly practices may be very strong in the wake of some ecological disaster. Although this is not the main topic of the present book, such issues will surface quite frequently in the course of these pages. It should always be borne in mind that what the company says is one thing, but the opinion that stakeholders may form using evidence from different sources is quite another.

1.3 What is corporate discourse?

We have considered who the audiences of corporate discourse might be, but I have not spelled out exactly what corporate discourse is. On the basis of what we have just seen, I take corporate discourse to include the set of messages that a corporation chooses to send to the world at large, and to its target markets or existing customers. Moreover, my understanding of corporate discourse also includes messages that are intended for internal consumption only, such as those used to communicate with employees, or those intended for a predefined set of stakeholders, such as those who hold shares in the company. However, this inclusive vision of corporate discourse is not shared by everyone, so it is worth taking a moment to consider why I feel that it is useful to understand it in this way.

Discourses and audiences

Much of the earlier research on corporate discourse centres on the messages that organizations send to external audiences, particularly to customers or to the general public. Recently, however, a blurring of organizational boundaries has been noted. Companies are paying more attention to their communication with both internal and external audiences, and are developing discourses that seem to be directed towards both, sometimes at the same time. This seems to fit with wider social trends. Scholars have pointed out that the complexities of the present economic system and the omnipresence of the modern media mean that roles which may in the past have been defined in more exclusive terms are now harder to separate: the employee who receives a message in a training session or inhouse journal will go home and see a general corporate message on the television, or buy a product on the internet and receive a message directed at customers through Facebook. Similarly, the investor who owns shares in the company may also be a customer, and the employee may also be a shareholder.

This is not just what we as outsiders might see as a blurring of roles or proliferation of composite identities that reflects the intricacies of the postmodern landscape. It is also the result of an intentional bid to organize corporate communications along more consistent, more homogenous, more persuasive lines. Recent trends in corporate communications are moving towards a coherent, overall corporate communications strategy that groups all the different aspects of communication under one heading, perhaps placing them all under the authority of a single department. From the company's perspective, it is increasingly seen as desirable to have (Goodman, 2000, p. 70):

> A strong corporate culture; a coherent corporate identity; a genuine sense of corporate citizenship; an appropriate and professional relationship with the press; a quick and responsible way of communicating in a crisis or emergency situation; an understanding of communication tools and technologies; a sophisticated approach to global communication.

If all of this can be forged together clearly and consistently in the company's global communications strategy, all the better, say the pundits. According to business communications expert Christensen (2002), twenty-first-century corporate communication seeks to bring all the company's different communicative activities together under one heading, in order to 'project one uniform and unambiguous image of what the organization is and stands for' (p. 162). This approach is consistent with the ongoing tendency, mentioned above, for forms of corporate communication that have traditionally been separate to merge together, so that communications with investors also contains messages aimed at potential customers, or information about sponsorship activities formerly aimed at the media also have a prominent position in direct communications with clients.

The importance of this turn of events should not be underestimated. Whereas previously, roles were more clearly defined, they are now more diffuse, and they tend to flow into each other in such a way that it is difficult to delimit the precise boundaries. Is it useful to tell the shareholder about improvements in company quality standards because he/she, as an investor, needs to know about advances made in the company in order to assess whether it is worthwhile to maintain his/her investment? Or is this useful because the same shareholder might shop in the company's store or purchase its products? It is really not easy to say. But this is not the only point. Underlying the corporate communications strategy there is also an awareness that by communicating something in a particular way, especially if the message is consistent, the company can go a long way towards building and shaping the public perception of that company, that is, its 'image', and thereby also build and shape the future of the company itself.

We know that discourse builds a particular representation of reality. But discourse is dialogic, inviting its audiences to participate in the realities that it represents. People construct their world through discourse, and other people enter these constructed worlds, adopt their language and participate in the transmission of their representations to others. The social worlds that are built partly through language are held together by sets of structures, values and roles that are defined and negotiated mainly through discourse. Of course, these worlds are not static. The agents who participate in them can introduce new representations or reinterpret older ones. But they cannot entirely discard the structures that have been created: to a great extent, they have to work within the existing system. However, they are also part of this system and whatever they do, their actions and discourses will have an effect on the way the system is carried forward to future players.

Let us take the view that the modern corporation is a social system in the sense explained by Giddens (1984), that is, a specific patterning of social relations across time and space, usually understood as being maintained through the reproduction of social practices. From this starting point, we can go on to examine the way in which that system is generated, maintained and perhaps modified, by considering how discourse is used within that system. According to Giddens (1984, p. 25):

> The social systems in which structure is recursively implicated (. . .) comprise the situated activities of human agents, reproduced across time and space. Analysing

the structuration of social systems means studying the modes in which such systems, grounded in the knowledgeable activities of situated actors who draw upon rules and resources in the diversity of action contexts, are produced and reproduced in interaction.

The production and reproduction of systems through action, particularly discursive action, involve the participation of individual and institutional agents, with interaction between them, and with other entities and systems outside the institution itself. This interaction may result in stability and reproduction of the existing system, or it may generate change – change that is possible within the framework of internal or external constraints operating on the agents at that time. What happens in encounters between agents within institutions is moulded by what the institutional orders permit, by the resources that are available, but also by the knowledge and intentions of the agents involved. One classic example of this is to be found in business meetings, where discourse may be used to reproduce a pre-existing value system, but also perhaps to negotiate a change in that system or even set in motion a thorough-going alteration in the structure or activity of the company. Since the board is the company, and the company's objects and structure can be redefined by the board, the discourse of the board members is a constitutive discourse which shapes the reality of that company. In this sense, the social world is formed by situated actions, often discursive actions, produced in specific situations, which become available for use and reference for future actions.

However, it is extremely important to remember that such systems are also characterized by a power imbalance, by a hierarchy in which some discourses have more importance, prestige and authority than other discourses. The constitutive discourse of the board meeting is more important for the company than the discourse of disaffected employees, for example, because the former is imbued with socially endowed power whereas the latter generally is not. Against this background, we can see that the discourses of the corporation are discourses of the powerful, which are directed at creating and controlling the internal and external perceptions of the company and what it does. The massive growth in corporation communications activity over the last 30 years has been fuelled by the recognition of the importance of discourse in the current economic and political scenario – not just to persuade customers to buy, or inform investors in the hope that they will invest, but to legitimate the company in the eyes of the public, and to build a positive image that will help to secure popular and political acceptance.

Discourse and discourses

We have considered corporate discourse as the overall communicative activity of the company on a variety of levels. In this broad definition, discourse is any kind of communicative action, of any sort. If we try to break this idea down into smaller categories, we will see that the different types of communication issued by companies obviously include a range of spoken and written genres, as well as certain identifiably distinct 'discourses', such as promotional, informative or legitimatory discourses. In Gee's words (1996, p. viii), such discourses are 'ways of behaving, interacting, valuing, thinking, believing, speaking, and often reading and writing, that are accepted as instantiations of particular roles'. These discourses are 'ways of being in the world'. Taken together, all these rather variegated forms of communication or 'discourses' undoubtedly constitute what we might term a 'discourse system' (Scollon and Scollon, 2001). Such a discourse system is self-sufficient, in that it comprises everything that can be said or talked about within a particular domain, and supposes acceptance of a common ideological position, a process of socialization of members, a set of preferred discourse forms (genres, strategies, lexicon) that act as symbols of membership and a structured system of relationships, both inside the domain and with outsiders.

Corporate discourse is therefore more than a set of texts and or genres. In fact, it is, in the terms explained above, more than just one 'discourse', if this is understood as the instantiation of a 'role'. Corporate discourse would most properly be understood as a discourse system, a set of social practices which includes a range of texts and genres, but which is not limited to them, because at any time it may generate new realizations that will still recognizably embody corporate discourse. This discourse system is constantly being renewed and revised, but it is none the less a system of considerable size and complexity, which means that any sweeping change will take time to work its way through the system. Along these lines, we may observe how discourses of social responsibility or sustainability originating in other areas of public life have gradually been appropriated by the body corporate, at least in its communications with important external agents such as the media, but also, increasingly, in its dealings with its own investors, as these issues have gained greater importance in the perceived social consciousness of our generation.

Moreover, corporate discourse can also be understood as being underpinned by a cohesive, though not explicit, ideological system. When approaching Western corporate discourse it is of fundamental importance to understand that it is a voluntary discourse system grounded in utilitarian ideology (Scollon and Scollon, 2001), based on individualism, empiricism and rationalism, but which accommodates a democratic view of organizational relations (Lanham, 1974). At the same time, corporate language incorporates features of technologism, scientific materialism and consumerism. As in other discourse systems where membership is voluntary, members express their identity by showing that they participate in its ideology. This is made manifest in a multitude of details. For example, the all-pervasive use of 'we' and 'our' in corporate literatures reflects democratic ideals of equality that are compatible with utilitarianism, as well as expressing the solidarity system of face which supposedly underlies interactions in Western corporations.

On the other hand, we must always bear in mind that the construction of corporate identity is constrained by the external, profit-seeking goals of the corporate world, and that these may change from time to time as new economic problems or opportunities arise. Unlike traditional family businesses or, perhaps, companies in other parts of the world, the Western corporation has generally operated on a basis that is impersonal, individualistic, empiricist and rational. These underlying premises tend to influence corporate discourse systems in the west, but they are also likely to undergo modifications over time in response to other social changes, as corporations have to justify their actions or account for their very existence using what we can term 'legitimatory' discourses.

One example of such a change has been observed recently in the area of corporate discourses concerning social responsibility towards the environment and the human community. Changes in social expectations regarding issues such as public safety, environmental awareness and social responsibility, and scandals such as Enron, have meant that Western companies have come to recognize the need for a change in their primary culture or at least, a change in the image of this culture that is projected to employees and the general public. To take one concrete example, initiatives such as the UN agreements on environment and climate change (World Climate Programme, 1979; World Meteorological Organization, 1979; Brundtland Commission, 1987; Kyoto Protocol, 1997) have brought sustainable development into the public arena and made it impossible for companies to ignore these issues completely. Those companies which are most directly implicated in the climate change debate, such as oil corporations, are driven by public pressures to take a stance towards these movements, either by mounting a rearguard propaganda action against initiatives such as the Kyoto Protocol, or by showing the public how they are themselves adapting to a changing scenario by reducing harmful emissions and investing in green technologies. Similar discursive operations are also mounted to demonstrate to public opinion that companies act ethically, adhere to safety standards and aspire to accountability.

In general, if we look at corporate discourse systems, we can observe various ways in which they can be broken down for analysis. One possibility is to take specific genres or text types, either from one company or from many, and explore how each genre is the instantiation of a particular social function that is realized through discourse. Along similar lines, we could use our understanding of each genre to map the corporate genre system, taking account of all the different genres that might be used in a particular company, and fitting them together on a conceptual diagram to show a cross-section of discourse in that company at a particular time. A further, complementary approach would be to document the 'natural history' of discourse through a range of material instantiations in genres, from the dialogues of a meeting where a decision is made, to the minutes of that meeting, to the policy documents, plans, reports or brochures that come into being as a result, and ultimately to the reception of these by their intended audiences or readers.

A genre-based approach is not the only means of approaching corporate discourse. A different method would be to start from the audiences or addressees of corporate discourses and investigate the way in which companies direct their messages towards them. It is thus possible to talk of 'corporate discourse intended for employees', or 'corporate discourse aimed at investors', each of which would reflect the company's role in that relationship, and the role or roles of the addressees. Since this approach foregrounds the dialogic purpose of discourse, and avoids some of the fragmentation inherent in an approach centring entirely on genres, this is the approach which will be adopted in this book. Far from sidestepping the issue of genre, we shall look in detail at the most important genres in corporate communication, grouping them together in terms of who they are intended for. This means that we will consider genres in their most essential sense as socially grounded instantiations of communicative action between particular agents for a particular purpose.

Finally, I will also consider a third way in which discourse systems can be approached, which also impinges on both of the previous understandings, and which will be used where appropriate in this book. This involves an understanding of discourse not primarily as something contained in genres, or as something used in a dialogic relationship with other parties, but rather as something that can be classified into types or categories according to its functions. We can thus talk of 'promotional discourse', as a type of discourse

Table 1.1 Corporate discourses

Defined by origin	Corporate discourse – discourse generated by corporations			
Defined by addressee	Corporate discourse to employees	Corporate discourse to customers	Corporate discourse to investors	Corporate discourse to general public
Defined by genre	Employee handbook Employee website Job interview	Advertisement TV commercial Advertorial Customer website	Annual Report Shareholders website	Website Press releases Sponsorship activities
Defined by discourse type	Promotion Information Control	Promotion Information	Information Promotion	Promotion Information Legitimation

which is most characteristic of advertising or of public relations activities, and which has the primary purpose of presenting its object in a positive light and persuading the audience to accept or perhaps purchase it. We could similarly define 'informative discourse' as the type of discourse that is fundamentally concerned with conveying information, facts or news. On the other hand, if we try to define discourses by their functions, we may well find ourselves coming up against a fundamental problem. By classifying discourses into broad categories defined by their general purpose, we will run the risk of missing what is genuinely interesting about each manifestation of corporate communication, because the interest lies precisely in the adaptation and fine-tuning of general discourse types to connect with different addressees, and in the blending or hybridization of discourse types in the attempt to make a particular effect on the target audience. What is interesting about promotional discourse is not so much the lowest common denominator that is common to almost all variants of promotional communications, such as the absence of lexis with negative connotations, but rather the specific features of the promotional discourse of, say, oil corporations when they communicate with a general audience that is ecologically aware. Table 1.1 represents an attempt to show visually the different ways that we can understand and classify corporate discourse and discourses: by speaker or 'origin', by presumed recipient of 'addressee', by customary textual manifestation or 'genre', or by more general discourse function or 'discourse type'. Of course, this does not exclude the possibility of other divisions or categories, such as a classification based on a more fine-grained exploration of origin, for example. The purpose is merely to provide a broad, very general overview of the ways that corporate discourse and discourses are going to be identified and analysed in this book.

Since all of the aspects of discourse included in Table 1.1 are important, I shall try to keep them all in mind as I examine the different areas of corporate discourse. For the sake of clarity and convenience, the book will be chiefly organized in terms of the second row of the table, namely, with regard to the people to whom the corporations address their communications: employees, consumers, shareholders, the general public. I shall therefore examine corporate discourse aimed at employees, for example. However, in this analysis, I will base my explorations on the concrete genres in which this communication is realized: on employee websites and handbooks, for example, which are issued by the corporation to convey the messages that management wish to transmit. In this, we shall inevitably find ourselves looking at different discourse types – some genres will show evidence of discourse that is mainly promotional, while others will yield evidence of more than one discourse type.

In all of this there is inevitably some overlap: the company's discourses directed at its employees may merge with those aimed at customers or investors, for example. Yet this is itself significant. It is through the exploration of how corporations strive to strike up, foster and subtly alter their relationships with stakeholders that we will begin to see the importance of discourse in constructing, reproducing and reinventing the corporate world.

2

Approaches to Corporate Discourse

Companies participate in a vast amount of language-related activity, generating huge volumes of text of different kinds. Over the years, there has been enormous growth in this area, and most companies now employ inhouse corporate communications professionals, as well as engaging specialized agencies to deal with public relations and advertising. As I have explained in the first chapter, in this book I will refer to the kinds of language used across a vast range of social functions within companies as aspects of 'corporate discourse'. This chapter sets out my understanding of what corporate discourse is, and maps out some of the ways in which we can approach this phenomenon analytically.

2.1 Roles of discourse

The term 'discourse' is often taken to mean language in action, as distinct from language viewed as a system or structure in itself. Because language has a crucial role in almost every area of social life, the notion of 'discourse' is extremely wide. It is currently used in a number of different ways, ranging from a value-neutral consideration of how speech and writing function in different social situations, to a much wider analysis of the patterns of thought and communication that define our society in a particular philosophical or historical context, which is often accompanied by a critical evaluation of this phenomenon (Hyland, 2009, p. 21). In this sense, we can observe a panorama of discourse studies ranging from the research of linguists like Swales (1981, 1990), who analyse text in detail to show how meaning is conventionally made through the choice and organization of language in specific contexts, to the work of thinkers like Foucault (1972), who focus very broadly on the role of discourse in constructing social systems and perpetuating social injustices or inequalities, rarely descending to the level of concrete textual features. In this book, we shall look at different ways of approaching the discourse of the corporation, some of which approximate more to one end of the scale, others to the other. In my view, it is vital to understand that there is an unbroken line extending between detailed textual studies and broad interpretations of the role of language in society. Against this background, it is possible not only to take advantage of different methods for gathering data, but also to benefit from the interplay of different interpretations which add depth and complexity to our vision of the phenomenon of corporate discourse.

In my understanding, there is a continuum extending from the surface of the text, through the roles that this text performs in social contexts, to the structures and ideas that configure whole societies, and there is two-way influence along this line. A change at one level in this system will provoke a set of reactions that may travel both up and down. In other words, discourse both shapes and is shaped by the specific contexts and by the whole society in which it is used. A particular society makes certain ways of using discourse available to its members, but proscribes or discourages certain other ways. Constraints are exerted, either deliberately or through an unexpressed consensus, on what may or may not be said. However, this should not be understood in the terms of a crudely understood 'Sapir-Whorf' hypothesis, which posits that our minds are so shaped by the cultures in which we have been socialized that we cannot imagine or relate to anything not contained in that thought-world (Widdowson, 1998a, p. 139; Breeze, 2011c). In fact, we are able to understand ideas from beyond our immediate cultural sphere: were we not able to do so, our world would be a very different place, and cultures would stagnate rather than grow, interact and change. We have the capacity to imagine new ways of thinking and speaking, and to act in accordance with these so that, over time, social structures develop in different ways. Social practices shape discourse, but discourses may also shape social practices. As Giddens said, social structures, and the orders of discourse that maintain them, make social action possible; but this very social action creates, maintains and changes those social structures over time (1984). The institutions, practices and codes that underpin social structures can simply be reproduced uncritically, leading to social stasis and replication of the status quo. But they can also be modified, for better or for worse, when people combine them in different ways, or consciously adapt them to convey new concepts and relationships (Giddens, 1984; Fairclough, 1995a). Against this background, discourse analysis aims to identify the ways in which linguistic and other semiotic resources are used, to understand better the patterns that emerge in different contexts, to explore ways in which language is used to serve ideological ends and to trace changes over time. To do so, it may make use of a wide range of analytical tools, which will be explained further below. Before this, however, it is worth considering three rather different groups of people who all study corporate discourse, but who investigate the same phenomenon to different ends.

2.2 Corporate discourse studies

The large-scale development of corporate discourse has been reflected in a growing theoretical interest in corporate communications from three different angles: first, many professionals involved in these activities engage in applied research with a view to developing more effective practices; secondly, independent researchers from fields such as applied linguistics, discourse analysis and ethnography of communication have opened up more theoretical lines of enquiry designed to explain and interpret what is happening; thirdly, in the area of English teaching, there has been enormous interest in equipping non-natives to take on an active role in an international business world which is dominated by the English language.

Commonality and divergence

Although the first and third of these areas (professional groups and English teaching specialists) tend to have a specifically practical focus, while the second (applied linguists and discourse analysts) may often be more theoretical, there is a significant interplay between them. They all share certain underlying understandings of corporate discourse and its functions, and they are all concerned, albeit in different ways, with certain central issues that arise in this context. Some of the points that form common ground between the three groups are:

- Corporate discourse is concerned with communication between a company and specific audiences, ranging from well-defined interest groups to 'public opinion' at large.
- Corporate discourse seeks to present the company's point of view, and to depict its activities in a positive light.

- Corporate discourse is dialogic in that it constructs and projects particular types of reader, engaging their support or pre-empting their criticisms. To be effective, communicators try to understand these audiences and learn how to establish a relationship with them.
- Corporate discourse is dominated by the English language, yet intercultural differences play an important role. Corporations therefore take cultural factors into account when devising their communications strategies.
- Corporate discourse is closely bound up with corporate practices, to such an extent that we can say that a discourse is an expression of a particular practice. Corporate practices are discursive practices, and yet these discourses are far from transparent. To understand them, it is necessary to read between the lines, and to analyse both what is said, and what is left unsaid.

However, there is also considerable divergence, particularly on the level of what researchers and interpreters might seek to achieve. In the following paragraphs, I shall outline some of the differences in their interests that colour the type of research and analysis that they produce.

The professional groups are committed to their employers, and tend to highlight the practices and strategies that are most likely to benefit the company. Their concern is with effective ways of putting the company's message across, increasing its market share, winning the support of external players such as the media, the government or social pressure groups, building commitment among the workers, inspiring better performance and 'managing' crises. This means that the research conducted under their auspices, and published in journals such as the *Journal of Business Communication* or the *Journal of Advertising* tends to be focused on what works best and how practices can be improved. Although such journals sometimes include articles on ethical issues relating to these activities, it is fair to say that most such articles are about how to improve corporate communication from the company's perspective, and they rarely adopt a profoundly critical approach. Few of these authors might be quite as outspoken in their stance as Brummett (1995, p. 22), who provocatively advocates using 'scandalous rhetoric' to put across the company's point of view, and recommends corporate public relations departments to use any rhetorical device that comes to hand in order to convince the audience in a 'free for all, swashbuckling mode'. Yet most of the people who actually work within the corporate sphere, or in business schools, are professionally committed to the corporate world and have its interests at heart, which means that their assessment of the situation is not likely to show great critical detachment from the interests of the enterprise.

The applied linguists, discourse analysts and ethnographers of communication have a central interest in language and its workings in society. This means that they can study corporate communications from a neutral perspective, focusing on how language seems to work in these contexts, without expressing any commitment as to whether it is serving the company's interests as well as possible or not. Moreover, this also means that they can adopt a critical approach. Since they are not primarily committed to any particular company, or even to the corporate world as a whole, they can stand back to assess whether the company is attempting to whitewash its image in the face of criticism, or manipulate other entities. Some researchers in this area focus in a neutral sense on language forms and their observable functions, linking this to our knowledge of how language works in other areas of life. Others tend to foreground aspects such as the role of language in creating and maintaining social power structures. These analysts may endeavour to place the discursive phenomena they have observed into a wider sociological or philosophical context, linking them to developments in late capitalist society that have been studied by specialists in other fields.

In the language teaching perspective, the main underlying objective is to make knowledge of business language accessible to non-native English users. The focus is therefore on 'typical observable practice' and on acquisition of sufficient competence to function in real-world contexts. Although it might be assumed that both of the above approaches (the professional one and the critical one) have something to contribute to the teaching of non-native users, most of the textbooks and materials on the market tend to rely on the findings gathered by applied linguists rather than by professional communications specialists or critical discourse analysts. Perhaps because of the sectorial links between applied linguistics and language teaching, most 'business English' textbooks use insights from neutral language-focused studies, and are less concerned with evidence about 'good practice' from professional fields such as public relations. Two important factors which may contribute to this tendency are the relative inaccessibility of the professional journals in comparison with applied linguistics and English for specific purposes journals, and the understanding that it is hard enough for second language learners to cope with standard business language, and that the subtler details of corporate communications that are visible to first language practitioners might be beyond their reach. None the less, this situation is likely to change, particularly as second language learners acquire greater competence and take on more active roles in business education. On the other hand, critical discourse studies also tend to be avoided by the writers of language teaching material, perhaps because their critical stance makes them less immediately 'usable' in the classroom, or because teachers are concerned that their students would not respond positively to an approach that criticizes the sector in which they hope to work.

To illustrate the differences between the three approaches, let us consider the following brief extract from a 'letter to shareholders' published in a company's Annual Report:

1. This is my first full year review as Chairman . . . I have been immensely
   impressed by the energy, knowledge and commitment of our staff, whom I
   would like to thank for their continued efforts on Abcam's behalf. (Abcam
   Annual Report)

Researchers who work within corporate communications would probably consider this extract as an example of positive, persuasive communication which sets a constructive tone in a high-profile text. They might centre on the use of intensifiers such as 'immensely', and positive nouns like 'energy' and 'commitment'. They might also consider the impact of this type of language on readers, or analyse its role within the company's overarching corporate communications strategy. Applied linguists would also pick up on these features, but might be more critical, placing these items within the lexical range of conventional 'corporate buzz words'. They would probably also note the curious relationships established through the pronoun structure: it is logical enough for the chairman to speak in the first person, but when he talks about 'our staff' and thanks them, we begin to perceive something about the power structure that underpins such texts: here, the chairman is definitely assigning the employees to an inferior role. Applied linguists might also consider the addressees of the text, but with a view to understanding how such texts are composed and read, rather than in order to improve them next time round. Finally, researchers from the area of teaching are more likely to look at such a text as a typical manifestation of the 'letter to shareholders', and thus also as a genre which shares many features with a conventional letter (use of first person, beginning with orientative statement, transactional elements such as thanking). By making students aware of these aspects, they try to help them to become more efficient readers or better business writers themselves, and although most students are unlikely to write a 'letter to shareholders' in the near future, it can do them no harm to discover different manifestations of the letter genre.

Although the three approaches outlined above differ in their aims and their understanding of what research is for, the methods they use to carry out that research often overlap. In what follows, I shall explain some of the different tools used to analyse corporate discourse. Although these tools do not differ greatly from those applied in other areas such as the language of education or science, I shall illustrate them here by using examples from studies carried out on corporate discourse.

2.3 Starting from the text

If the object of our study is discourse, that is, how language functions in real contexts, then it is clear that this object can be studied through the analysis of concrete examples of language from particular contexts. Such examples will be described, for our present purposes, as texts. This itself begs a question, because some of the examples of corporate discourse that we shall examine are spoken, and some authors might consider that spoken language does not constitute a text in the traditional sense, while others might contrast text (the written word) with paralinguistic material (gesture and facial expression, typefaces and so on). Still others might challenge the tendency to consider text (language in whatever form) on its own, and insist on the need for a multimodal approach in which text is regarded as one mode coexisting with modes such as visual images or music, or with a range of even more detailed subdivisions of modes. Each of the approaches described below tends to have a slightly different attitude to what constitutes a text that can be analysed, and so rather than providing a categorical definition here, I shall try to bring out what text means for linguists working in each of these approaches.

A second complication arising from what follows is the extent to which scholars working in each of the areas outlined below attempt to explain and interpret the features that they identify. Some may confine themselves to the description of texts and/or discourses, either because they feel they lack sound epistemological bases for explaining and interpreting their data, or because they are mainly concerned with teaching people *how* to write particular texts, assuming that those people will supply their own answers as to *why* they need to do so. Others may choose to offer explanations of textual and discursive features in terms of the immediate context within the company and the wider business culture in which this is embedded. Still others may go beyond explanation to attempt to interpret the phenomena that they have found in the light of social and cultural theory. A full synthesis showing exactly how all these approaches might fit together would go far beyond the scope of this book. My aim here is only to set out some of the main approaches used in analysing discourse, all of which are reflected later in this book. Although tentative explanations and interpretations will be proposed in Chapters 3 to 6, I shall attempt to gather together my principal conclusions on the nature and meaning of corporate discourse in Chapter 7.

Analysing genres

The term genre is used to mean the characteristic types of text that are used in given situations. In Western culture, the concept of genre was originally applied mainly to works of literature that followed particular conventions: the sonnet, the ode and the epic, for example, have an ancient history, yet prove surprisingly robust and resistant, providing a framework within which poets across the centuries have been able to express their creativity. The application of the notion of genre to the analysis of non-literary works is relatively recent, but has also proved extremely fruitful. Social life is organized around recurring situations and typical communicative needs. Ever since writing has existed, people have been using it to draft laws, to write letters of invitation or condolence or to give instructions. These recurrent situations have given rise to conventional written forms which encapsulate the necessary transactional elements, often complementing this with features that are purely social or interactional. In the business context, we might think first of typical business correspondence, or of reports and memoranda. All of these are transactional, that is, they are intended to fulfil a particular social purpose. And all of them have features that are conventional, which enable the reader to recognize them for what they are, and to place them in a real-world context. A moment's reflection, however, will tell us that the range of corporate genres extends far beyond these familiar text types, and incorporates a huge amount of variation. Reports themselves come in a multitude of formats, and contain an array of different sections, each with its own purpose, style and conventions. Corporate websites and brochures are also complex phenomena containing multiple genres. The world of advertising presents an even greater panoply of genres, with the complication that advertisements often play on our knowledge of other genres to achieve their effect. Even conventionalized spoken interactions, such as job interviews, can be thought of as genres, since their linguistic parameters are confined by their social purpose. Examples 2 and 3 below show two instances of what must be the shortest corporate genre: the mission statement. Both are concise, and both share the form of a positively framed forward commitment, even though one verges on the visionary while the other is more down-to-earth.

2. To unlock the potential of nature to improve the quality of life. (ADM)
3. We will be the easiest pharmacy retailer for customers to use. (CVS Corporation)

Current approaches to genre analysis have a varied intellectual background. It has often been said that there are three distinct traditions regarding the understanding of genres in discourse analysis, all of which acknowledge the primacy of the social uses of language. Although there is considerable interplay, or even convergence, between the three, let us consider them separately in order to see what each one contributes to our general discussion. The first of these approaches has a conceptual background in the rediscovery and revival of classical rhetoric, and the recognition that rhetoric pervades language use in mundane as well as elevated contexts (Burke, 1950; Perelman and Olbrechts-Tyteca, 1969). This view was taken up by writing experts such as Bazerman (1988), Freedman and Medway (1994), and Coe (2002), and became identified as the so-called new rhetoric movement. These authors recognize the usefulness of the tools of rhetoric to examine real-world uses of language, but place a heavy emphasis on the need for writers (and analysts) to understand the multiple pressures and opportunities of the situation, rather than focusing on the more mechanical aspects of rhetorical organization. In fact, the insistence on genre as social action here tends to overshadow the conceptualization of genre as text, to the extent that contextualization is accorded priority over textual analysis.

A slightly different approach to genre was developed within the fold of systemic functional linguistics (Halliday, 1994). Its practitioners seek to bring together the consideration of the social purpose of the genre with the details of its concrete realization in a particular text type. In other words, they scrutinize the text to find out how different aspects of social purpose are given a material linguistic form. This approach is especially important in its emphasis on close analysis of the linguistic realization of generic stages, which opens up the way to micro-analysis of texts in consonance with serious examination of their social functions (Rothery, 1996; Christie and Martin, 1997; Solin, 2001). Genres are understood as 'staged goal-oriented social processes' (Martin, 1997, p. 13): texts unfold through stages as complex social action is performed through language in order to achieve a particular goal. Such close investigation of text in context is also compatible with ethnographic research into discourse communities. Texts carry out real tasks and fulfil real functions, but they also bear traces of power structure and prestige systems.

A third approach to genre, which has undoubtedly been influenced by the other two, but which has gained enormous momentum of its own because it has proved particularly fruitful for research in applied linguistics and languages for specific purposes, is the type of genre analysis advocated by Swales (1990) and Bhatia (2004), sometimes known as the 'ESP approach' (Solin, 2011). This is influenced by both systemic functionalism and pragmatics in its insistence on the relationship of form to function, and its hands-on attitude to text analysis, but also takes in aspects of rhetoric in its analysis of text structures beyond surface level.

Despite differences in their approaches, what the 'ESP school', systemic functionalists and new rhetoricians would agree on is the importance of genre as a social phenomenon, and the need to analyse real writers and communities to gain access to insider accounts and expert understandings of what genres are about. In their different ways, all would agree that:

- Genres are shaped by conventional practices and by collective interests.
- Genres may also be influenced by the private intentions of experienced writers who negotiate the challenges of the business world by skilled use of rhetoric.
- Genre are located within genre systems: groups of genres which cluster around a particular social context or professional situation.

Following these approaches, students of corporate discourse can carry out close study of texts to establish what linguistic functions are used in sales letters in general, or to explore what features to make a sales letter or letter of application persuasive to a particular readership. Our examination may reveal particular lexical choices that shed light on the system of values which operates in that situation. Scrutiny of the pronouns, possessives and verbs used in the text may show how the writer positions herself with regard to the reader, and reveal the particular kind of relationship that she is trying to build. Our investigations will be considerably enriched if we can also compare this information with interview data or ethnographic research about the context in which the texts were used. The main principle here is that there should be an attempt to match the concrete discursive manifestations found inside the text with a social situation and purpose outside that text. This offers enormous potential for the study of corporate discourse. Moreover, within this approach, taking in both context and genre, we can also open our field of gaze to examine the existence of hybrid genres such as the 'advertorial', and look critically at the related phenomenon of 'genre bending', in particular cases where genres seem to have been subverted for purposes other than those for which they originally came into being (Bhatia, 2004).

Across and beyond genres

What the genre analysis approaches have in common is an understanding that language is used in typical patterns and forms in order to fulfil social functions. A genre is both a sample of language and a social action. However, all the genre analysis approaches outlined above place the genre itself in the foreground: they insist on the product, the artefact. There are other approaches to analysing discourse that situate their standpoint elsewhere. This is important, because the genre is an embodiment of discourse, but discourses transcend the genre. We need to be able to see beyond the confines of the genre to find out what speakers or writers are doing and why. This will both complement and complete our understanding of genre, but will also lead to a deeper understanding of discourse.

If we look for an explanation that will anchor our enquiry into discourse to something other than genre, we might turn to classical rhetoric, which tells us that the key elements of 'logos', 'ethos' and 'pathos' are combined to achieve the particular desired social effect. We can search for embodiments of these three elements in the way arguments are constructed ('logos'), the credibility of the author is built up ('ethos') and a relationship is extended to the reader ('pathos'). Searching for more direct, recent antecedents, we may prefer to adopt Halliday's view that our purposeful use of language has recourse to three interconnected meta-functions: the ideational function, in which language reflects our surroundings and influences them; the interpersonal function, which covers relationships between participants; and the textual function, which is about the internal organization and coherence of texts. These systems – the classical and the Hallidayan – both offer a way of talking about discourse in terms of abstract categories, a 'metadiscourse'. In their concrete application, they are not the same, because 'logos' can be understood as both ideational and textual, for example, while 'ethos' and 'pathos' both reflect something of the relational. None the less, there is a curious confluence between the ancient and the modern, in the need to find a system and a language for talking about discourse.

In the direct context of professional and academic language, one system that has been developed in great detail is that of Hyland (1998, 1999, 2005), who identifies aspects of metadiscourse in different types of text, or similar texts from different fields. On the basis of previous studies concerning interactive and interactional resources (Thompson, 2001), Hyland concentrates particularly on the 'interactional' dimension, that is, the way that writers involve their readers in the text. Within this, he develops two overarching categories which he terms 'stance' and 'engagement'. Stance refers to the writer's textually constructed 'voice' or social or professional persona. It is conveyed through devices such as hedges and boosters, attitude markers and self-mention, particularly the use of the personal pronouns 'I' and 'we'. Engagement, on the other hand, includes items that are more directly aimed at the reader, such as use of 'you' or inclusive 'we', directives (use of imperatives such as see, consider), direct questions used to provoke dialogic involvement, asides (as we all know) and references to shared knowledge (of course, obviously).

This conceptual structure has proved robust enough to identify differences between academic writing from different fields which shed light on the way the writers understand their role as scientists and researchers (Hyland, 2005). The presence or absence of self-mention, for example, may reveal the underlying epistemological basis that determines how knowledge is understood to be constructed in a particular discipline. As we shall see, the same approach also produces interesting findings when applied to corporate discourse, though arguably the differences between sectors and genres are not as conventionalized, because their conceptual grounding is less secure. Let us consider the following example from a Corporate Social Responsibility report:

4. In a resource-constrained world, we must use innovation as a driver to conserve water, increase our energy efficiency, reuse and recycle our products. (NIKE)

Here, the use of 'we' might seem ambiguous: does it signify the company, or is it inclusive, intended to rope in the world at large? In fact, this blurring of identities is a strategy through which the writer both signals solidarity with readers and attempts to involve them in the corporate agenda.

Although the framework of stance and engagement has proved extraordinarily fruitful in the field of applied discourse analysis, particularly in the context of academic and professional language, it is far from being the only possible approach. Some researchers have explored other constructs, such as the notion of polyphony (multiple voices) and the key role played by *verba dicendi* (verbs of saying) in the reporting of sources when constructing an argument or relaying business information to the media (Maat, 2007), or the use of argumentation theory (Perelman and Olbrechts-Tyteca, 1969; Toulmin, 1969) to analyse the argumentation used in corporate discourse (Corvellec, 2001, 2007).

All of these text-based approaches to research bring insights, but they also result in fragmentation: if, instead of considering a whole text and its functions, we take one feature of a text (such as metadiscourse) and compare this feature across genres and sectors, we will learn a lot about metadiscourse. If our objective is to learn more about metadiscourse per se, because our object of study is the linguistic system itself, then our mission has been accomplished. But if we want to know about particular genres, we will then have to extrapolate back from these comparisons to the texts that we started with. Then, if we are interested in teaching students, we will have to assemble the facts about pronoun use, say, with what we know about other features of the text, in order to provide clear guidelines about how students ought to write, and why. The fragmentation brought about by use of an increasing number of analytical methods has led some scholars to search for a system, a way of putting the different methods together that is both meaningful to linguists and analysts and useful to teachers and practitioners. Appraisal analysis (Martin and White, 2004) builds on a Bakhtinian view of text as dialogue with readers, systematizing aspects such as lexical choice and argumentative rhetoric, and working towards an all-encompassing framework for studying and classifying real language samples. Verschueren's balanced multidimensional approach (Verschueren, 2012) has similar aims, focusing systematically on how ideology is conveyed through text by working up through different layers of meaning to show how facts, ideas and relationships are constructed and communicated through language.

In short, a wide variety of text-analytical approaches are available that are suited to the analysis of corporate discourse. Some have been used frequently, while others have had fewer immediate applications. What they have in common is a focus on the actual wording and structure of the text as such, usually in the context of whole texts from identifiable sources, whose function is known and understood.

Corpus approaches

The above approaches are often used in qualitative exploration of manageable samples of text that are taken to be representative of particular genres or areas. Many of them can also be complemented and enhanced by use of corpus linguistics, which potentially offers a greater degree of objectivity, because it makes it possible to handle much larger quantities of text and submit them to more rigorous analyses.

Corpus linguistics takes as its object a 'corpus', that is, a collection of texts which are thought to be representative of a particular genre, register or language variant, or which were written by a particular author or group of authors. When a corpus is compiled, the aim is usually to create a corpus which is maximally representative of the language variety or text type under examination, so that it can provide an accurate picture of the tendencies in that variety. By working on a corpus of this kind researchers will be able to test out intuitions that arise during a normal reading of the text. However, they will also be able to conduct other searches that may bring to light patterns that are not visible on a qualitative reading, perhaps because they are not particularly frequent, or because they are subtle in nature and only become visible in large volumes of text.

Two of the key concepts that can be researched in corpus linguistics are frequency and association. Frequency refers to how often a word, combination of words or grammatical pattern occurs in the corpus. If a feature is frequent, then we can surmise that it is significant in the way that kind of language (genre or register, for example) functions. For example, in his major study of the language used in university contexts, Biber (2006) was able to substantiate many patterns of word use that we might sense intuitively but would find it more difficult to test in small samples. He confirmed that word categories coincided with discourse types, so that modal verbs were found more often in procedural discourse, whereas adjectives were more common in content-focused discourse, nominalizations more frequent in written than oral discourse and so on.

In general, corpus linguistics has been less widely applied to corporate discourse than to areas such as academic or scientific texts. However, there are some large-scale studies of lexis from the wider area of business, such as the findings from the Business English Corpus (Nelson, 2000), which examines a corpus of authentic business texts. To investigate the nature of business English, Nelson compared his real business texts with the much larger and more general British National Corpus, in order to obtain 'keywords', that is, words that are more frequent in the smaller corpus than would be statistically probable on the basis of the frequency of the same words in the larger one, often measured in terms of 'log likelihood'. As might be expected, he found a high frequency of words relating to the business context. Table 2.1 shows the top ten keywords from Nelson's BEC corpus (Nelson, 2000).

Such results might seem predictable (we already know that business is about companies, management, customers and sales). Moreover, they also

Table 2.1 Top ten keywords from Nelson's BEC corpus

N	Word	% in BEC corpus	Keyness Log L
1	Business	0.28	3557.7
2	Company	0.29	3118.6
3	Market	0.23	2056.1
4	Customer	0.12	1763.0
5	OK	0.09	1635.1
6	Product	0.14	1377.2
7	Sale	0.12	1239.4
8	Fax	0.06	1085.0
9	Management	0.10	989.6
10	Price	0.13	941.5

date surprisingly quickly (where would we now find such frequent use of the word 'fax'?). None the less, a deeper exploration of such quantitative findings brings more interesting patterns to light. For instance, the key lexis of the BEC corpus contained a large number of positive and few negative words, and a preponderance of 'action words', particularly what he terms 'dynamic public verbs'. Such findings are of relevance to discourse analysts, who can try to map these discoveries about business lexis into the broader landscape of the ideology of corporate communication.

Interestingly enough, authors from within the professional sphere have also been keen to explore the potential of corpus linguistics. In a different corpus study focusing exclusively on Annual Reports, Rutherford (2005) found a similar emphasis on positive lexis, even in the supposedly more technical sections of the report dedicated to financial statements. However, few studies exist which explore corporate discourse through corpus tools beyond the level of word counts: corpus linguistics holds considerable promise for the study of corporate language, and is still relatively underexploited.

Multimodal approaches

Most of the approaches described above involve an acceptance that language serves social and personal needs, and that it fulfils certain functions. In the real world, language (in the sense of words and phrases) is not the only way that people communicate. What we loosely call 'texts' are, in fact, often multimodal phenomena: even something as seemingly 'textual' as a newspaper contains a considerable degree of paralinguistic information, not to mention images. If it is an online newspaper, it will probably also contain moving images, videos with integration of sound, music and images, or even interactive options, so that readers can leave their own comments on the page, vote in reader surveys, upload their own photographs, or click through to other, related texts or sites. The realization that 'texts' function on a multitude of levels through many media, and that the whole is more than the sum of the parts, underlies the social-semiotic approach to multimodal texts developed by Kress and van Leeuwen (1996). Here, the object of analysis is not the text as a merely linguistic phenomenon, but the entire phenomenon as it is represented across a variety of semiotic modes. To do justice to complex multimodal artefacts, these authors increasingly speak in actional terms of 'semiotic practices' rather than in terms of unidimensional texts or modes (Kress and van Leeuwen, 2001).

In multimodal social semiotics, the notion of the 'semiotic resource' is of crucial importance. Van Leeuwen (2005, p. 3) explains that this concept originated in Halliday's view that the grammar of a language is not a set of rules, but 'a resource for making meanings' (1978, p. 192), and that other resources also contribute to this process. Multimodality classically refers to the messages conveyed in different types of print and sound, images, colour, material objects and so on, through which meaning-making takes place. This understanding has now given rise to multimodal transcription analysis and 'cluster' analysis involving hierarchies of modal items operating across different levels (Baldry and Thibault, 2006; Djonov, 2007). It is hardly surprising that the complexity of the phenomenon as a whole, and the interactions between modes and messages in particular, present a considerable challenge to discourse analysts. To all of this, we must add the increasing dimension of interactivity, which radically alters the basic parameters of the way in which readers can react to texts.

In the area of corporate discourse, the multimodal phenomena which have received the greatest attention have been advertising, in general, and the corporate website, in particular. Advertising has been multimodal since its birth, and many studies explore the use of different modes and the interaction between them in what is the most creative area of corporate discourse (Cook, 1992). The more recent phenomenon of the website has been analysed by some researchers, who have investigated how qualitative and quantitative methodology can be extended to take in interactive and multimodal elements (Evangelisti Allori and Garzone, 2010):

- Overall structure
- Hierarchy and accessibility of sections

- Texts
- Images (photographs, graphs, graphics) and colour schemes
- Sound and video
- Interactive elements (interactive maps, questionnaires, online purchasing)
- User discussion groups or comments pages
- Devices for contacting the company itself (chats, email)
- Links to social networks

As if this were not enough, none of these features operates in isolation. The essence of multimodality is that different modes interact with each other, and if analysts set out to study a multimodal phenomenon, they need to take account of the ways that messages sent in different modes complement and reinforce each other, or cancel each other out. This is particularly challenging, because although web genres may now be consolidating somewhat, websites are still often an unstable configuration of modes which integrate traditional business genres in a new context, thereby destabilizing and reconfiguring them. As people visit sites, they tend to create their own pathways, and new meanings emerge from these interactions. This points to the growing importance of multimodality and interactionality in corporate discourse, and suggests that the existing tools of linguistic and semiotic analysis need to be updated to take account of what is still an emergent phenomenon.

Critical approaches

Our overview of approaches cannot be complete without a brief review of what is perhaps the most ambitious type of discourse analysis in terms of aims and scope. Critical discourse analysis, or CDA, can be described as an approach or attitude towards analysing language which is particularly concerned with power as a central conditioning force in social life. The name CDA is frequently used interchangeably with the term 'critical linguistics', but seems to have acquired precedence over it. CDA is not a method or a theory of language, but rather an attitude to handling language data, a way of thinking about texts.

Like many of the areas outlined above, CDA takes an intense interest in the context, in the way that texts form part of their own environment. However, it can be distinguished from these other approaches in its particular focus on the power relations that exist in society and the way that discourse operates ideologically to underpin these invisible power structures (Wodak, 2011). The underlying assumptions of CDA are therefore fully in line with Habermas's view that 'language is also a medium of domination and social force. It serves to legitimize relations of organized power' (Habermas, 1967, p. 259). The questions that preoccupy critical discourse analysts concern how dominance is legitimated through language, how the powerless are excluded by discursive means, how ideology and power imbalances are 'naturalized' and 'consensualized' in the social order through language, and (less frequently) how disempowered groups can make their concerns heard or change the established discourses.

CDA is quite openly and unashamedly eclectic in its methodology, admitting a plurality of different approaches including corpus analysis, systemic functional linguistics, qualitative text analysis, ethnography, multimodal studies, conversation analysis and so on. On a theoretical level, too, it is open to many influences, including postmodernism, feminism and the Frankfurt school. In practice, its approach tends to be problem oriented, setting out from a perceived social problem such as 'racism', to analyse the ways in which the situation of inequality is produced and reproduced through discourse, drawing on a wide range of methods and theories to account for what is observed. This very openness has sparked a considerable number of criticisms (Breeze, 2011c). None the less, CDA is a powerful movement within the academic community, not least because it addresses certain problems that have sometimes been observed in mainstream linguistics, such as an apparent lack of relevance to social affairs, or a passive attitude towards the role of language in injustice and manipulation.

One trend in CDA which is promising for the study of corporate discourse is represented by Fairclough (1985, 1993) and Chouliaraki and Fairclough (1999). These authors analyse discursive events in terms that would be familiar to linguists with a background in systemic functionalism, but focus particularly on the Foucauldian notion of 'orders of discourse' (Foucault, 1981). An 'order of discourse' is the entirety of the discursive practices within a social domain, and the relations between them. The order of discourse of a society is therefore the set of the various smaller orders of discourse operating within that society (school discourse, home discourse, workplace discourse) and the relationships that prevail between these different discourses. As society changes, discourses from one area of life may 'colonize' other areas, or alternatively particular areas may 'appropriate' discourses from other ones. The direction of the relationship (colonization implies invasion and subjugation, while appropriation implies a form of 'borrowing') will be influenced by the way that power relations are structured in the given context. Importantly for our present subject, Fairclough has shown how the discourse of consumer culture that prevails in 'post-traditional society' is influencing other areas of life, such as the universities, which are now presenting themselves to their 'customers' in a manner which radically reconfigures the relationship that was traditionally assumed to exist between centres of learning and their students (Fairclough, 1995b). Such a reconfiguration is also taking place in the corporate world. Consider the following example from a job advertisement:

5. At M, we offer exceptional careers to people with exceptional talent (. . .) To continue our unprecedented growth, we need people with a natural flair for sales and entrepreneurship (. . .) The ideal candidate will be motivated by working to targets, being pushed outside their comfort zone and developing their business through cold calling (. . .).

All companies have to recruit, and the genre of the job advertisement developed to alert suitable applicants to a position that is available. To this end they traditionally give a brief description of the position and the type of person required. Why, then, are superlatively phrased examples such as 5 are increasingly common? A critical discourse analyst might point to the colonization of transactional genres by promotional ones, and to the all-pervasive promotional tone that now permeates all aspects of corporate discourse. They might also note the subject position offered to the would-be worker, couched in conventional 'dynamic' terms ('natural flair', 'entrepreneurship'), with euphemistic representation of what is expected of employees ('pushed outside their comfort zone'). Critical analysts might argue that the corporate socialization process begins precisely here, in the job advertisement.

Another extremely influential author in CDA is van Dijk (1998, 2008), whose ground-breaking work on racism in the press in the 1980s has been followed by a serious and complex endeavour to understand the role of context in the dynamic representations of communicative events. His concern with the socio-cognitive aspects of communication gives his work a solidity that is sometimes lacking in CDA, since authors in this field all too readily assume that readers are influenced in a particular way, yet are unable to explain or show exactly how social structures influence discourse structures or suggest how social structures are enacted, legitimated or reproduced through discourse. One particularly relevant aspect developed by van Dijk is the area of 'legitimation', that is, the discursive means used to justify the company's actions, or indeed, its very existence. As van Dijk points out (1998, p. 255), legitimation is a social and political act, which is typically accomplished through discourse. Although it is obviously related to self-defence, it does not necessarily pre-suppose real past or present attacks, but often simply pre-empts possible future ones. Institutions are particularly likely to use legitimatory discourses, since all those who have no absolute power may need to justify their actions as a matter of course. We should note that legitimatory discourses are top-down, emanating from the elites or institutions and directed at their members, clients, workers and so on. Thus after a major ecological disaster, the 'letter to shareholders' published in BP's Annual Report states:

6. Clearly, after a very troubled and demanding 12 months, BP is a changed company.

To legitimate the company's ongoing activities, the CEO has to distance the company from its recent past. Following familiar techniques of crisis management, he acknowledges the problem, but emphasizes the changes that have now taken place. In the course of the letter, through skilful use of discursive manoeuvres and careful handling of metadiscourse, the company will actually emerge as a survivor rather than a wrong-doer. To the critical analyst, such instances shed considerable light on the workings of language and power in the current economic system.

Critical discourse approaches will play an important role in the present volume, since they offer considerable scope for interpretation of data in a broader social and ideological context.

2.4 Starting from the context

All of the approaches mentioned in the previous section can be grouped under the heading of applied linguistics, and generally take the text itself – be it oral or written, multimodal, interactive or whatever – as their starting point. However, some approaches to analysing communication go beyond this, looking instead at the wider picture within which the text plays a role. We have already seen some movements within genre analysis that place a major emphasis on the social role of texts. Many of their methods and findings overlap with those used by ethnographers of communication, or even by workplace psychologists and sociologists.

Ethnographic approaches

Discourse is a form of action, and as we have seen in the section on genre, the use of language in specific areas of life can be conceptualized as part of 'disciplinary practice' within a 'discourse community'. In this view, genres are produced within a wider system of social interaction in a particular situation, company, discipline or sector. It is, of course, perfectly possible to begin our analysis by looking at the environment as a whole, rather than focusing immediately on the immediate environment of the text. Such approaches to research can be grouped together under the heading of 'ethnographic approaches'. Ethnographic approaches usually concentrate on obtaining as much information as possible about the environment that is being studied. Although quantitative data can be obtained, there is often an emphasis on qualitative material, which may be obtained by observation or interviews, which can be compiled to provide 'thick descriptions' of the situation (Geertz, 1973). This approach is often informed by the ideas that underlie 'grounded theory' (Glaser, 1992). It is generally characterized by a commitment to the belief that local contexts instantiate large-scale social phenomena, so that a detailed observation of one context will enable the researcher to draw conclusions that go far beyond that immediate context, shedding light on the nature of the society in which it is embedded.

Ethnographic methods put a premium on capturing the 'inside view', that is, the ways that participants themselves understand their experiences (Silverman, 1993). Texts and genres are important in such an analysis, but the habitual starting point for ethnographic enquiry is the observation of a situation or group of people, which may be conducted over a fairly long period of time. The observational material obtained, including notes, recordings and video, will be complemented by interviews and text analysis, but the text is generally regarded as an artefact or exhibit, rather than as the primary object of study. None the less, some researchers working in the area of professional writing have used ethnographic approaches to provide insights into the discourse communities within which the texts were produced and used (Swales and Rogers, 1995; Gollin, 1999).

Intercultural approaches

One point that is becoming increasingly obvious as discourse analysts explore the material produced by companies across the world is the variation between cultures, even if the same product or industry is targeted and the same language is used. This has led some authors to draw on wider cultural theories to help interpret their findings. Social anthropologists working in the corporate world have drawn attention to systematic differences in the way that people think and relate to each other in different cultures, which are often reflected in aspects of corporate communication. One of the most influential figures in this area is Hofstede (2001). In the 1970s he conducted a large-scale project based on data obtained from 100,000 self-report questionnaires given to IBM employees in over 70 countries. The results enabled him to hypothesize that cultural differences can largely be accounted for by consideration of five 'dimensions': power distance; collectivism/individualism; masculinity/femininity; uncertainty avoidance; and short/long-term orientation. This approach has proved particularly fruitful in studies of advertising discourse and webpage design (de Mooij, 2010), but may also be relevant to other aspects of corporate communication. There has also been interest in strategies for overcoming cultural differences. For example, Spencer-Oatey and Franklin (2009) look at the cultural dimensions of corporate communication within the perspective of pragmatics, and rather than analysing differences, focus on ways in which rapport can be built and maintained between businesspeople from different cultural backgrounds. Approaches directed at describing and explaining features of different cultures can shed light on corporate discourse, and can help us to interpret our findings, particularly in cases where cultural elements are particularly salient, such as in advertising.

2.5 Explaining and interpreting corporate discourse

The question that arises out of all of this is perhaps whether it is possible for these diverse approaches to be brought together in an all-round research programme on corporate discourse, and whether indeed this would be desirable. The overview presented here reflects my understanding that all these approaches are stages along the same path, but as we progress along this path, different criteria come into play. Analysis of text and textual features must be objective and rigorous, whereas explanation and interpretation are of their nature more speculative. If we want to understand the discourse of the corporation better, all of these methodologies have something to contribute. If we could somehow bring them in together under one roof, ordering them to show exactly where each one stands in the global edifice, this might be beneficial. Yet it is not really necessary. What matters is that the different aspects studied and findings obtained should be integrated into a coherent vision. In this sense, it is important for those using empirical approaches and critical-interpretive approaches to understand each others' methodologies and heed each others' conclusions.

It is impractical to suggest that a researcher should examine all the possible linguistic and extralinguistic phenomena associated with a particular professional activity. Apart from being extremely time-consuming, such an enterprise would probably produce an indigestible quantity of data. What really matters is that the methodology that researchers choose should be appropriate to their goals, and that they should try to integrate their findings into the broader picture of what we already know about corporate discourse, and so interpret them in the light of the more theoretical approaches developed by critical discourse analysts, sociologists and philosophers. This book brings together previous research from many different areas of discourse analysis. It also applies a range of different methodologies, sometimes in coordination with each other, and sometimes on their own. What holds this together is the theoretical underpinning, the emergent understanding of corporate discourse as a powerful force in late capitalist society, which enables us to interpret different aspects of our empirical findings in the light of social theory.

3

Communicating with Employees

From the moment when a company places an advertisement in the newspaper or a stand in a recruitment fair, to the moment when it hands over the handsome retirement gift, there is ongoing communication between the corporation and its employees. The roles of each party and the relationships between them are shaped, or even constructed, through discourse. This chapter will look at this process sequentially, beginning with job advertisements and recruitment processes, then moving on to induction seminars and guides or videos for new employees, before turning to inhouse newsletters and ongoing forms of internal communication. It will conclude with a brief outline of the major trends in company–employee communication in European and US companies today.

3.1 Job advertisements

Although job advertisements might seem to be almost inconsequential in the vast panorama of corporate discourse, they have several important functions. First, advertisements for specific jobs, or the more general type of publication targeting graduate recruits, are often the first contact that young people have with the world of business and employment as potential participants. This encounter is important, because through the advertisement or recruitment page, the business or institution sends particular messages to potential recruits. Not only does it state the formal requirements for the position and promise particular rewards, but it also sets the parameters of the future employee's relationship with the company, and projects an image of the business itself, its workers and the nature of the collaboration that is expected. Advertisements targeting more experienced professionals are also important, but have a slightly different discursive function, in that they have to provide a rationale that might lead someone to change company in mid-career. This again is usually couched in language which is both flattering and enticing to the candidate, and which promotes the company's own image. We must note that both types of advertisement serve an additional purpose of bringing the company to the attention of a wide audience and generating a positive impression: recruitment advertising plays a part in the general public relations activities of the company and the publicizing of its corporate image.

Since many job advertisements are now found in the form of recruitment pages on the internet, where space is not the limiting factor that it is on paper, the genre of the job advertisement has flourished in recent years. Advertisements and postings now typically incorporate a large amount of information about the kind of candidate who is being sought, as well as more details about the position and the company, supported by other discursive features intended to enhance the company's image in the eyes of potential candidates and the general public. The examples in what follows are from a corpus of job advertisements compiled from webpages such as www.gradjobs.co.uk. The following advertisement is fairly typical of what we find on webpages of this kind:

Location: UK
Salary: Competitive
Application Deadline: ASAP

At M, we offer exceptional careers to people with exceptional talent. Through our Sales Leadership Programme, our consultant company plays a pivotal role in the delivery of information to over 20,000 global household brands, with successful people moving into global management roles!

Every successful Managing Director and Area Director for M (we have over 50 offices globally with Sydney, Hong Kong, New York, to name a few) started on this programme within the last 4 years. With even more expansion across the US, Australia, Africa and Europe in 2012, this really is an exciting time to join the M Group. To continue our unprecedented growth, we need people with a natural flair for sales and entrepreneurship – who want to become inspirational leaders. In effect, we are looking for our next line of Managing Directors to train up from Sales Consultants. This is a great first step for anyone seeking a career in business and sales. The skills and market knowledge you will gain as a sales consultant and manager open up exciting opportunities throughout M Group. This is a proactive sales-based role. You will need to be driven by results and have excellent communication skills, a professional attitude and the ability to think around a problem. The ideal candidate will be motivated by working to targets, being pushed outside their comfort zone and developing their business through cold calling, client meetings and business pitches. You should have a good degree and a proven interest in current affairs. Previous commercial experience, ideally in a sales or management, will be an advantage but not by any means a pre-requisite.

In November 2011 we'll recruit for our UK offices for roles with a January 2012 start: Edinburgh, Manchester, London, Cardiff

If you would like to apply, then polish your application and send it to: recruitment.uk@meltwater.com.

In what follows, we shall look in more detail at some of the discursive features that are characteristic of advertisements of this kind.

Transactionality and impression management

Although expectations as to what a job advertisement should contain vary between sectors and between countries, we can say that there is a limited range of possible contents. At bottom, job advertisements are designed to attract suitable candidates so that companies can recruit the people they need to keep their business going and, if possible, improve it. They also serve a general public relations purpose, but if they fail to provide appropriate applicants, they will have failed to fulfil their main communicative aim. Job advertisements therefore have a significant transactional dimension, and their social purpose goes beyond merely providing information or enhancing the company's image.

To attract suitable candidates, the typical advertisement will contain a brief description of the post, perhaps with information about the location, salary and fringe benefits. This is often accompanied by a short profile of the company or department. However, an increasingly prominent position is now being given to information about the kind of candidate that the company is looking for, which in English-speaking countries generally goes beyond paper qualifications, such as 'graduate' or 'mechanical engineer', to include lists of skills or personal qualities. In the longer advertisements or postings found on the internet, this aspect tends to be more developed. For example, one large-scale content analysis of job advertisements on graduate recruitment databases (Bennett, 2002) showed that in the United Kingdom, in addition to sector-specific and job-specific qualifications, employers are now extremely likely to ask in their advertisements for personal qualities and abilities such as communication skills, initiative, creativity, the capacity to solve problems and leadership. This trend has raised some questions, because there seems to be a fuzzy line between what is stated because it is genuinely desirable for the post in question, and what is stated mainly for public relations purposes. In fact, it has sometimes been suggested that demands for particular skills appear in advertisements merely for the purpose of 'impression management', that is, engaging in positive self-description and expressing preferences that are currently in vogue (Baron and Byrne, 2000, pp. 68–71). However, there is objective evidence that this is not the main reason for including such descriptions. The results of the follow-up survey to the content analysis of job advertisements conducted by Bennett (2002) suggested that the skills requirements specified in the job advertisements were actually determined formally, logically and systematically by personnel experts. The respondents in the companies in question felt that skills such as communicative abilities or creativity were especially important because they would enable new recruits to make an immediate contribution to the company. The skills mentioned in advertisements appeared to have been carefully selected (e.g. by psychological profiling and careful analysis of the role to be fulfilled), and were not designed simply to enhance the image of the position or make it appear more challenging.

In fact, the particular emphasis often found on 'personal skills' in the latest generation of job advertisements reflects developments in the sociocultural environment: changes in employment patterns have led to a greater need for recruits with good personal skills. In London, for example, around half the workforce now works in 'higher level' occupations linked to the knowledge-based economy (LDP, 2000). It is a matter of some concern in the bibliography of management studies that graduates are often deficient in key skills, such as teamworking, decision-making and communication, at the time when they enter the labour market (LDP, 2000; Bennett, 2002). This is particularly important today, owing to increased competition for a dwindling number of posts. This situation, alongside our increasingly sophisticated understanding of psychological aspects of the workplace, has led to a general acceptance that 'qualitative considerations' should have an important role in the selection process (Gush, 1996, p. 6), which in turn finds expression in the long lists of desirable qualities often provided in advertisement. It is therefore clear that much of what a job advertisement contains is actually intended to be an accurate description of what the company requires, so that it can optimize its chances of finding the right candidates.

None the less, the language of such job advertisements and postings does have a dual function, since the immediate need for recruits is tempered by the need to pursue general public relations objectives. It is becoming increasingly rare to find factual postings like the following one, which simply states the requirements in basic terms. Perhaps the fact that the post is an internship implies a low degree of commitment on both sides:

1. We are seeking engineering interns for Summer 2012. Our internships are fully structured and competitively paid. You should be studying Engineering (ideally Chemical or Mechanical), be predicted a 2.1 or higher in your degree and be fluent in written and spoken English.

It is now more usual for the texts found in recruitment literature to provide a list of personal qualities like those given in the following example, which casts a flattering light on the candidates, and reflects positively on the company that employs such committed professionals:

2. There are certain qualities and competencies that are common among our most successful consultants: passion for their work, desire to build and share their expertise, determination to be the best, drive to exceed targets and commitment to deliver exceptional customer service.

Although these attributes may be the fruit of careful analysis, the promotional dimension of such texts is evident. The message being transmitted to the candidate (and any other reader) is that the company itself is providing 'exceptional customer service', and that by employing people who are determined to be the best, it is itself 'the best'. The company is thus 'roped in' to the description of its potential employees in highly positive terms. Certain aspects of the job advertisement can thus be seen to be promotional, in that they seem to do more than merely inform prospective candidates about the vacancy, alluding to positive attributes of the company or its activities and enhancing the corporate image. The intention is not specifically to promote the company's products, and so this type of discourse appears to belong within the general type of promotional activity aimed at generating a positive corporate image or 'brand image', which plays an increasingly important part in corporate communications today.

This type of double message is now found in most recruitment messages, and may sometimes take the form of a 'direct sell', as in the following example which praises the company directly, in the context of a search for 'talented people':

3. M Group is a global specialist in online media monitoring, social media monitoring and SEO. We're looking for talented people to help our

global expansion! M Group is recognised as one of Britain's Top
Employers as well as Europe's 25th fastest growing software company in
2010.

In other examples, the message about the company is transmitted more subtly, as
in the following case which highlights the nature of the 'environment' in which
the new employee will work:

4. Quick and independent learner, paying attention to detail

    Desire and flexibility to learn and grow in an ever-changing environment

    Ability to effectively multi-task in a fast-paced environment and must possess
    the ability to work independently and to be a self-starter.

    Team player willing to take on a wide variety of tasks.

Although this advertisement ostensibly focuses on the candidate ('quick',
'independent learner', 'desire to learn', 'ability to multi-task' and so on), the
company's own environment is presented in a positive light, as a stimulating
'fast-paced environment' where recruits will find themselves learning quickly
as they take on a variety of different tasks. The association of lexical items with
positive connotations, including nouns ('flexibility', 'self-starter', 'team player'),
verbs ('grow', 'multi-task'), adjectives ('fast-paced') and adverbs ('effectively',
'independently'), generates an enhanced view of the company and the life that
the raw recruit is likely to find there. We might note that what is meant by the
'ability to effectively multi-task in a fast-paced environment' could alternatively
be conveyed in terms of 'ability to cope with stress' or even 'you have to do several
jobs at the same time under extreme pressure'. In this sense, the wording of the
advertisement, though not strictly euphemistic, is carefully judged, sending the
message that those who do not like stress need not apply, but doing so in a way
that enhances the company's image and provides a mirror in which candidates
may see themselves in a positive light.

As we have seen, corporate advertisements and postings generally depict
both candidate and company in a positive light, endowing them with qualities
that form constellations around what we might term 'corporate values'. In
addition to sector-specific requirements (engineers should be 'analytical', sales
representatives are supposed to be 'persuasive' and so on), we should note the
ample presence of particular 'buzz words' or 'key words' in texts of this type.
The small sample used here abounds with lexical items that cluster around the
concept of dynamism (pro-active, self-starter, exciting, fast-paced, passion),
growth (thrive, grow, expansion), originality (outside the box, flexibility, bright,

creative, flair), challenge (problem-solving, pioneering, trouble-shooting, being pushed outside their comfort zone, incredibly demanding, fiercely competitive), specialness (unique, exceptional, transform, magic, inspirational), as well as ideas associated with the knowledge economy (know-how, intelligence, expertise) and with the culture of quality management (high degree of service, exceptional customer service, high calibre).

Earlier writers have commented on the prevalence of superlative words and action verbs in business language in general (Nelson, 2000). The repeated use of such words in advertisements from the corporate sector projects what we might call a value system, in which particular sets of similar words are used to construct a mental framework that establishes the parameters for what is 'good' (special, dynamic, challenging, intelligent, high-quality) and, by implication, for what might be 'bad' (ordinary, relaxed, easy, average, run-of-the-mill). Underlying this framework we can perceive an ethics of competitive elitism, a constellation of values that is quite unlike, say, the framework that might be found in advertisements for positions in the caring professions. Moreover, even though it might be imagined that many of the posts advertised also require a great deal of stamina, determination, and sheer hard work, or even, in more traditional terminology, constancy and fortitude, these less exciting values are underplayed, being referred to indirectly as the action of 'managing challenging workloads', or explained in competitive terms as a 'drive to exceed targets'.

This brings us back to the point made at the beginning of this section, that the research suggests that the qualities and skills mentioned in advertisements are a reflection of what is really required in the job. This may well be true. However, in the wording of the advertisements, these requirements are at once shaped by the corporate culture (which requires use of terms that sound competitive, dynamic, creative, etc.) and presented in an optimistic light (i.e. in terms of challenge rather than difficulty) to create a positive overall impression. Recruitment publications thus increasingly serve a double purpose: to attract suitable candidates, and to promote the company's image in a more general manner.

Building a relationship

One key feature of these texts is the way they attempt to set the parameters of an incipient relationship with potential future employees. We have seen that the choice of word is vital in establishing the tone of company-recruit communication. Another range of discursive resources comes under the heading of metadiscourse, specifically in the categories of engagement and self-mention

(Hyland, 1998, 2000). In this context, metadiscourse is used to construct the relationship between the company (writer) and the job seeker (reader), and between either or both of these and other entities (customers or clients, the business environment). It is most characteristically represented in English in the use of first-person pronouns and possessives to convey the writer's presence in the text. In academic texts, for example, first-person pronouns are often used to communicate a sense of competence and authority, particularly in combination with emphatics and epistemic verbs of judgement such as 'we genuinely believe' or 'I consider' (Hyland, 1998, 2004). In corporate documents, 'I' tends to be used sparingly, except in texts that are presented as personal statements, such as personal testimonies, or some kinds of CEO letter, while 'we' is common when representing the body corporate. Job advertisements, and material targeting employees in general, represent an interesting discursive development on this, because in addition to making abundant use of the first-personal plural in order to build a 'we' to 'you' relationship, they also contain considerable numbers of statements in the second person, which have the effect of projecting an idealized 'you' to 'us' position. In other words, by telling the reader what he or she is, or wants, they construct an 'ideal reader' (Bakhtin, 1981), or in cognitive terms, 'induce a reciprocal process of identification' on the part of potential recruits (Russell-Loretz, 1995). Such a direct second-person strategy is relatively unusual in published text, and is often associated with directive texts such as guides, manuals and instructions (Biber, 2006), as well as with promotional discourses (Afros and Schryer, 2009).

The job advertisements and postings examined here were rich in personal pronouns and possessives, providing ample examples of metadiscursive strategies. A straightforward example of a direct 'we' to 'you' employee-recruit relationship is exemplified in the following extract where the applicant 'you' is invited to explain how he/she proposes to contribute to 'us' as a specific company (Essar Group) and as an industry ('the oil industry'):

5. Your letter should explain why you want to work in the oil industry and what you can bring to the Essar Group.

The following example goes further in defining the 'you' to which the advertisement is addressed, discursively constructing an 'ideal' employee subject position in terms of motivation, competences and attitudes that fit with the corporate value system:

6. You will need to be driven by results and have excellent communication skills, a professional attitude and the ability to think around a problem.

The ideal candidate will be motivated by working to targets, being pushed outside their comfort zone and developing their business (. . .)

Relationships between the corporate 'we' and the aspiring applicant 'you' are also often implicit, as in the following example which flatters the reader with the implicature that he/she might be a 'talented' person of the type that 'we' need:

7. At M, we offer exceptional careers to people with exceptional talent

   We're looking for talented people to help our global expansion!

   Taking a different strategy, some companies position themselves alongside their future employees in a composite 'we' that is committed to a common cause – in this case, that of helping others.

8. That's why we want the very best people to join our business as consultants – experts (or aspiring experts) – who are driven to help individuals, companies and industries to flourish.

A similar type of relationship that we encounter frequently in these texts is the 'generous offer', which positions a talented and fortunate 'you' as a fellow pioneer working alongside 'us' at the cutting edge of technology:

9. It's not every day you get to explore new worlds. Unless of course you secure a place on our graduate programme, in which case that's exactly what you'll be doing over the course of 18 months. You'll join us at the frontiers of technology – the outer reaches of innovation. It's not easy, which is why we need graduates with a pioneering spirit to help us explore.

Finally, another relationship that is sometimes projected in advertisements and postings is that of the interested and welcoming 'us' who are open to 'you' as you are, with all your potential and attitude:

10. We are more interested in who you are and the attitude you bring to work every day.

Arguably, this open-ended approach cannot be sustained for long, because advertisements almost always have to provide some concrete information about the job, or a description of the target candidate which narrows down the range of roles on offer. This strategy would seem to be designed to maximize the number of applicants, giving the impression that their different qualities will be welcome in a flexible business environment through a 'you'-centred discourse.

In some contexts, companies have used videos to attract graduates to apply for positions with them. For budgetary reasons, these videos are less specific than advertisements, because it is unlikely that many companies would go to the lengths of making a video to fill one specific post. They therefore primarily have a public relations function, in that they convey positive ideas and feelings about the company to a wide audience, with the aim of attracting talented recruits across a range of fields. They basically set out to establish the company as an employer worthy of consideration by promising job seekers. In other words, since there is no one particular target post, these videos construct their claim along the lines that 'X is a good employer': the company presents a positive image in order to attract recruits.

However, this is far from simple, because as Russell-Loretz (1995) points out, many such generalized organizational self-representations seem to epitomize the inherent paradox of institutional identity management, in which the organization asserts a 'distinct identity', yet bases many of its claims on a fundamental 'sameness' to other institutions of its kind. She analyses a corporate recruitment video, drawing attention to a focal paradox that seems to underpin the entire rhetorical strategy: 'we are unique/we are the same'. This central paradox is reflected in four other paradoxes that form sub-themes: 'we are old/we are new', 'we are big/we are small', 'we are people/ we are technology' and 'we are our products/we are not our products'. The company is multifaceted, and so it can choose particular facets – which may be mutually contradictory, at least if we apply a strictly logical analysis – to project itself to a target audience. If the target audience consists of potential recruits, the function of the identity that is projected tends to reflect 'familiar values cherished by its audience' (Russell-Loretz, 1995, p. 171), in a way that is likely to maximize its appeal. The corporation highlights those very general values that it identifies as a part of itself, encouraging candidates to identify with it by offering them a role that enhances their own self-image, in either specific or general terms.

In short, the more general the advertisement, the more it has to rely on transmitting intangible aspects like 'corporate culture' and 'values', which may be intrinsically vague or even contradictory. Simply because of the production costs involved, companies have to formulate a general message that will attract a broad cross-section of the type of people they are looking for. The result is a kind of corporate 'self-portrait' (Russell-Loretz, 1995) which serves a general public relations purpose, but which cannot provide the specifications of a particular post.

3.2 Recruitment processes: The job interview

The job interview is crucially important, because it is the point at which two discourses meet, the point at which the personal language and experience of the candidate are held up to the discerning mirror of the company's expectations, the point at which it becomes apparent whether the candidate senses his or her potential role in the company and can adapt his or her discourses to those that are expected, or not. In the worst case, the candidate's communication skills will appear to be hopelessly inadequate to the roles that are offered. In the best case, the candidate will seem to 'fit' seamlessly into the subject positions on offer. In between the two, situations can be envisaged in which there is a partial match. To analyse these scenarios from the point of view of discourse, we need to have recourse to the tools of pragmatics. The job interview is a particularly interesting area as far as pragmatics is concerned, not only because interviewers appear to violate the normal rules of conversation by asking face-threatening questions, but also because interviewees often find it hard to fit into the discursive role that they are being offered. Particular aspects such as Grice's 'quantity maxim' (1989) and Leech's 'modesty maxim' (1983) prove particularly difficult for candidates to negotiate, particularly if there are added complications due to different cultural expectations (e.g. when a German or Spanish speaker of English as an L2 is interviewed by a native speaker from the United Kingdom or the United States).

According to Grice's theory of the cooperative principle in conversation, listeners and speakers must cooperate mutually, and accept and adapt to the purposes and rules of the interaction if communication is to be effective. In his pragmatic scheme, the maxims of 'quantity' and 'relevance' are closely related. Speakers are supposed to know how much to say ('quantity') in terms of how much is considered to be relevant. In job interviews, candidates often underperform by saying too little, or by saying things that are irrelevant. There is also often a problem with a third of Grice's maxims, that of 'manner', which among other things determines how clear and concrete one should be, or how much vagueness is admissible. In a corpus of transcriptions made from recordings of simulated job interviews carried out with LLM students at a Spanish university (Breeze, 2011b), we find examples such as the following:

11. Interviewer: *Tell me something about your qualifications for this position.*

    Candidate: I think I have different skills to be a lawyer.

12. Interviewer: *Tell me something about your qualifications for this position.*

Candidate: For this position you know what I got, you know, what I offer you it's em I got some experience, I've been working abroad and I got, you know, a good background, I studied law and you know I've studied tax law.

The first of these is inadequate in that it is very short, yet vague. The second is longer, more wordy, but also extremely vague. To give a good answer to this type of open question, the self-help manuals for surviving the job interview tell us that one should 'use specific examples, show how the skills, attributes or knowledge you've developed through school or work relate to the requirements you believe are necessary for the position' (Suntrust, 2012). These candidates' reluctance to use specific examples can perhaps be attributed to insecurity and a misunderstanding of the discursive role that they should be playing, which is probably exacerbated by cultural factors (Sancho Guinda, 2001; Birkner and Kern, 2004; Spencer-Oatey and Franklin, 2009). Candidates often say that 'the interviewer has my CV, so he/she already knows all about me', to excuse their own lack of communicativeness. In fact, even if the interviewer does already know what they have studied from their CV, he or she would expect the candidate to 'tell the story in his/her own words', in order to reveal something about his/her personality, preferences, life-history and so on. The candidate who fails to come up with a personal narrative risks seeming taciturn and uncommunicative on this 'easy' question.

A second area of difficulty is related to what Leech terms the 'modesty maxim'. Example 2 above also appears to indicate difficulty with the kind of 'ritual boasting' expected in job interviews in many cultures. The candidate appears quite diffident about his achievements, as though he were trying to play them down. Arguably, in normal conversation, particularly with a person who is perceived as 'senior' to oneself, it is not usual in many cultures to indulge in lengthy self-praise. However, to succeed in the job interview one has to be able to sing one's own praises in an appropriate manner. The art of the successful job interview is to know how to show one's achievements in a positive light without seeming boastful and arrogant. The kind of answer regarded as appropriate in the context of the job interview is illustrated by example 3, which is both relevant and sufficient, and shows a becoming degree of modesty by placing the stress on 'preparing' and 'learning'. It should be noted that despite using superlatives, the candidate situates him/herself relatively humbly as a person who has learnt from experience, and that he/she locates the hoped-for high achievements in the future, as an aspiration.

13. Candidate: My background to date has been centred around preparing myself to become the very best financial consultant I can become. Let me tell you specifically how I've prepared myself. I am an undergraduate student in finance and accounting at X University. My work experience has been in the retail trade, where I learnt a lot about working with other people and keeping to deadlines. That really taught me a lot!

One final point that is worth considering about job interview discourse is the issue of showing that one belongs to the relevant discourse community. Lipovsky (2010) conducted a study of job interviews and reached the conclusion that more successful candidates tend to be better at signalling membership of the professional community through language. Thus a law or engineering student who talks like an 'insider' within the profession will tend to be regarded as a more suitable candidate than one who positions him/herself as a 'student' or 'outsider'. Ways in which candidates can signal membership of the professional discourse community include using specialized terminology, talking 'as a lawyer' or 'as an engineer', rather than 'as a student', and showing adherence to what are perceived to be the key professional values. Even the notorious 'tricky' questions like 'tell me about your greatest strengths and weaknesses' are best negotiated within this perspective: thus your main 'weakness' will be accepted if it is one that is fairly typical in your profession. For example, an engineer who confesses to being 'a bit nerdy' is likely to be met with a certain degree of understanding, rather than condemnation (Lipovsky, 2010).

3.3 Induction seminars and guides for new employees

Socialization through discourse

Of course, the story does not end when the company decides who to hire. New employees have to acquire new skills, develop their existing knowledge and may receive further training of a formal or less formal nature. They have to get to know a new set of people, develop new contacts, learn how to work as part of the particular team that they will belong to. They have to learn how their new company functions, become familiar with the accepted ways of thinking and working. In some way, they will have to adapt their previous ways of thinking and working to the 'corporate culture' of their new firm. As we have seen, this process has been likened to a process of socialization, in which people learn how they are expected to behave in their new environment, at the same time as they learn how to do the things they are expected to do. Although many companies provide in-house training to cover some of the formal aspects of what needs to be learnt, most of what the new recruits learn is acquired in the workplace. This usually takes place through a form of 'apprenticeship', in which trainees or new workers start by taking on a peripheral role in the professional activity of the company, and gradually assume a more central role, until they come to participate fully in that community of practice (Lave and Wenger, 1999). This learning process will continue through the employees' time with the company, as they attend training and updating sessions, learn about changes in company policy, language and image, keep abreast of product developments and so on (Jablin, 1987). As they are promoted through the company hierarchy, they may undergo further forms of situated learning, in which they develop managerial or consultancy skills as they take on senior roles. Such changes in position require the employee to adapt once more to the new environment and develop new technical and organization skills, different ways of communicating and so on.

The need for conscious management of the 'induction process' for new employees has been a matter of concern to management theorists for a considerable time. Fifty years ago, Schein expressed concern at the 'considerable waste of human resources' (1964, p. 68) that occurs when graduates do not adapt to the realities of company life, and advocates 'the giving of immediate responsibility to the college graduate *but under a supervisor who is sensitive to the new man's* (sic) *needs and capacities*' (1964, p. 72). This supervisor should engage the trainee in 'a secure father or older brother relationship. This calls for a supervisor who is more competent than the new man but who is anxious to teach because he is secure in his own knowledge' (1964, p. 76). Since that time, considerable attention has been paid to the induction of new employees, both among management theorists and in social psychology (Zahrly and Tosi, 1989). The need for an organized 'induction process' for new employees is now widely recognized, and the programmes that exist are much more extensive and complex than 50 years ago. Most medium-sized and large companies in the Western world have established formal procedures (courses, mentoring, evaluation and self-evaluation schemes) that facilitate the process by which new recruits adapt to the company. It is important to emphasize that the process, at least in theory, is precisely this: the idea is that the people who are hired should adapt to the company, and not the company to them. An intermediate process of mutual integration is not envisaged. A range of different theoretical frameworks have been applied to understand this process, from study of personality traits or prior learning experience, to work role orientation and the ability to cope with transitions. However, it is generally agreed that the early stages of anyone's life in a new company amount to a process of socialization, in which the employee has to accommodate to his/her surroundings.

The role of language in this ongoing socialization process can hardly be underestimated, yet the discourses of employee induction and communicative actions designed to foster company loyalty and encourage employees to 'buy in' to the corporate image have received relatively little attention from analysts. In early examples, public relations experts such as Cheney (1983) emphasize that language has an important role in this process, yet are unspecific about how this actually occurs. Experts in organizational communication like Jablin (1987) come close to the actual realities of language, to make claims along similar lines. In Jablin's view, a new employee's assimilation period is a crucial time in which he or she learns his/her role and finds out what is considered 'normal' or 'appropriate' in terms of thought and behaviour. An employee who fails to respond positively to the signals that are being sent as to how he/she should behave in his/her new environment is likely to have a more difficult time in the company (Jablin, 1987, p. 695).

The discursive means used to support employee induction are varied. Leaving aside personal conversations with mentors, or meetings with superiors, which fall better into the scope of 'workplace discourse', we can find many areas in which the company uses discourse in order to send particular message to its employees and, particularly, to those who have just started work. Many companies now provide face-to-face initial training or briefing sessions in the form of 'induction' or 'orientation' seminars or weekends. Videos are very commonly used, particularly when recruitment takes place throughout the year, or in different places. Moreover, large companies now often have employee websites in which they provide useful information, but also communicate more diffuse ideas such as 'company values', and display testimonies from contented employees. These companies have an ongoing company–employee communication strategy designed to create and maintain the type of relationship that the company hopes to encourage.

Managing the relationship

The official messages from management to recruits may be published or presented in the form of the 'new employee handbook' or orientation sessions. Given the technological changes of the last 20 years, much material of this nature is now presented in internet/video format. In what follows, I shall examine the discourses of the 'employee websites' and 'employee induction videos' of some major corporations.

To see how this works, let us look at corporate employee websites, induction brochures and videos from large multinational companies. It is possible to track the discursive means through which employees are socialized into the company.

The discourse of induction material is usually framed in terms of 'helpfulness' to the new recruit. It is felt to be important in corporate 'team-building' that the company should express concern for the participants (McKinney, 1995, p. 182). This promotes positive identification with the corporate ethos, and encourages the employees to make an active contribution. Thus one corporate website promises:

14. This program is designed to share valuable information about Unilever, help you navigate through the first critical weeks and provide an overview of commonly used resources.

A high degree of pseudo-personalization is achieved through use of second-person pronouns:

15. Getting to know people and establishing close working relationships is important to help you settle in. During the first few months, you'll meet colleagues from your immediate area and from different functions across the business.

Moreover, in addition to offering an individualized approach to training and career development, the firm promises to recognize its employees' achievements. This is important, because people feel more satisfied if they think they are working to the common good, and their motivation usually increases still further if they believe that their efforts will be rewarded both materially and in terms of recognition and respect (McKinney, 1995). Thus one company explains the framework within which employees 'achieve their aims':

16. Once you're familiar with the company and your role, the next step is to discuss and agree a personal development plan. This will identify your learning requirements as well as the support you'll need to achieve your aims. (. . .) As part of your development plan, you'll be given personal targets and team goals and a time-frame within which to achieve them. Over regular meetings with your manager, you'll evaluate your progress and address any issues.

At the same time, the company promotes itself, while flattering and motivating its employees:

17. We have gained our reputation as one of the world's most admired employers by providing an environment where individuals can achieve their goals, both professionally and personally. We are aware that to attract and retain the best people, we must offer them more. More ways to take advantage of the opportunities, more room to succeed and grow, and more directions in which to pursue their careers.

Such discourses establish the company as an admirable entity which 'provides' an excellent environment for its employees, offering them 'more' than others might. Thus between the promotional discourses used about the company ('most admired') and the flattering descriptions of the employees ('best people'), a kind of discursive win-win agreement is set up, in which both parties are contructed as benefiting. It is a common theme in these discourses that 'we' the company are constructed as 'investing in', 'helping' or 'supporting' 'you', the employee. Moreover, we may note that the pact is typically projected in terms of 'we' and 'you', generating a discursive 'closeness' which tends to engage the reader. The affective dimension of this relationship is reinforced in declarations of the following kind, which project a relationship in which both 'we' and 'you' contribute to a common project:

18. We hope you are as excited as we are about our future and the opportunities that lie within Unilever to create the future you want. We invite you to come and explore what a career at Unilever will mean for you!

Other characteristic features of such employee induction material include the emphasis on specific 'values' that are supposed to characterize the company and its ethos (related, of course, to its 'brand'). Thus Unilever, in this case, stresses 'freedom' and 'empowerment', and ostensibly promises scope for the employee's own choices and initiatives.

19. Our success depends on innovation, so we do everything we can to ensure that enterprising people have the freedom to act. We give them all the support and encouragement they need. At the same time, we empower them to make tough decisions, implement new ideas and use their initiative.

Other companies state that they recognize the importance of 'family', or of 'serving the community'. This is thought to generate resonance between the employees' own values and those apparently held by the company, which has a positive effect on employees' attitude to their firm. In fact, this is a further aspect of the 'epideictic' rhetoric discussed elsewhere (see Aristotle, 1991), which extols values that are (supposedly) held in common between speaker and hearer. In such rhetoric, 'the speaker tries to establish a sense of communion centered around particular values recognized by the audience' (Perelman and Olbrechts-Tyteca, 1969, p. 50), with a view to strengthening the audience's beliefs and loyalties, perhaps to prepare the way for a future exercise in persuasion or call to action, or perhaps merely to reinforce social cohesion. Although epideictic rhetoric may sometimes be used to spur the hearer on to action, in this case, the function is mainly that of building up premises that cement employees' loyalty to the firm, and reassuring them in aspects of their own self-image that the company deems appropriate (McKinney, 1995).

Interestingly, in the discursive construction of the relationship between large corporations and their employees today, it is increasingly common to see that standard terms such as 'salary' and 'promotion' are being replaced by other words. Thus 'salary' is often described in terms of 'rewards' and 'compensation packages', or as part of an 'incentive programme'. The use of 'reward' is particularly interesting, since its connotations would appear to give it a greater appeal than the prosaic term 'salary', and its meaning would seem to imply that the employee had deserved something special, rather than merely collected his or her pay cheque. In fact, the highly developed 'reward systems' sometimes encountered, with multiple salary grades and bonuses linked to the acquisition of particular competences, are a product of recent thinking on employee motivation based on studies of organizational behaviour (Edwards, 2005). These incentives combine an element of control with an element of motivation, thus carefully managing the relationship with employees.

None the less, it should be noted that underpinning the discourses of 'responsibility' and 'initiative', there is a hint of control. Here, people are allowed freedom, but it is expected that they will make a contribution to the company's aims. If you perform well within this framework, you will do well. If your aim is just to be promoted, you are not welcome. The company will reward those who have the right 'attitude'.

20. We believe that individuals should drive their own careers and that life at work should be a continuous learning journey. Seizing the opportunity to make a difference is more important than simply progressing up the ladder. People with this attitude and approach will find Unilever challenging, inspiring and highly rewarding.

As we have seen, the website for new employees continues the relationship between company and employee that is first generated through the discourses of the job advertisement. This relationship is also fostered through a variety of other means, which we shall now examine.

Testimonies

One particular feature of company recruitment websites is the testimony, which gives the company a 'human face' for potential recruits to relate to. Such testimonies are provided in the form of printed text or webpages, or increasingly, on video embedded in the company website. Most of them follow a similar pattern, which can be analysed as a genre using the standard tools of genre analysis (Bhatia, 2004).

First of all, what do these testimonies contain, and how are they structured? The main features of these first-person accounts of life within the company are a brief description of day-to-day activities; a positive evaluation of in-house training schemes for new employees; a description of a project that the writer has completed for the company; and an expression of satisfaction and personal fulfilment.

The discursive features of these testimonies vary, but they tend to transmit very much the same value system as the advertisements or postings, using the same rather formal register, but in the first-person singular. The message is transmitted in a slightly more personal way, although the 'voice' tends to be formal and lacks intimacy, despite the use of 'I':

21. I have progressed from the challenging and rewarding Customer Project Manager role and moved into the field of marketing. I find this an exciting area of the business that is giving me visibility and knowledge of a key facet of the global organization.

Thus the company is positioned as showering benefits on the recruit, who is being shaped in order to realize his/her potential. This process of inculturation or socialization into the company is sometimes described:

22. And then there are the courses, each designed to develop graduates like me into future leaders. These have been hugely beneficial, especially the 'human' skills courses. It's proof of Ericsson's commitment to a culture of high performance, transparency and respect for its people.

There is often a heavy emphasis on the company's achievements, sometimes in terms of important numbers, such as in this testimony from the recruitment website of J. Sainsbury plc:

23. I'm serving in excess of 40,000 customers per week, in a business that's turning over in excess of 50 million pounds per annum.

Other videos of this kind are ostensibly intended purely for recruitment purposes, such as the 'Day in a life' video made by the London law firm Allen and Overy, which focuses on a graduate applicant and explains the selection process. Surprisingly, the young interviewee declares that all the people he met there are friendly and put him at ease.

24. I chose A and O because it's a great mix. International cutting edge work, with a genuinely friendly atmosphere.

A different perspective comes from the US company, Suncor Energy. This employee emphasizes his need for 'challenge' and 'growth'.

25. They'd been very happy with what I provided them during my initial eight months and they were hoping I'd choose to stay on with them – that made me feel very valuable. (. . .) I am excited. I think there will be a lot of opportunity here. (. . .) There's lots of room for me to grow.

However, in both cases it is clear that the company is highlighting certain key values, offering models of the kind of employee it considers appropriate who embody these qualities.

If we analyse the discursive position taken up by the givers of such testimonies, we find that they are constructed as the humble and grateful recipients of the company's help, perfectly at ease with the notion that they are being shaped into useful members of the company, and satisfied with the rewards that they have been promised. Moreover, they subscribe eagerly to the company's value system, praising its 'culture' in glowing terms. In short, the employees who give these testimonies do not usually shine out as individuals, but rather epitomize the 'company values' which they have made their own. In them, the socialization process appears to have been accomplished to optimum effect.

Failing to manage the relationship

To see these productions in perspective, it is useful to look at a contrasting example in which a video made for employees proved to be counterproductive.

One early study that addresses the area of employer–employee communication through video is that by McKinney (1995). He presents a critical analysis of what he calls an 'indoctrination video', that is, an induction video, intended for the employees of a midwestern pharmaceutical company, made in the mid-1990s. In his appraisal of the video, McKinney analyses a number of ways in which it fails to achieve the desired effect. These are worth considering, since they offer many points of contrast with the type of discourse used in the examples quoted above.

The first half of the video centres mainly on the founder of the company's own rags-to-riches story, and on the rapid expansion of the company in terms of buildings and physical locations. In this lengthy section, the company founder himself is the only protagonist. After this, some executive managers appear, and make various comments on the remarkably rapid growth of the company, or the high quality of the buildings and equipment. The main message of such a video seems to be that the most valued resources at Midwest Pharmaceutical are its buildings. 'For example, when showing scenes within the various buildings, employees are highlighted only in relationship to a particular machine which they appear to be serving: in most instances, employees, who usually appear in masks and gloves, are shown feeding chemical materials into a machine or packaging products' (McKinney, 1995, p. 182). The final section of the video focuses on products, with long lists of drugs announced against a background of masked lab technicians bottling drugs with gloved hands. As McKinney observes, in this presentation 'it is not the dedicated workers that make Midwest Pharmaceutical memorable, but rather it is the organization's hero and his wonderful buildings, marvellous equipment and innovative products that are worthy of praise (. . .) the hardworking individuals who staff the buildings, skilled workers who operate the machines, and great minds who develop the products are completely ignored' (1995, p. 183). Oddly enough, the video concludes with a panegyric of praise to the 'spirit of Midwestern', and exhorts employees to 'work together as a team' and say to themselves 'I work for the best company in the world. I'm a Midwest Pharmaceutical associate' (1995, p. 184). The last few minutes thus offer a complete contrast to the preceding 30 minutes, as though the producer has had a sudden realization of what the video might be for.

In his analysis of this curious production, McKinney outlines what he (as an expert in corporate 'indoctrination') feels to be the major problems. In a fundamental sense, it ignores, and thereby delegitimates, the role of the individual in the organization (1995, p. 189). In fact, the video devotes considerable efforts to praising the buildings and equipment, but the employees only appear as shadowy figures operating machinery. Importantly, the only person who is extolled is the founder, alone in charge of his vast empire, which is hardly conducive to promoting fellow-feeling or encouraging commitment among the staff.

It would be unusual today to find an inhouse induction video of the kind described by McKinney, at least in the English-speaking world. If we take a look at more recent websites and videos intended for employees, we can observe that the industry has moved on. The positive strategies alluded to above by McKinney tend to be used to positive effect, and there is a prevalence of positive strategies intended to persuade the employee to 'buy in' to the corporate culture. It is rare for the latest generation of employee induction videos and websites to fall into the trap of projecting an image of the company in which the role of employees is belittled and delegitimated. Rather, the tendency is to weave discourses in which employees are welcomed and their contributions are valued, but in which they are also nudged in the direction of what will be most beneficial for the company. Such discourses function ideologically to produce, maintain and reproduce the company culture and the power structures that underpin it.

Creating and maintaining a community

Once employees are fully fledged members of the company, other discursive devices exist to shape and consolidate the developing relationship and foster loyalty to the firm. Inhouse journals also contribute to what is termed as 'community building', transmitting positive stories of achievement, providing the information that is thought to be opportune, inculcating key ideas, generating a sense of belonging to an important and attractive entity and encouraging employees to identify with the 'corporate spirit'. In other words, a vast discursive web is woven that not only persuades employees of the merits of the company, but also positions employees within the system, and convinces them of the benefits of contributing to the good of the company in their allotted position. In their multiple persuasive and coercive functions, the inhouse discourses of the company bear a strong similarity to political discourse.

Cheney (1983) investigated the identification strategies in employee newsletters, and concluded that four particular strategies predominated: 1. use of common ground, emphasizing shared interests between employees and their employer; 2. identification by antithesis, that is, identification in common cause against a common enemy; 3. implicit identification, a much looser concept generated through use of the pronoun 'we'; and 4. unifying symbols, including logos and other devices intended to build identification with the organization, its values and actions. Since that time, inhouse journals, newsletters and webs have become the norm in all large companies, and have made increasingly creative use of different media to raise employee morale and encourage them to adopt corporate values.

If we stand back from all these tendencies and try to make out a general pattern, we will probably notice a growing desire to manage the employee–employer relationship, to send discursive messages that invoke a positive relationship and yet also manipulate or even control. These trends have not escaped the attention of observers in other fields. One interesting angle of the issue of employee induction is to be found in connection with the concepts of 'employee branding' and 'employer branding'. Managers, PR specialists and human resources experts have become increasingly interested in the question as to the interaction between the company brand and the company's present or future employees. 'Employee branding' focuses broadly on ensuring that employees reflect or embody company values or the company image. 'Employer branding' refers to the way that the company itself is seen by its employees.

The latest tendencies in human resources management show the all-pervasive effects of branding, and states that employer and employee branding are 'an important activity that a modern HR department should focus on for the organization to be competitive' (Edwards, 2005, p. 266). In this new world of employer and employee branding, the socialization process has taken on increasing importance. The recruitment experience is now branded from the very beginning, from the (carefully branded) advertisement, to the application and induction packs, induction courses and so on. In the training provided for new staff, there is an increasing emphasis on aspects of branding, in addition to aspects of the job itself. Recruits are told what attributes are associated with their brand, and how it differs from that of the competitors. Product launches are organized in such a way that employees are not only informed about the product, they are 'sold' the product and its merits.

One factor that underlies the movement towards employer branding is that job applicants are widely believed to have an interest in applying for positions with companies whose values they admire or share, particularly companies with a strong corporate social responsibility record. Some studies suggest that young recruits are more likely to work hard for a company if they believe in what that company is trying to do, that is, if they subscribe to its mission (Ellsworth, 2002; Dentchev, 2004). Employer branding activities centre on how the company is seen by actual or potential employees, with a view to recruiting and maintaining talented staff. The organization is the branded entity, and the employees are the recipients of the message. Employer branding is also broadly conceived of as including aspects such as the management style within the company, and promotion of loyalty to the firm throughout the employee's career. It embraces 'the package of financial, economic and psychological benefits provided by employment and identified with the employing company' (Ambler and Barrow, 1996, p. 187).

Employee branding is rather different, since it covers the way employees behave in relation to the company's brand values: ideally, customers should have a consistent 'branded' experience through all their dealings with the organization. Companies have long been interested in promoting certain attitudes or types of behaviour among their staff. This can be seen to have an important role, particularly in view of the increasing importance given to branding and the management of corporate identity in order to compete more effectively in the market place. Employee branding has sometimes been seen as an extension of the management of corporate culture. The norms, values and goals of the organization are made explicit, and are presented as an ideal that all staff should identify with in their work behaviour. It thus contains elements of control, since we can imagine that some employee behaviours or ideals would be rejected and others promoted. As Edwards (2005, p. 271) puts it, 'with employee branding, the employee is part of the brand, they are exemplars of the brand, they have been branded'.

It is evident that there is some overlap between the two types of employee-related branding. Edwards defines the relationship as follows: 'A focus on organizational values is an inherent part of employer and employee branding activities' (2005, p. 268). Thus the 'values' that attach to the brand and which are embodied by the employees should mesh with the 'values' that should be reflected in company practices affecting those employees. This broad picture has also been linked with the growing interest in corporate social responsibility, which also reflects and defines the brand both internally and externally. The two types of branding are supposed to feed positively into each other, since both are shaped by the same values, and both ultimately general a positive brand image, the internal image reinforcing the external one, and vice versa.

What is particularly striking here is not the general idea, but the increasing sophistication with which companies now seek to put these ideas into practice. It has been suggested that the human resources department of the company should work closely with the marketing department to manage the firm's corporate identity and brand. In the past, public relations dealt mainly with the outside world, with customers and other external agents. There is now an increasing emphasis on internal public relations, and on how to get employees to identify with the company to the extent that they are willing to 'go the extra mile' on the organization's behalf (Rousseau, 1998, p. 218). In this, it appears to be important for the company to be understood as having a strong identity, with strong, recognizable values (Ashforth and Mael, 1989; Ashforth and Saks, 1996). As a result, experts believe there will be 'a series of positive linkages between an employer brand, a strong organizational identity and employees that link some aspect of their identity to the organization' (Edwards, 2005, p. 270). We have seen that employee websites and induction material go some way towards pursuing this goal.

The type of case found in the professional bibliography of human resources management is epitomized by the following example. The US low-cost airline Southwest Airlines chose 'freedom' as the key to its corporate brand, with the tagline 'At Southwest freedom begins with me'. This theme was used to shape the material (posters, leaflets, webpages) given to employees, who were told that their employment experience was structured according to eight freedoms, such as 'freedom to learn and grow', 'freedom to make a positive difference' and so on. Positive examples were provided, such as that of a Southwest reservations agent who took the initiative to meet an elderly patient himself and take her to the hospital where she was to undergo treatment (Sartain, 2003, p. 3). Here, not only is discourse used to shape the way employees understand their role, but 'role models' are provided to make the message even more explicit.

Further examples show how companies make use of multimodal discourse strategies to socialize their employees into appropriate working habits and bring them into line with the brand image. In many cases, employees are required to represent the brand physically through their appearance, by wearing company ties or uniforms. Sometimes this approach extends further, into aspects of employee behaviour which is conceptualized not only as 'appropriate' or 'professional', but as an 'embodiment' of the brand. One prominent campaign along these lines was carried out by Orange, which encouraged its workers to take in the brand ethos through use of symbolic means. A large and colourful 'orange wheel' was used in an employee consciousness-raising campaign to represent various aspects of behaviour, such as 'openness' and 'listening loudly', which employees were supposed to be learning.

We have seen that employers frequently emphasize corporate 'values' and brand-associated qualities throughout their dealings with employees. There is some discrepancy as to whether such attempts at branding are wholly successful, or, as the specialists put it, 'whether the attempted socialization fundamental to internal branding activities has a substantive effect on employee values' (Edwards, 2005, p. 277). There is some evidence suggesting that this is the case. For example, Ashforth and Saks (1996) looked at the way graduate recruits understood the companies for which they were working, and found that those working at companies with organized socialization tactics had a stronger sense of what the company was supposed to stand for. However, it is also fairly obvious that if the employee's values are at variance from the company's values at the outset, the socialization process will be uphill work. If an employee's attitudes and expectations 'fit' what the company has to offer, he or she will find it easier to adapt (Kraimer, 1997).

Interestingly, the bibliography on this subject rarely considers the ethical dimensions of employee branding. As Edwards points out (2005, p. 280), 'no consideration seems to be given to what this actually might mean to the individual who is being branded'. He relates this issue to the question of emotional labour, discussed by Hochschild (1983), who analyses situations in which the employee's feelings are commercialized or used to present a particular image, perhaps at a cost to the employee. He calls this a transmutation of the emotional system, in which feelings fall prey to 'social engineering' (1983, p. 19). Employee values, in this system, are a commodity which the organization can use to obtain high commitment and good performance (Bunting, 2004) – which, of course, benefit the company by ensuring greater customer satisfaction. In Edwards's view (2005, p. 282), 'it could be argued that the very nature of employee branding emasculates employees, it highlights the idea that they are a resource to be moulded and it is very unlikely that they would be treated as legitimate stakeholders'. Moreover, this recent trend appears to lead companies back into a position where they can be accused of paternalism, that is, by telling employees what to think and attempting a form of 'moral conversion', the company is acting as though they had diminished responsibility and inferior values and beliefs (Flanders, 1970). However, it should be noted that this is not a return to an earlier model of paternalism, but rather to a form of 'sophisticated paternalism' in which employees are disempowered, but through manipulation rather than authoritarianism (Warren, 1999, p. 53). Of course, as Edwards points out (2005, p. 283), employees are in some sense free to choose whether or not they subscribe to company values. But the stronger the organizational culture, the harder it will be to resist. On the one hand, close identification with the company brand may be good, because employees might be happiest in a company whose values they share. On the other hand, if the company tries to coerce its employees into changing their deeply held values, the attempt is likely to be doomed to failure, and the outcome is unlikely to be positive. What is particularly alarming about this scenario is that if such 'corporate branding' activities become widespread to the extent that they are wholly embedded in business practice, then management of employees' values and beliefs, of their 'inner selves', may well be accepted as the social norm and will not be questioned from an ethical point of view.

3.4 Constructing employees

As management analysts have documented, the last 30 years have seen a shift in the way that the relationships between managers and employees are understood in the Western world, with a move away from what might be termed straightforward authoritarianism towards a more participative framework in which the employee is expected to buy into the corporate culture and contribute more actively to the company's well-being. In the words of Thompson and van den Broek (2010, p. 4):

> Employers, in their search for competitive advantage through consistent service quality, are changing the balance of controls from the direct towards the unobtrusive: seeking to incorporate employees' tacit, inter-personal, affective skills and a *degree* of self-direction compatible with maintaining overall managerial prerogative.

This tendency is allied to contemporary changes in the labour market, in which there has been a shift away from manufacturing to the tertiary sector and knowledge-intensive work, which in itself has been said to 'generate a tendency towards info-normative controls' (Frenkel et al., 1995, p. 786). This fits with the increasing importance of 'soft' human resource management strategies, in which the management seeks to shape employees' identity, colonize their subjectivity and transform their values. Although it has been well documented that this bid to 'win hearts and minds' often goes hand in hand with increased surveillance, in the form of electronic observation or the bureaucratic paraphernalia of quality control, which even seeks to monitor qualitative dimensions of worker performance (Cooke, 2006), there is considerable evidence that companies have indeed increased the efforts they make to 'bring the workers on board' and persuade them that the companies' actions are not just expedient or useful for the common good, but also essentially right and worthy in themselves (Thompson and van den Broek, 2010, p. 5).

The extent to which this strategy is successful might be questioned (Kunda and Ailon-Souday, 2006), particularly against the current background of sectors in crisis and corporate restructuring. In fact, one could even ask whether such a strategy is even necessary, since employees will probably meet targets if it is in their interest to do so, whether or not they share the company ethos. None the less, there is a persistent belief in management circles, at least in the Western world, that it is worthwhile to invest in attempts to win employees' hearts and minds, in addition to exerting control and offering material incentives. This appears to be here to stay, as part of a hybrid organizational system which combines 'authoritarian bureaucracy with an ostensible commitment to enterprise and empowerment' (Cooke, 2006, p. 240). It is striking that the public and private sectors, which traditionally offered quite different paradigms within which one could live out one's working life, now appear to be converging, so that, for example, public sector employees are subject to 'productivity' reviews, while company workers have to submit to the bureaucracy of quality management. The truth is probably that there is an increasing flow of ideas and practices between the two sectors. In many countries, private companies and public institutions alike obtain funding from state or European institutions. An increasingly complex business panorama provides ample evidence of mergers, spin-offs, subcontracting, privatizations and public acquisitions. The major division that was once made between the two sectors is no longer valid, against the background of hybridization and the blurring of differences. It is therefore hardly surprising that hybrid systems of communication and control should also be arising, and that these should be oriented towards engineering compliance and consensus, with an emphasis on types of 'ideological' or 'normative' discipline that underpin the system.

Daskalaki (2000) has shown how companies see employees as increasingly important in the company's quest for excellence. Companies are seeking new forms of 'hegemonic' interaction based on the reproduction and manipulation of cultural events (du Gay, 1996). In this context, the rhetoric of 'team work', 'empowerment' and 'self-actualization' are used to create and promote corporate cultures that socialize workers into work tasks and habits, and that aim to change their inner perceptions, values and identity. Advertisements and interviews offer carefully moulded 'subject positions' to recruits. Induction processes are used to operationalize the business culture and to 'delineate, normalize and instrumentalize the conduct of persons' in order to achieve the ends that are perceived to be desirable (du Gay, 1996, p. 61). If employees have internalized company or sectorial values, this will tend to make it easier for corporations to operate in general, and will certainly help to harmonize employment relations and minimize disputes. In this chapter, we have traced the material realization of this process in the discourse of large Western corporations, from the recruit's first contact with the company through the job advertisement, through the interview, induction and training, to full participation in the corporation community. Further studies are needed to explore the extent to which these patterns resemble or contrast with practices elsewhere in the world.

4

Communicating with Investors

This chapter will look at company communication with investors, centring on the classic vehicle for this: the Annual Report for shareholders. Beginning with an exploration of how these documents meet the requirement to supply reliable information, we shall then examine the more rhetorical aspects of shareholder literature, including the kind of warmly optimistic discussion of the company's past performance and future prospects found in documents like the letter to shareholders. Special attention will be focused on such letters in sectors that have been the object of negative publicity. Although other documents, such as annual reviews and corporate social responsibility reports, are also at least partly directed towards shareholders, these potentially have a much wider readership, since they form part of the company's general public relations activity that addresses the public at large, including customers, interest groups and the media. For this reason, these will not be discussed here, but will be handled in detail in Chapter 6.

4.1 Annual Reports

The Annual Report is generally understood to be 'the principal document used by most public companies to disclose corporate information to their shareholders' (Securities and Exchange Commission, 2002). In most jurisdictions, the legal framework of the public limited company stipulates that companies must publish an Annual Report containing, at least, the basic information about the company and its directors, and the audited accounts. This must usually be sent to all shareholders, or at least made available to them in some format. In most countries, considerably more information must be made available in the Report.

For example, in the United Kingdom, the Companies Act of 2006 states that public limited companies that are listed on the London Stock Exchange must publish a report and accounts that include: 1. main trends and factors that may affect the future development, performance and position of the business; 2. information on environmental matters, employees and social issues; and 3. information on contractual and other arrangements essential to the company's business (Companies Act, 2006).

The main reason for the existence of the Annual Report is therefore the legal requirement to inform shareholders about the company's financial performance, so that they can learn at first hand how the company is performing, what new investments or commitments it has made, whether it has made a profit or a loss in each of its activities and so on. In short, its purpose to give the investors who have a stake in its capital the relevant information about how the company is doing, so that they can take informed decisions as to whether to keep or sell their investment in that company, and make the appropriate choice if they are required to vote at the Annual General Meeting.

None the less, from the company's point of view, the existence of a document that has to be made available to all shareholders – and to a wider public interested in the company's activities – provides an excellent opportunity for corporate communication in a wider sense. It forms part of what is known as 'financial public relations', a range of activities designed to communicate with stockbrokers, financial analysts, institutional investors and private investors, financial journalists and the financial press in general (Malavasi, 2010). In fact, Annual Reports are increasingly being viewed as promotional documents which are intended to spread a positive image of the company and its products, in addition to providing reliable information about its performance (Dolphin, 2004; Tosun, 2004; Malavasi, 2006a, 2006b). They are one medium through which a positive institutional identity and image can be engineered for a company, in the sense that positive attributes are emphasized, relationships with investors and other stakeholders are strengthened and confidence in the management team is enhanced.

Annual Reports thus have a close affinity to other types of corporate communication that are intended to establish and maintain long-term relations with important audiences, particularly with those that can help the company to further its aims (Dolphin, 2004, p. 27). Their audience consists first of shareholders and potential investors, but secondarily also of financial experts in general, employees or creditors who have a stake in the company, the media, government agencies and society at large. We may add that these different groups may also have varied levels of financial literacy and diverse social concerns. In view of this situation, the goals of the Annual Report overlap, at least partially, with those of corporate communication in general, which are to forge a strong corporate culture and a coherent corporate identity, with a view to propagating a positive corporate image to many different audiences. In the words of Preston, Wright and Young (1996), the Annual Report is 'the calling card of a company': companies use it to communicate their financial position and performance to their shareholders and potential investors, and to the world at large.

The Annual Report has not always had these functions. It came into being as a strictly informative document intended to provide hard data for people who had invested in it. Diachronic studies covering different periods of time (1965–88; Lee, 1994, 1970–90; Bartlett and Jones, 1997, 1965–2004; Beattie et al., 2008) have provided valuable insights into the evolution of the Annual Report. In a recent study, Ditlevsen (2012) traced the development of the Annual Report in one company, the Danish food company Danisco since 1935. She found that the reports she studied had become more voluminous over the years, with a large increase in the number of pages and visual content, and a somewhat smaller increase in the amount of text. For example, in 1935 the Danisco report had 12 pages and one image, while by 2007–8 it had 128 pages and 123 images. It had turned into a complex and colourful publication, where public relations objectives seemed to play an important role alongside informational ones.

Although Ditlevsen links these developments to changes in Danisco's management structure, we may speculate that wider contextual influences are also at work. It has been shown that the pattern she documents is fairly typical of developments across many countries (Droge et al., 1990; McKinstry, 1996; Stanton and Stanton, 2002). At least in the United Kingdom, legal changes between the 1930s and 1990s certainly led to a tightening of the regulations governing the type and quantity of information to be included in the Annual Report. However, recent changes in legislation and information technology have now altered the parameters of the Annual Report again. With the increasing use of the internet, it is now often enough for companies to make the Pdf files of the Annual Report available to shareholders on their websites. For example: the Companies Act of 2006 states 'A quoted company must ensure that its annual accounts and reports are made available on a website (. . .) that is maintained by or on behalf of the company and identifies the company in question' (430, 1, 2). It is no longer necessary for the company to send a hard copy of the report to all its shareholders. Moreover, when the shareholders visit the section of the website intended for their use, they will find not only the Annual Report with all its legally required contents, but also various alternatives in which key information is presented in a more attractive or dynamic style, and mandatory aspects like the auditor's report are sidelined or omitted. These parallel genres include the 'annual review' or 'illustrated annual review', as well as the 'interactive report' (see Chapter 6).

In what follows, we shall look first at various aspects of the classic Annual Report genre, which includes information and promotional material, but importantly, never omits the auditor's report, which is subject to stricter limitations. A special section will be devoted to the 'letter to shareholders', a genre which has attracted considerable critical attention.

Information and persuasion

Previous researchers analysing the Annual Report have approached it from a variety of viewpoints. Authors working within the professional areas of accountancy, marketing and corporate communications have centred on the efficacy of the report in pursuing the different objectives they have in mind (clarity and accountability on the one hand, general marketing and image management objectives on the other) (Stanton and Stanton, 2002). On the other hand, some applied linguists have focused critical attention on the use of specific rhetorical strategies and hybrid genres to present company information in a positive light (Hyland, 1998; Bhatia, 2004; Breeze, 2011a). A few researchers on both sides of the divide have also looked at the persuasive functions of images and imagery in the Annual Report (Douglis, 2000; Stanton and Stanton, 2002). Both business-focused researchers and applied linguists have investigated the way in which Annual Reports have adapted to new concerns, such as social responsibility and environmental awareness. Both groups have researched, sometimes critically, into how companies have sought to legitimate their activities by discursive means (Gamble et al., 1996; Cerin, 2002; Callan and Thomas, 2009; Degano, 2010). However, as Stanton and Stanton (2002) point out, in their review of ten years of (professional) research into the Annual Report genre, most of these studies focus selectively on particular parts of the Report, usually the first part, or the 'letter to shareholders'. They generally fail to address the document as a whole, in terms of the variety and integration of messages contained within it. In what follows, although it is impossible to discuss all the possible perspectives involved, we shall try to present a balanced view of the report and its many sections, and draw some conclusions about current tendencies.

What is generally recognized as the dual purpose of the Annual Report – to fulfil the company's legal requirements by presenting accurate information for different stakeholders, and to play a part in the firm's broader public relations activities – is reflected in the structure of the document itself. Bhatia (2004) analyses the Annual Report as belonging mid-way between promotional and reporting genres, since it seeks to inform readers about financial performance, but also, more subtly to persuade readers to maintain or increase their investment, use the company's products, support its actions and ascribe to its worldview. The Report as a whole can be thought of as a hybrid genre, containing different sections with different origins and different communicative purposes. In this, the different sections of the Report have slightly different roles. Some, such as the 'operating and financial review', are devoted mainly to providing information, while others, such as the highlights section, are intended chiefly to promote the company's image, but most provide a blend of the two. This leads to a certain amount of confusion, and so particular attention needs to be paid to sections which purport to be informative, but which are essentially promotional.

Typically Annual Reports contain a large number of sections that fall into two very broad categories: the review of the year, and the operating and financial review. It is important to realize that the 'review' is the company's 'self-description', which is generally written in a positive light, and will include: an overview of the year, perhaps including financial or other highlights, the Chairman's letter or statement, the CEO's letter or statement and reports about corporate governance. It may contain a section on corporate social responsibility, or this may be the subject of a separate report. The operating and financial review, which are usually found towards the end of the Annual Report, consist of information such as the balance sheet, income statement, cash flow statement, notes to the financial statements, etc., as well as other information for shareholders. These are accompanied by a statement from the auditors, reproduced verbatim, confirming that this information is trustworthy.

There is thus an important distinction to be made at the outset between the parts of the Annual Report that are composed freely by the company itself, and the parts that are vetted by the external auditor. It is quite natural that the sections in which the company has a free hand are going to be more positive, more likely to encourage shareholders to maintain and increase their investments, and generally more optimistic about every aspect of the company. These parts of the Annual Report obviously fulfil a public relations function. The sections containing audited financial statements are expected to be both more objective and more technical, since their main function is to provide a true picture of the company's performance and general financial situation over the previous year.

In what follows, we will look at these parts of the Annual Report using two approaches that are particularly revealing in this context: a multimodal approach, examining Annual Reports in terms of image and text; and an investigation of features related to lexis and stance, informed by corpus studies. We shall then pay special attention to the genre of the 'letter to shareholders', which has been widely discussed by applied linguists and discourse analysts. The emergent genre of the annual review and the interactive Annual Report or review will be discussed in Chapter 6, where I will explore the changing nature of company-shareholder relations mediated through these new genres.

Multimodality

In visual terms, most Annual Reports fall into two clear halves. The front and back cover, index pages and first sections generally make ample use of the options that the high-quality full-colour format offers. However, the financial sections towards the end of the Report present a much more sober image, with page after page of dry tables displaying numbers, dense text with technical-sounding headings, little colour and few graphs. This contrast is important for our understanding of both parts of the Report. The abundance of images, colours and visual information in the first half is indicative of the 'public relations' purpose underlying these sections of the Report. But the lack of images and visual dullness of the second half also stress the 'hard' and 'dry' nature of the material that is presented, adding to the air of seriousness and authenticity created by the technical language and numerical data. The 'visual rhetoric' of this second part of the report emphasizes its dryness, its factuality, and, by implication, its reliability.

Although this is interesting, it is inevitable that the first half of the report should occupy most of our attention when we are focusing on multimodality. As Preston et al. (1996) explain, the cover of the report is particularly important, since it is often designed with regard to the 'brand image' that the company is trying to develop. They cite the example of a PepsiCo report with a dramatic image of a grim-faced Sumo wrestler on the cover, showing how the image relies on metaphor to connote a correspondence between a 'powerful' Sumo wrestler and the 'power' of PepsiCo's soft drinks brands. This metaphor is made explicit by the caption 'The power of big brands', which leaves little to the imagination. These authors contrast this with the more conservative Coca Cola Annual

Report covers of the period, which tended simply to show photographs of young people drinking the product. The choice of image by each of these companies reveals something about the nature of its marketing strategy, and perhaps about its relative market position.

An examination of 40 Annual Reports from 2010 reveals a wide range of different multimodal strategies, which shed light on the company's strategy for self-promotion.

- Metaphor: Many reports use images that represent some attribute that are supposed to be associated with the company. In some cases there is also a real connection, such as a sponsorship agreement which links a sport or event to the company in a real, as well as a metaphorical, sense. One clear example of this is the 2010 Aberdeen Asset Management Annual Report, which has a dramatic photograph of three rowers, taken from above against a dark water background, with the slogan 'Global strength. Local knowledge.' blazoned across it in a white sans serif font. The associative link is obvious, but there is also a factual link, which is explained on page 3 as 'Aberdeen signed a four year agreement this year which saw it become the title sponsor of Dad Vail Regatta, the largest collegiate regatta in the United States.'
- Iconicity: A second approach is to use images that show the company's real activities. For example, Anglo-American Mining Corporation has a report with a white cover, on which it places six faces of miners, of varying ethnicity and including one woman, and the text 'Delivering real excellence', with the small tagline 'Real Mining. Real People. Real Difference' in the bottom right-hand corner. This report highlights the human form in almost all the images it includes, projecting the image of a company where people work hard, in difficult physical surroundings, to generate wealth. The 'realism' of the images in this report, despite the glossy presentation and attractive colours, generates a sensation of ruggedness which is presumably felt to be appropriate to the company's activities and general image, and which is likely to be attractive to readers. The inclusion of a woman, for example, as one of the six faces in a mining helmet on the cover, sends a message of inclusiveness and equality that is presumably felt to be appropriate to a 'modern' company.
- Faces or things: As the example from the Anglo-American Mining Corporation illustrates, the human face or figure is important in some companies' multimodal presentation. We might contrast this report with

that produced in the same year by the Gem Diamonds Group, which has an elegant black and white image of two huge unpolished diamonds on its cover, and a colour photograph of an excavating machine on the back. This report only contains photographs (of the small, square, passport variety) of the board members, plus one colour image of some gemstones. We may not only note the sobriety of this company's self-presentation, but also the underlying message that diamonds just 'appear' on a table, instead of being arduously dug out of the earth by human beings.

- Magazine design: The visual presentation of some reports is close to magazine design, in the use of colour for photographs, graphics and headings, and the collage-style page layout. Examples of this can be found in the report for J. Sainsbury plc, where the inside cover sets out the firm's 'values' with eye-catching illustrations and statistics in large type. Information is provided (in red and orange company colours) such as 'As a leading food retailer we focus on being best for food and health', which is accompanied by a photograph of shiny, colour-coordinated apples on a shelf, the number '5,000' in large print, and the somewhat opaque information that 'Over 5,000 of our own brand products are labelled with front-of-pack Multi-Traffic Light Labelling'. This style of design is far away from the sober presentation of facts and figures favoured by some other companies, which presumably feel that such an approach is either inappropriate or liable to be counterproductive.

- Highlighting key information: As in the above example, many of the reports for 2010 highlight words, phrases or numbers, which are interspersed with, or printed on top of, photographs and other images. Information from the text is often presented again, in the form of 'highlights', which consist of sentences, sentence fragments or keywords that are given special visual emphasis by use of different font sizes, different colours, bullet points and combination with photographs or other images. For example, an image of workers operating machinery in the Anglo American Mining Corporation report has the text '$9.8bn operating profit' printed on top of one corner, while the report for BSkyB places similar snippets of information, such as '9.86m Total Sky TV Customers' in white lettering on blue blocks arranged along the left margin of the text. Other reports include shaded boxes positioned across photographs, such as the phrase 'Highlights. Profit before tax up 26.6% to £20.3m (2010: £16.0m)', found across an image of a shelf of wine bottles in the report for Majestic Wine plc.

- Displaying numbers: As we have seen, numerical data are often picked out in large type, highlighted by a colour contrast, or blazoned across photographs. Some reports devote considerable space to the visual display of important figures using brightly coloured pie charts or diagrams. The first few pages of the Vodafone report illustrate the data about their customer base, segments, employees and so on, by pie charts scattered around the text in block colours, followed by similarly brightly coloured bar charts and maps.

- Photographs of board members: Almost all the Annual Reports examined contain photographs of the board members, and all accompany the 'chairman's statement' or 'letter' and the 'CEO letter' with a photograph of the writer. The more colourful reports (such as J. Sainsbury plc) tend to favour dynamic poses or action shots, with the executive shown talking to customers or smiling (presumably in reaction to the company's excellent results). Others are smaller, less colourful and present a more serious air (AstraZeneca plc). Sometimes the Chairman and CEO appear side by side, sober faced and heavily suited, as in GlaxoSmithKline plc. As we shall see, it is important that the 'human face' of the 'boss' should appear, not least because this is the figure who will be associated in the media with the company's success or failure, and who may have to ritually 'take the blame' if any disaster should occur.

The multimodal features of Annual Reports have provoked criticism from various quarters, not least because their presentation is felt to distract readers from the information they contain. Simpson (2000, p. 231) contends that 'the level of imagery in company Annual Reports is linked to maintaining levels of ignorance in society which are essential for companies to maintain their existence, and for society to maintain stability and order'.

Representing the corporate self: Stance and lexis

If we take a glance at a few Annual Reports, we may be struck by the way in which the reports tend to present a 'positive' image to their readers in the choice of words used to explain their subject matter. We know that words matter: it is not the same to say that 'the company is having a bad year because of the recession' and 'the company is adapting to challenging market conditions'. We will probably also notice another common feature of these reports which is grammatical rather than lexical, namely their use of personal language, with many prominent statements made in the first-person plural. These two phenomena might appear to be only tenuously related. However, if we test out these intuitions in a more scientific way, we will find that they open up an interesting line of enquiry into the way discourse is habitually used in the Annual Report.

One promising approach to the language of Annual Reports is through corpus linguistics, which makes it possible to detect patterns that might not be obvious to the average reader, and gives us quantitative data that may support – or disprove – any hypothesis we may have about vocabulary choices, personal pronouns and so on. Annual Reports are easy to analyse in this way, as companies usually supply them in PDF format, which can easily be stored in the form of text files and analysed using standard corpus tools such as WordSmith or SketchEngine. These can provide lists of word frequencies, keywords, multi-word combinations, and more sophisticated information such as typical lexical patterns, grammatical patterns or words used in similar contexts.

The most obvious use of corpus tools with specialized texts is to establish word frequencies. Using WordSmith tools (Scott, 2007) on a small (800,000-word) corpus from Annual Reports, we find that the ten most frequent words are much the same as would be expected in general corpora, but that the pattern then diverges rapidly from general language.

This striking divergence can be approached in another way, by using the keywords function on WordSmith to calculate the extent to which the word frequency list generated for the Annual Reports differs from the general frequency list for the BNC.

Keywords (Table 4.2) are calculated by comparing two lists of word frequency to find out which words are more prominent in one than in the other. The aim is to find out which words most characterize a particular genre or text, by comparing it with a larger and more general corpus, such as the British National Corpus (BNC). Calculation of keywords is thus useful to determine what a particular text is about, sometimes known as its 'aboutness'. The Annual Reports studied here are evidently 'about' money, which is hardly surprising. It is more interesting, however, that these written texts of a semi-technical nature give great prominence to the item 'our', which has a statistical 'keyness' value of 7,003, that is, 'our' is very much more likely to occur here than in the BNC.

As we see from Table 4.1, 'we' and 'our' both make it into the top 30 most frequent items in the Annual Reports. However, although 'we' is more frequent in the Annual Reports than in the BNC, the difference between its relative positions (22 vs 37) is not as great as the difference for 'our' (15 vs 102).

To understand why 'our' is so prominent, and how 'we' and 'our' are used in the Annual Reports, we need to use other corpus tools. WordSmith itself provides

Table 4.1 Top 30 words in ARs and in BNC

ARs	BNC
the, of, and, to, in, a, for, on, is, are	the, of, and, to, a, in, that, is, it, for
at, group, financial, as, our, by, with, year, million, that	was, I, on, with, as, be, he, you, at, by
or, we, from, other, value, company, share, be, which, have	are, this, have, but, not, from, had, his, they, or

Table 4.2 Top 20 keywords in ARs

Keyword	Frequency %	Keyness
Financial	0.57	22,149
Group	0.57	15,579
Million	0.44	13,403
Assets	0.28	13,169
Statements	0.23	10,803
Directors	0.23	10,531
Share	0.30	9,929
Value	0.31	9,369
Shares	0.23	8,112
Annual	0.22	8,078
Remuneration	0.13	7,939
Cash	0.22	7,631
Year	0.46	7,594
Liabilities	0.13	7,487
Governance	0.11	7,227
Our	0.51	7,003
Profit	0.18	6,720
Risk	0.22	6,709
Income	0.22	6,580
Impairment	0.10	6,516

the option of using a concordance to locate all the instances of a particular item in the corpus. If we examine these, certain patterns emerge which point to an interesting feature of the Annual Report genre: the writer emphasizes a collective identity, one which may include the company itself, or even the company and its shareholders or the company and people in general. This is possible because the use of 'we' and 'our' is vague and inclusive. So even though in general, frequency use of the first-person plural points to what Hyland (2001, 2009) calls an 'author-saturated' style, it also sometimes functions to 'rope in' the readers and include them in the ideas that are being expressed. In many cases, 'we' is the 'conceptual starting point' (Chilton, 2004, p. 160) of the discourse, the point at which writers and (compliant) readers coincide, the point from which all other things are measured. Let us examine the typical functions of 'we' in the Annual Reports corpus.

The uses of 'we' and 'our' in Annual Reports include instances that are clearly promotional, which can hardly be distinguished from advertising. Such examples indicate that the company is adopting the relationship of 'company to consumer', even in the Annual Report:

1. We stock wines for every occasion. Our range is innovative, vibrant and diverse whilst representing the best quality and value. (Majestic Wine)

However, many 'we' statements emphasize the 'company to investor' role, in which the investor's interests are foregrounded and the investor is 'roped in' as part of the corporate 'we':

2. In 2010 we continued to expand our presence across Europe as we realize our vision to 'Turn Europe Orange', building on our strong positions at major airports and adding two new countries to our network at the end of the year. (Easyjet)

Other instances of 'we' align the company with positive achievements in areas such as the environment and social responsibility. Here, we could say that the company is adopting a 'company to citizen' role:

3. As a result of our work, we are the first brewer and pub operator in the UK to achieve the coveted Carbon Trust Standard after cutting carbon emissions by 7.8 per cent (11,941 tonnes) in the last three years. (Greene King)

There are also instances in which the 'we' seems somewhat defensive, and the writer is almost positioned in the role of justifying the company to its critics:

4. We deeply regret that 14 employees and contractors lost their lives while working at Anglo American in 2010. We take the view that any loss of life is unacceptable and we believe that all injuries are preventable. We therefore continue to be unrelenting in our efforts to keep our people safe. However, we are encouraged by the significant progress in our safety performance over recent years. Since 2006, the total number of workplace deaths has declined by 68%, and 30% year on year. (Anglo American Mining Co)

None the less, the high frequency of 'we' across a range of uses tends to blur the referents, leaving a vague sensation of commonality rather than delineating a clear relationship to each particular set of addressees. This pervasive use of 'we' doubtless also reflects the 'solidarity face' that has been associated with corporate discourse, which is thought to reflect its underlying utilitarian value system (Garcés-Conejo, 2010).

Another prominent feature of the non-technical sections of the Annual Report is their use of a particular range of vocabulary that generates a positive image for the company, even when the circumstances are not particularly encouraging. Examination of the word frequency list for the Annual Reports shows that adjectives with positive connotations are fairly frequent, whereas those with negative connotations are rare. To go more deeply into the type of adjectives used, the corpus tools offered by SketchEngine (Kilgarriff et al., 2004) provide a different range of options, such as the 'thesaurus' function, which can identify a selection of positive adjectives in the corpus. By putting the word 'good' in the thesaurus function, we obtain words that act as synonyms or partial synonyms, as shown in Table 4.3.

The information provided in Table 4.3 obviously requires further explanation. For example, it is clear that 'strong' may function as a synonym of 'good', since we know that 'good performance' is much the same as 'strong performance'. However, it is obvious that 'long-term' and 'global' do not have the same meaning as 'good'. To understand what is happening here, we need to look at how the thesaurus tool works. The thesaurus detects words that appear in the same grammatical relationship to other words in order to find out which words are

Table 4.3 Thesaurus for 'good' (F=493) in Annual Reports

Lemma	Score	Frequency
Strong	0.285	386
Excellent	0.225	64
Great	0.221	210
Local	0.198	287
High	0.196	468
Positive	0.167	106
Significant	0.143	516
Long-term	0.139	319
Global	0.138	265
Effective	0.130	369
Overall	0.129	173

Table 4.4 Collocates of 'good' and 'strong' in Annual Reports

Pattern	Frequency	Pattern	Frequency
Good growth	9	Strong growth	50
Good performance	7	Strong performance	41
Good progress	19	Strong progress	3
Good governance	13	Strong governance	5
Good year	4	Strong year	10
Good flow	3	Strong flow	9
Good value	8	Strong value	2

used in a similar way in the corpus (Lin, 1998; Kilgarriff et al., 2004). Although this method tends to throw up a large number of inconsistencies, it enables us very quickly to identify a large number of adjectives that help to give the texts their peculiarly 'positive' flavour.

To obtain further insights into the functioning of these words, we can use the SketchEngine Difference function to identify patterns of usage. For example, if we take the obvious pair consisting of 'good' and 'strong', we can find out whether their use in the reports actually overlaps, or whether they actually have distinct functions.

This shows us that in this particular set of texts, 'good' and 'strong' do overlap, but there are major differences (see Table 4.4). 'Growth' and 'performance' are more likely to be found in the company of 'strong' than 'good'. On the other hand, 'progress' and 'governance' are more likely to collocate with 'good'.

It is important to note that some words only go with one or the other. So 'practice', 'people', 'understanding' and 'quality' are only found with 'good', whereas 'platform', 'base', 'culture' and 'demand' are only found with 'strong'. Interestingly, 'strong' is also encountered in the company of a number of adverbs, some of which are intensifiers: 'particularly strong', 'exceptionally strong', 'consistently strong' and 'significantly strong'. The same does not hold for 'good', which is only modified by 'very'. 'Strong' thus has a particular tendency to be gradable in this context.

Another pair of adjectives that can be compared using this method is that formed by 'strong' and 'high'. Here, we see that the overlap is much smaller, consisting only of five nouns that may be modified by either ('value', 'process', 'base', 'performance' and 'position'), and two adverbs used to modify them ('significantly' and 'very'). 'High' is particularly common in combination with 'standard', 'level', 'price', 'quality', 'degree', 'proportion', 'return' and 'probability', none of which is found with 'strong'.

Examination of the negative adjectives used is even more revealing. There are only 17 instances of 'bad' in the entire corpus, and these are almost all found in the context of 'bad debts' (i.e. debts that other entities have not repaid to the company itself).

The following table (Table 4.5) shows some of the more appropriate synonyms provided for 'difficult' in the SketchEngine thesaurus function.

The most frequent of these 'negative' words is 'challenging', which appears in combinations like: 'challenging climate', 'challenging conditions', 'challenging conditions', 'challenging consumer economy', 'challenging economic climate', 'challenging economic environment', 'challenging market conditions', 'it has been a challenging year'. It is evident that in the corporate discourse of the report, what we might naturally call a 'bad year' is represented as a 'challenging year', while the grave 'financial crisis' that has engulfed most of the world is referred to as a 'challenging economic climate'. Unlike the media, which tend to emphasize the negative and regard the worst results as the most newsworthy, corporate language is resolutely positive and, true to the principles of positive thinking, presents difficulties as challenges. The following example is typical of the way that company performance is reported in difficult times:

5. Notwithstanding a tough consumer environment and a highly competitive market place, the Company has delivered another year of strong performance, increasing both its customer base and market share. (J. Sainsbury plc)

All of these features seem to be common to Annual Reports from different sectors. However, if we examine reports from each sector separately, we find that different types of company tend to focus on different attributes which are held to be 'positive' in that sector. In her study of the Annual Reports published by 47 large European banks, Malavasi (2010, p. 217) shows how banks strive to demonstrate that they are 'solid, durable and long-term', by constructing a

Table 4.5 Thesaurus for 'difficult' (F=20) in SketchEngine thesaurus

Lemma	Score	Frequency
Prevailing	0.439	18
Uncertain	0.378	23
Challenging	0.295	41
Inappropriate	0.216	16
Volatile	0.085	14

trustworthy institutional identity and projecting a positive corporate image. She carried out a corpus analysis of banks' Annual Reports, and found that a particular range of lexical items is used to build up the banks' image. A large number of evaluative adjectives feature throughout the first sections. She classifies these into three types: those referring to the importance and competitiveness of the bank (*leading, dominate, top, growth, large, expand*); those used to describe the activities it carries out (*excellent, profitable, optimize, success, achieve, outperform, prosperity*); and those which denote the values that underpin its operations (*transparent, client-oriented, support, flexibility, integrity*). The last set of items is particularly interesting, since words of this kind are most likely to occur in the corporate governance section, and in the directors' report. Malavasi (2010, p. 220) points out that three types of lexical item are particularly important in these sections. First, there is a prevalence of 'humanized adjectives which highlight managers' attention towards clients', such as *customer-related* or *client-focused*. Secondly, frequent use is made of nouns that stress operational values, such as *flexibility, integrity, responsibility* or *transparency*. Thirdly, she identifies a further set of verbs which underscore the company's priorities, ambitions and dedication, for example, *aim, foster, aspire, strive, safeguard, ensure*. These often have an orientation towards the future, and may be accompanied by more neutral items including *will, would* and *plan*, which refer to positive future actions. Examples like the following are particularly characteristic of the management report sections:

6. The new Group will have the resources to pursue a strong and profitable growth strategy and will rapidly become one of Europe's powerful world-class groups. (Credit Lyonnais, 2002, quoted in Malavasi, 2010, p. 221)

However, although these features seemed to be general across the banking sector, Malavasi also detected differences between 'traditional' banks and banks with a particular 'ethical' commitment. Thus 'ethical' banks such as the UK Co-operative Bank were seen to be more interested in explaining their corporate ideology: the Co-operative Bank's report emphasizes how it avoids investing in repressive regimes or the arms industry, and shows concern about issues such as quality of life.

In our corpus of Annual Reports, those from the food sector are characterized by a high frequency of words like 'quality' (0.04%) and 'health/y' (0.04%), and also make frequent use of the word 'British' (0.02%), presumably because of the perceived quality factor attaching to home-grown produce. In those from the mining sector, we find a different range of frequent words, including 'risk/s' (0.17%) and 'safety' (0.04%). However, both food and mining sectors make frequent use of 'standard/s' (0.06% in the food sector, 0.05% in the mining sector), which reflects the pervasive nature of statutory or self-imposed standards in many areas of business, particularly those which entail a certain amount of risk to people's well-being.

In other cases, differences in lexical patterns may also be due to particular situations that have arisen over the year. For example, in the wake of a disaster, reports from the oil sector may show a heightened insistence on safety (Breeze, 2012), and when there is public concern about corruption, reports from companies in the financial sector may stress adherence to correct practices, or commitment to socially responsible governance (Poncini and Hiris, 2006).

Reporting facts or building confidence?

It is easy to see why the non-financial sections of the Annual Report have taken on many of the characteristics of public relations discourse. Many of these sections are non-obligatory add-ons to the report itself, which have been designed with promotional aims in mind. However, we might expect the sections devoted to the financial statements themselves to be much more informative or objective in the sense of providing the true facts, approved by the auditors, which will tell investors the truth about the company's situation.

In fact, the situation is not so simple. The auditor's statement is subject to legal obligations to veracity. However, as we shall see, this does not apply in exactly the same way to the rest of the section where this report is usually situated, namely the Operating and Financial Review. Although it is obviously vital for the writers of this financial review to align their account with the numerical data, they typically do this in a way that is beneficial, or at least not damaging, to the company.

Let us first take a look at the auditor's statement. This is the formal guarantee that the financial statements published in the report are reliable, and although we know that auditors may not always be trustworthy, this still constitutes the final check on the company's information for shareholders. Auditor's statements are generally reproduced verbatim alongside the financial statements in the Annual Report. Interestingly enough, the 'independent auditor's statement' is often heavily hedged and fenced around with disclaimers. The following example is typical of the way such statements generally begin:

7. We have examined the group's summary financial statement for the year ended 31 December 2008. This report is made solely to the company's members, as a body, in accordance with Section 251 of the Companies Act 1985. To the fullest extent permitted by law, we do not accept or assume responsibility to anyone other than the company and the company's members as a body, for our audit work, for this report or for the opinions we have formed.

The statement then goes on to delineate still further the precise nature of the auditors' responsibility, and the duties that fall on the shoulders of the directors of the company, stating clearly what legislation has been followed:

8. The directors are responsible for preparing the Annual Report in accordance with applicable UK law (. . .). Having made the requisite enquiries, so far as the directors are aware, there is no relevant audit information (as defined by Section 234ZA of the Companies Act 1985) of which the group's auditors are unaware, and the directors have taken all the steps they ought to have taken to make themselves aware of any relevant audit information and to establish that the group's auditors are aware of that information.

The following example, from the auditor's statement published in the Annual Report of Anglo American Mining PLC, is also illustrative, in that the opinion is couched in two classic legal phrases which represent a time-honoured professional way of indicating that the writer thinks, on balance, that the information is probably true, at least for the time being: 'a reasonable expectation', and 'the foreseeable future'.

9. The directors have, at the time of approving the financial statements, a reasonable expectation that the Company and the Group have adequate resources to continue in operational existence for the foreseeable future. (Anglo American)

From a discursive point of view, these examples are interesting in several ways. First, although the language is formal, there is a clear 'we' to 'you' relationship ('our responsibility is to report to you'), and a clear statement both of action ('we have examined') and of the limitations of responsibility ('we do not accept or assume responsibility'). Although the language is framed within a direct 'we-you' relationship, the curiously detached tone characteristic of legal correspondence and documentation is maintained. The text is made up of long sentences, with repetition of key phrases. Moreover, it is characterized by semi-technical vocabulary and characteristically legal terms, such as the reference word 'thereunder' and the adjectives 'reasonable' and 'foreseeable'. The following example illustrates these features:

10. We read other information contained in the Annual Report and consider whether is it consistent with the audited consolidated financial statements. (. . .) We consider the implications for our report if we become aware of any apparent misstatements or material inconsistencies with the consolidated financial statements. (BP)

The writer is telling us in impersonal terms that if the auditors find something that is wrong or misleading in the financial statements, they bear this in mind when they write their report. We should note that this is not the same as guaranteeing that they have *not* found any such misleading or erroneous information. Other researchers have noted that auditors' reports make extensive use of indirect language expressed through modality ('might', 'might have') to hedge their statements (Flowerdew and Wan, 2010, p. 87). Moreover, the combination of hedging ('apparent') and a formal, even semi-technical register ('misstatements of material inconsistencies') has the effect of creating a distance between the reader and the meaning or implications of what is being said.

It is also interesting that even this brief, even laconic statement by the auditors is also hedged, because at the bottom of the same page there is a note to the effect that:

11. Legislation in the United Kingdom governing the preparation and dissemination of financial statements may differ from legislation in other jurisdictions.

Elsewhere in the financial statements sections of the Annual Report, lengthy and detailed disclaimers are also found, such as the following:

12. In order to utilize the 'Safe Harbor' provisions of the United States Private Securities Litigation Reform Act of 1995, BP is providing the following cautionary statement. This document contains certain forward-looking statements with respect to the financial condition, results of operations and businesses of BP and certain of the plans and objectives of BP with respect to these items. These statements may generally, but not always, be identified by the use of words such as 'will', 'expects', 'is expected to', 'aims', 'should', 'may', 'objective', 'is likely to', 'intends', 'believes', 'plans', 'we see'

or similar expressions. (. . .) By their nature, forward-looking statements involve risk and uncertainty because they relate to events and depend on circumstances that will or may occur in the future and are outside the control of BP. Actual results may differ materially from those expressed in such statements, depending on a variety of factors, including the specific factors identified in the discussions accompanying such forward-looking statements; the timing of bringing new fields onstream; future levels of industry product supply, demand and pricing (. . .) (BP)

The auditor's statement and the cautionary statements represent one extreme of the Annual Report. These are the points at which the discourse is most 'official', where commitments are spelt out and, importantly, hedged and delimited. In all these features, the statement belongs to legal, rather than specifically financial, language. In this, it contrasts with the other sections of the report: a discursive fault line demarcates these sections from the other parts of the text. Their carefully worded legal phraseology marks them as 'different', and they stand out clearly from the body of semi-informative, semi-promotional texts that make up the rest of the report.

However, the rest of the section in which the auditor's statement appears is composed in a spirit of greater freedom. This is the Operating and Financial Review section, where the profit and loss accounts, balance sheets and financial results are set out in table form, accompanied by explanations and background information presented in texts and in graphic form.

At least in the United Kingdom, the Operating and Financial Review is subject to certain standards and restrictions set out in the framework of guidance provided by the Accounting Standards Board, whose status is 'persuasive rather than mandatory' (Accounting Standards Board, 1993, p. ii; Rutherford, 2005, p. 351). The guidelines state that it is essential for the Operating and Financial Review to be 'balanced and objective, dealing even-handedly with both good and bad aspects' (Accounting Standards Board, 1993, parag. 3). The existence of these semi-authoritative guidelines means that all British-based companies tend to cover similar ground in their review, but that there is also a certain degree of freedom within which they can operate.

A corpus-based study by Rutherford (2005) examined the Operating and Financial Review from 70 Annual Reports of companies listed among the Times UK 1000. His study was based on simple word frequency counts, from which function words, numbers, times and so on were eliminated. From these, he identified what he termed 'charged words', that is, words which seemed to be carrying a positive or negative connotation. Thus the words 'profit' and 'profits' were categorized as 'positively charged words', while 'loss' and 'losses' were negatively charged. He then examined the data to find out whether companies that were making a loss, or had very low profits, used a different type of language from companies that were profitable.

The results of this study confirmed what Rutherford calls the 'Polyanna principle', that is, the phenomenon that 'positive, affirmative words are used more often than negative words' (Hildebrandt and Snyder, 1981, p. 6), even in what are ostensibly objective accounts of financial data. Approximately 80 per cent of all the 'charged' language in the reviews in his study carried a positive charge. In all groups, companies used words like 'profit' or 'assets' more than they used 'loss' or 'liabilities'. They also tended to use 'up' words, such as 'increase' or 'rise', at least three times as frequently as they used 'down' words, such as 'decrease' or 'reduce'. Rutherford notes that the loss-making companies in his study still referred to profits more frequently than to losses. Low-profit companies mentioned losses no more frequently than high-profit companies did. The overall balance between positive and negative vocabulary was not significantly different between loss-making companies and highly profitable ones. Even loss-making companies still used the words 'profit' and 'profits' considerably more than they used 'loss' or 'losses'. In Rutherford's words, 'the most profitable companies are less "positive" in their language than the least profitable, suggesting that the least profitable display more Polyanna-ish tendencies than the most profitable' (2005, p. 372).

However, although the prevalence of positive and negative vocabulary was similar across all levels of company performance, there were some other differences that might shed light on what is happening. For example, the word 'market' was significantly more frequent in the reviews published by the largest companies, while the words 'customer' and 'customers' had similar frequencies across groups. Such a difference might, Rutherford speculates, mean that 'small or poorly performing companies focus narrowly, for example, on existing customers (. . .) whereas larger or better performing companies engage in a wider, more strategically oriented, discussion' (2005, p. 367). Another difference was the use of the term 'risk', which was, logically enough, more frequent in companies with considerable debt, or in the case of very large companies. On the other hand, the most profitable companies tended to make greater use of the word 'margins', which suggests that such sensitive topics might be discussed more openly when times are good.

Overall, the most striking features of Rutherford's results are the prevalence of positively charged vocabulary, and the fact that poor performance seemed not to be reflected in any way that could be detected by quantitative analysis. In fact, this effect seemed to be stronger, the weaker the company's performance.

Another facet of certain sections of the Operating and Financial Review is the proliferation of technicalities, as in the following example:

13. The following assumptions were made in calculating the sensitivity analysis:

All income statement sensitivities also impact equity.

No sensitivity is provided for interest accruals as these are based on pre-agreed interest rates and therefore are not susceptible to further rate changes.

Changes in the carrying value of derivatives (from movements in commodity prices and interest rates) designated as cash flow hedges are assumed to be recorded fully within equity on the grounds of materiality. (Anglo American plc)

The piling up of financial terminology, and the use of concepts that are not transparent to the layperson, tend to make these sections of the report opaque to the majority of shareholders. Although companies are indeed acting correctly by presenting financial information in its full complexity, we may feel that such text does not invite any reader other than the fully qualified financial expert. Non-professionals will find it impenetrable, and its message will pass them by even if it is important for them. Discourse analysts have often commented on the plentiful use of technical language across different genres (Fowler, 1993; Potter, 1996). Such language suggests superior access to technical knowledge on the part of the writer, thus boosting his/her prestige and strengthening his/her power position with regard to the reader. It may even be applied deliberately to mystify or confuse the reader.

Along rather different lines, but to similar effect, there is an insistence in this part of the report on adherence to external standards and codes of practice, which again tends to build up the company's credibility and emphasize its trustworthiness:

14. The Ore Reserve and Mineral Resource estimates presented in this Annual Report are prepared in accordance with the Anglo American plc (AA plc) Reporting of Exploration Results, Mineral Resources and Ore Reserves standard. This standard requires that the Australasian Code for Reporting of Exploration Results, Mineral Resources and Ore Reserves 2004 edition (the JORC Code) be used as a minimum standard. (Anglo American plc)

Impersonal constructions tend to be used in this context, in order to foster a sense of maximum objectivity and reliability:

15. Anglo American Group companies are subject to a comprehensive programme of reviews aimed at providing assurance in respect of Ore Reserve and Mineral Resource estimates. The reviews are conducted by suitably qualified Competent Persons from within the Anglo American Group, or by independent consultants. (Anglo American plc)

Such statements are also accompanied by definitions which are also presented in impersonal, objective language with a register that verges on the scientific:

16. An 'Ore Reserve' is the economically mineable part of a Measured and/or Indicated Mineral Resource. It includes diluting materials and allowances for losses, which may occur when the material is mined. Appropriate assessments and studies have been carried out, and include consideration of and modification by realistically assumed mining, metallurgical, economic, marketing, legal, environmental, social and governmental factors. (Anglo American plc)

On the whole, we have seen that the texts from the operating and financial review section, even though they are theoretically written in accordance with official guidelines, tend to place a positive gloss on the company's situation. With the exception of the auditor's statement, these texts are not produced independently, even though auditors will have checked the accounts and balance sheets that accompany them. This suggests that there is not such a great divide between what is found in this section of the report and the rest of the text. Since this trend is widespread, and yet companies are presumably all subject to the same guidelines, we may assume that the 'positive framing' that we have observed is a legitimate way of presenting the company to its stakeholders. However, we might also conclude that those stakeholders ought to pay careful attention to the financial data, rather than accepting uncritically everything that the text says.

4.2 The CEO letter

If the technical, financial sections of the Annual Report are partly promotional in their intent, this is even more obviously the case with the 'letter to shareholders' or 'statement' issued by the Chairman and/or CEO which occupies a prominent position near the beginning of the Annual Report.

This is probably the section of the report that has received the most attention from discourse analysts (Kohut and Segars, 1992; Vázquez Orta and Foz Gil, 1995; Hyland, 1998). Bhatia sums up the main characteristics of the 'letter to shareholders' as follows (2004, p. 16):

> As an example of a letter, it has all the typical signals such as the opening address, the closing, and of course the body of the letter. Moving more towards treating this as a genre, one may claim that the communicative purpose of this letter is to inform the readers, who are the stakeholders in the company, about the performance of the company in the past year.

In fact, the letter to shareholders is framed just as a personal letter might be, often opening with 'Dear Shareholder' and ending with the signature of the writer or writers. Such letters are sometimes signed by the President or Chairman of the company, sometimes by the CEO, and sometimes by both. In some reports, both the Chairman and the CEO publish 'letters', while other reports contain sections entitled 'statements' that are very similar in style. It is currently common practice for particular messages in these 'letters' or 'statements' to be visually emphasized by subtitles, or by independent boxes that contain highlights from the text. They are also usually accompanied on the page by photographs of the writer, often smiling or posed in such a way that he (usually) seems to be interacting with the reader, which have the effect of fostering the relationship projected through the text.

In a detailed study of 137 CEO letters from Hong Kong-registered companies, Hyland (1998) documented the ways in which the writers used discourse to gain the reader's acceptance for the messages they wished to convey. He concluded that the rhetorical strategies these writers used had enormous importance in building credibility and inspiring confidence. Using the threefold structure of classical rhetoric, he argues that the CEOs use three main types of strategy. First, there are those relating to 'logos', or rational appeal to the readers reinforced by textual organizers that make the arguments appear clearer and more conclusive. The principal means for doing this is by use of discourse organizers and logical connectives, as in the following examples (Hyland, 1998, pp. 12–21):

17. *In conclusion*, the group is very optimistic about the prospects of the plastics industry.
18. This view must be tempered by the continuing delay in bringing about a successful conclusion to the Uruguay round of GATT talks which is so crucial to the world's free trade talks and *therefore* the well-being of our core business.

Secondly, the CEOs seek to create a credible and convincing 'ethos' for themselves as writers. To command respect, a CEO needs to present a competent, trustworthy and honest persona. To do so, Hyland argues (1998, p. 16) that he/she uses hedges, emphatics and relation markers to reinforce their statements. Moreover, they also sometimes appeal to external sources to underwrite their authority (Hyland, 1998, p. 16):

19. We're the top-rated underwriter of emerging markets debt, *according to* Euromoney, and International Financing Review *named* Chase 'Emerging markets debt house of the year'.

It is also interesting that the style of engagement in the letters and statements diverges from that of the rest of the text in the use of pronouns. In our sample, as in the study by Hyland (1998), whereas the Annual Report abounds in uses of 'we', the letters made frequent use of 'I', which is particularly common in the first and last paragraph, particularly when the writer wants to explain a personal situation, or communicate a personal message. It is often combined with emphatics or affective vocabulary to convey an air of sincerity and inject feeling into the relationship with readers:

20. This is my first full year review as Chairman . . . I have been immensely impressed by the energy, knowledge and commitment of our staff, whom I would like to thank for their continued efforts on Abcam's behalf. (Abcam)
21. Specifically, I would like to thank everyone for the role they have played in achieving another successful year. (Greene King)

This aspect also links with the third area of classical rhetoric, that is, 'pathos', or the effects of the text on readers and the way the writer seeks to involve those readers in what he or she is saying. This may be achieved through the expression of positive feelings in which the writer anticipates the reader's reaction, as in the following example from our sample:

22. It is pleasing to report that we were able to restore the dividend at the half year stage. (Anglo-American plc)

On certain occasions, the 'letters' also make use of 'you', in an attempt to engage the shareholders more closely in what is, legally speaking, their company.

23. In 2010, your company experienced a strong revival on the back of steadily rising demand. (Anglo-American plc)

We may speculate that since 'we' is so ubiquitous in all the sections of the Annual Report, as we have shown above, the 'letters to shareholders' require a heightening of the interpersonal temperature so that they can appear to be more direct and sincere, as befits a 'personal' message to investors, which would explain why 'I' and 'you' make an appearance here.

Information or promotion?

One striking feature of the 'letters' identified by previous analysts is the frequency of forward-looking statements with a large number of nominal constructions. Bhatia (2004, pp. 13–15) points out that such texts contain a very high incidence of three kinds of nominals: general words such as 'progress', 'objectives', 'growth'; nominals that express business concepts, such as 'operating efficiency', 'financial flexibility', 'free cash flows'; and noun phrases associated with positive future expectations, such as 'a world-class management team', 'strong leadership qualities', 'unprecedented flexibility', or 'commitment to find greater productivity gains'. He observes that these features cooperate to indicate that the text is embedded in a specific business context, and to project a strongly positive, forward-looking image of the company in question.

In view of this, one important issue that has occupied previous analysts is the question as to how objective or balanced the 'letter to shareholders' is. Some analysts have surmised that the language of the 'letter' can be correlated with the company's real performance. For example, Abrahamson and Amir (1996) looked at the proportion between words with negative connotations in the 'president's letter' and the company's subsequent performance, and found that high relative negativity was associated with poor performance both in the year of the report and in the following year. Along similar lines, Smith and Taffler (2000) analysed the lexis of 'chairman's statements' and found that heavy presence of nouns such as 'overdraft', 'loan' and 'closure' was associated with corporate failure.

However, some authors claim to have obtained contrasting results. Hildebrandt and Snyder investigated 'letters to shareholders' from Annual Reports and found that overall, 'positive, affirmative words' were always used more than negative words (1981, p. 6). Thomas (1997) analysed presidents' letters to shareholders at a time when their respective companies were not doing well. This study found that as the objective facts about performance became more negative, the language increasingly suggested an external, 'objective' situation caused by outside circumstances (1997, p. 47).

In order to account for the overwhelmingly positive tone of the letters to shareholders, Bhatia points to various important aspects of the context in which they are composed and deployed, which shed light on the type of message that is conveyed and the ways in which it is phrased (2004, pp. 16–17). In Bhatia's view, the inherent power imbalance between insiders who know the truth and investors who have limited access to information gives rise to a situation in which a seemingly harmless genre can be used to 'disinform, if not deliberately misinform' minority shareholders and mislead them as to the true financial situation of the company. In his opinion, this leads to what he terms 'genre bending', in which the parameters of an ostensibly informative genre increasingly make way to accommodate lexico-grammatical resources that would be more typical in a promotional genre.

However, other authors are less condemnatory, taking the line that it is natural for a company to present itself in the best possible light to everyone, and particularly to close stakeholders. Rutherford (2005) concludes that there is a significant level of 'impression management' in most 'letters to shareholders', but that this is not so successful that differences between good and poor performance can be camouflaged.

Legitimation strategies

One important aspect of the 'letters to shareholders' that has interested analysts is the extent to which they deal with negative issues involving their companies other than strictly financial problems. We know that corporate actors generally attempt to justify themselves and salvage their reputation as far as they can after perceived episodes of wrongdoing. The 'letter to shareholders' plays a particularly important role in this activity, not least because the 'personal' approach facilitated by the letter lends an air of sincerity or authenticity to the discourse. Another reason for this could be the fact that the CEO tends to be the figure who is framed as being responsible for corporate disasters, and that he/she is generally made to pay the price, functioning as a scapegoat that must be punished in order to redeem the company as a whole (Boeker, 1992; Lyons, 2011). It is thus logical that it should be the CEO who communicates directly with shareholders (and other interested observers) in the 'letter' or 'statement', in order to explain what happened and justify what has been done to make redress. Under normal conditions, the need to justify the company's actions may be perceptible as a thread running through some sections of the Annual Report, but this particular discursive activity reaches a significant pitch when a major crisis threatens the existence of the actors involved. Should such an event occur, institutions summon up a range of justificatory discursive strategies embodying ideological elements that resonate with socially accepted ideas, feelings or desires. This often finds particularly clear expression in the 'letter to shareholders'.

One case in which legitimatory discourse could clearly be perceived was in the 'letters to shareholders' published by the oil industry after the Deepwater Horizon catastrophe in April 2010, when a BP oil well cracked, sending thousands of gallons of crude oil into the sea. Like the Exxon Valdez oil spill 20 years before, it provoked a collective call to conscience. In the wake of the disaster, as the oil spread and the crisis appeared to be uncontrollable, public opinion turned on the oil industry. The negative publicity generated through the spill itself, the company's apparent inability to repair the leak, and its failure to respond appropriately in human terms led to a crisis in public opinion. It is not surprising that the messages to shareholders published in the Annual Reports of oil corporations during the following year all made reference to the incident, trying to justify both the individual companies and the sector as a whole. In the following year, oil corporations were at pains to review their safety procedures and cooperate in rescue operations. Not only BP, but also other oil companies unconnected with the spill, felt a need to present a cleaner image to the public eye. It is therefore not surprising that the Annual Reports published in spring 2011 should have taken trouble to stress improved safety measures and emphasize the companies' positive contribution to their physical and social environment. In short, the oil industry was faced with a need to legitimate itself on a massive scale, to the media, to public opinion in general, and to a range of other stakeholders, including its own current or potential shareholders.

In pragmatic terms, legitimation is related to self-defence, since the agent that seeks to legitimate itself generally operates by providing reasons, grounds or acceptable motivations for actions that have been or could be criticized by others. However, it differs from straightforward defence or justification in that it is not necessarily a response to a specific accusation or attack. Legitimation is a more complex discursive practice, which may involve a variety of strategies and a combination of different but interrelated discourses (van Dijk, 1998). Moreover, legitimation is usually understood to refer to defensive or justificatory practices of an institutional nature, used to bolster and defend the legitimacy of the actions of an entity or collective body. Institutional spokespeople stake their claims to legitimacy on a societal stage, and their assertions carve out a position for their institution as an actor in the social world (Verschueren, 2012). Their discursive actions can thus be said to be ideological in nature, asserting the rightness of the institution's actions, pre-empting criticism from other social players and marking out the boundaries of the institution's rights and obligations within society. Legitimation aims to create an ideological space within which the institution can operate, enjoying sufficient social acceptance to pursue its activities freely. Moreover, legitimation typically operates in a top-down manner, since power-holders tend to legitimate themselves to those on whose compliance they rely: governments to voters, institutions to clients and so on. Non-state entities, such as interest groups, institutions and corporations, increasingly participate in this type of self-justificatory activity, making statements in the form of press releases, corporate publications, brochures, etc., which are not precisely advertising, but which are intended to generate a positive evaluation and public image, combining classic promotional elements (self-praise, positive connotations) with aspects of explanation and self-defence designed to pre-empt or defuse criticism on concrete issues (Malavasi, 2011).

In this context, it is important to note that corporations are particularly vulnerable on two levels. In the strictly legal sense, they are subject to national laws and international conventions, and infringement of regulations concerning environmental protection or human rights could result in considerable fines or punitive damages. Secondly, since they are public limited companies which are listed on the stock exchange, they are susceptible to fluctuations in world markets, which often have a strong psychological base. On one level, if investors' confidence fails, share prices usually also fall. On a second level, some investors may be put off by negative publicity, and long-term wariness may damage the company's standing. Large corporations now invest a considerable amount of money in their public image, not only positively, by presenting their achievements in a rosy light through advertising and public relations, but also in a more defensive sense, by justifying their actions, and defending them against real or potential criticism. When damaging incidents occur, such communicative activity is often one ingredient in what is known as 'crisis management' (van Dijk, 1998; Lischinsky, 2011). However, the discursive phenomenon of legitimation extends beyond the attempt to extricate oneself from complex problems, since it extends to justificatory self-representation where no immediate defence is required. Thus companies in the oil sector may perceive themselves as being open to criticism because of the actions of other petroleum corporations, and seek to distance themselves discursively from that other entity or its actions, or to emphasize positive attributes that, they posit, offer an antidote to the shortcomings or misfortunes of their rivals.

Elsewhere, I examined the discourses of legitimation used in 'letters to shareholders' from oil corporations after the Deepwater Horizon catastrophe of 2010 (Breeze, 2012), showing how the specific context and situation in the oil industry in 2010 resulted in a significant heightening of legitimatory discourse on the part of oil companies, particularly those that were perceived as being closer to the disaster. The 'letters to shareholders' I studied reveal how their authors negotiate the complexities of legitimating their company's actions in both financial and environmental terms, on a moral, cognitive and pragmatic level focusing specifically on the roles assumed by the writer as scientist and environmentalist, as well as financial expert, and on the story-telling techniques used to present the events as a survivor narrative. The analysis discusses ways in which these writers endeavour to engage readers' solidarity by using the motif of the 'survivor narrative', while also appealing to readers' interests as stakeholders. The CEO of BP summarized his discursive reconstruction of the year's events in a phrase:

24. Clearly, after a very troubled and demanding 12 months, BP is a changed company.

The past is distanced and the company's present and future actions are legitimated by this sweeping programme of change: the result is 'a refocused strategy built on the pillars of safety, trust and value creation', in which 'checks and balances' have a prominent role. In the final section of the 'letter', the writer makes a new claim for BP as a world benefactor:

25. BP's ability to produce oil and gas from harsh environments means we have a vital contribution to make here.

He then sustains this by interweaving discourses of profit with discourses of responsibility:

26. Lower carbon resources remain central to this long-term strategy. BP is able to help meet the world's growing need for energy, but we can only do this if we have the trust of society. To achieve this, we must ensure that safety and responsibility are at the heart of everything we do.

In short, it can be seen that the 'letter' offers the company a special opportunity to present a 'personal', 'direct' statement to the people who have a financial stake in the company's actions. The 'personal' voice lends itself particularly to presenting justifications and to telling the story from an insider perspective – in other words, for transforming corporate actions into personal narrative in a bid to engage the reader. In this, these texts have a key ideological role in underpinning the workings of large corporations within the complex panorama of contemporary capitalism.

Of course, to what extent the company's promotional or legitimatory message is received uncritically by readers is doubtful. Readers are bombarded by other messages, especially from the media and from critical pressure groups. Yet some reader reception studies show that even sophisticated investors do not distinguish between high-quality and poor-quality information when analysing Annual Reports (Simpson, 2000, p. 239). As corporate communication strategies become more organized, it is important to adopt an increasingly critical stance to everything we receive from that quarter.

5

Communicating with the World: Advertising Discourses

One of the most important areas of communicative activity for a company is the one which is directed towards present and potential customers. The most obvious form that such communication takes is that of advertising. It is true that other aspects of public relations such as publicity events are also important, as are the activities of customer relations departments, and the increasingly sophisticated strategies designed to promote customer loyalty and so on. Of course, websites have also come to play a major part in the company's communications with consumers, but websites also serve other functions and address other stakeholders. But advertising remains the most emblematic expression of the company's discursive endeavour towards its markets.

5.1 Defining advertising

Of all the corporate discourse types, advertising discourse is the hardest to define and explain. We have seen that many corporate discourses and genres merge into one another, and that promotional discourses now pervade genres that were once purely informative, and may still be ostensibly so. In advertising, this promotional function takes precedence: advertisements exist primarily to promote something. In fact, the easiest way to define advertising is by its function: advertisements are intended to persuade a target audience to purchase a product or service, or, by extension, to persuade them to support a particular cause (such as an NGO or environmental group) or adopt a particular type of behaviour (discourage people from smoking or encourage them to drive more carefully). However, if we compare advertisements with other types of text, in which there is an ostensible function (to inform) that is usurped or 'colonized' by promotional interests, it is evident that in the case of advertising as such, this promotional purpose is obvious and accepted by its audience. Everyone knows that advertising is meant to promote something. That is what it is for.

But what is striking here is that apart from the common purpose which makes us recognize that something is an advertisement, there is remarkable freedom in the material manifestations of the genre. In its discursive manifestations, an advertisement can adopt almost any discourse function: it can inform, worry, amuse, flatter, tell stories, raise questions, provide answers and so on. The material form in which the advertising message is conveyed is open to almost infinite variation. It can be expressed just through an image, through an image and one word, or text of almost any kind, as well as through music, voices and video. It can be transmitted through almost any medium. There is arguably no single manifestation of advertising that we can say is central or archetypal, from which all others derive, and on which discourse analysts can ground their exploration of the advertising genre.

Parasite or creative genre?

The all-pervasiveness of advertising and its generic indeterminacy have led some authors to consider advertising to be a 'parasite' discourse. In fact, it can be said to be parasitic in several different senses. First, like a parasitic plant or animal, advertisements may, quite literally, attach themselves to other artefacts, as in the type of promotional packaging that is used for many commercial products. Secondly, they also invade the time and space of other genres, such as television programmes, newspapers, magazine and websites, in all of which they have a secondary, parasitic role, in the sense that viewers or readers are generally interested primarily in the programme or articles, rather than in the advertising spaces or slots that are fitted in around them. Thirdly, most importantly, they are parasites in the sense that they adopt discourses and genres from other areas of life and adapt them to their own ends. Although in an extreme sense, all texts and cultural artefacts might be seen to be reworkings of other, previous ones, in advertising this tendency seems to be taken to an extreme, and is exploitative in that the purpose of the original artefact is undermined as it is put to a new commercial purpose. For example, if an artist paints a picture that contains influences from and references to some earlier artist's painting, this is not considered to be parasitic because the new artist is developing these influences in the service of art. But if an advertiser takes images or ideas from art, he or she generally does not create a new work of art, but merely takes advantage of the cultural connotations or aesthetic effect of the 'parent' work to commercial ends. In fact, advertising is capable of picking up and using almost any genre, from scientific reports to poems, from abstract art to photography, from novels to songs.

This parasitic tendency has often drawn the attention of critics, who emphasize the lack of originality and exploitative nature of advertising. According to one authoritative volume (*Fontana Dictionary of Modern Thought*, 1988, p. 11), creativity in advertising is essentially second-rate and dependent on other genres: 'Creativity (in ads) means instant attention-getting, resulting in a glibness or lateral cleverness, not to be confused with creativity in, say, film, literature or art'. However, as Cook (1992, p. 34) points out, much modern literary work also uses techniques of bricolage, interweaving other discourses to such an extent that 'they have no existence independent of the sources they have plundered'. Since all discourse is the reworking of previous discourse, the distinction made above between advertising and 'art' is perhaps not as valid as it might at first seem. Moreover, there are many other types of discourse that can be said to be parasitic – from parody to literary criticism – none of which could exist without its 'source' discourse, but which may be thought to make a valid contribution to cultural life. Just as parasitic plants and animals may live in a kind of symbiosis that benefits their hosts as well as themselves, it is argued that advertising and other parasite discourses may benefit the manifestations that they exploit. Added to this, in a second, much more material sense, we know that many serious media enterprises, such as television channels or newspapers, can only exist in the current economic system thanks to advertising revenue. This means that the relationship of interdependence between the material host and its supposed parasite is even more complicated, since it may in fact be the parasite which is supporting the host. Thus the nature of advertising as a parasitic phenomenon, though undeniable, is much more complex than a straightforward analysis might suggest.

In what follows, we shall look at some aspects of the advertising carried out by companies of different kinds, and we shall offer an analysis of how such discourses function in different contexts. Our outline will cover issues such as product advertising in general, national and global advertising campaigns and use of hybrid genres, as well as the transversal question of branding. Intercultural issues in advertising will also be analysed. At the end of the chapter, the role of advertising as a social phenomenon will be assessed in the light of discourse theory.

5.2 Product advertising

We have seen that advertisements are defined by their purpose. In their quest to persuade, they may appropriate a vast range of discourses from the culture in which they are situated, adopting a multiplicity of strategies to bend these to a promotional end. It is impossible within the scope of this chapter to provide an overview of what is possible in advertising, or even a taxonomy of the resources that can be used. We shall therefore concentrate on examining advertisements from two very different spheres of life, which bring out central aspects of advertising discourse and demonstrate how it tends to function. These areas are cars and perfume.

It has often been said that the more similar a product is to its competitors in the marketplace, the more necessary it is to advertise, and the harder the advertiser has to work to make it appear different from its rivals (Hoshino, 1987). At the risk of shocking motor enthusiasts and perfume lovers, I take cars and perfume to be prime examples of products that are similar to, if not indistinguishable from, their competitors. In what follows, I will examine some of the tendencies of advertising discourse as they emerge from a small sample of advertisements for these products.

Information and association

The cars on the market are, of course, different from each other. There are small family cars, large people carriers, sports cars and so on. Yet within each of these ranges, the choice between the different makes and models that are available is not particularly great. Advertisers therefore have to exercise some imagination to find an aspect of the particular product that will appeal to the target market and distinguish the car in question from its closest rivals. Car advertisements are interesting in that they embody two clearly defined tendencies. One is to spell out the unique technological features in some detail, while the other is to create a set of associations that will appeal to the potential buyer for non-technical reasons. Let us look at these two tendencies in greater detail.

The following text is found in a full-page advertisement for a Ford Kuga, in white letters against a wintry sky background. Most of the page is taken up by an image of a snowy mountainscape with the car – which is also white – heading in from the left.

1. Can your car tell the difference between black ice and tarmac?

Intelligent all-wheel drive constantly monitors and instantly adjusts to unpredictable conditions. Traction is maintained by automatically applying the right amount of power to the wheels that need it most. It returns to two-wheel mode when you're on safe ground, using less fuel. Now that's even more intelligent. Ford Kuga.

At first sight, the discourse of this kind of 'techie' car advertisement seems fairly transparent. We might even say that compared with much of what we find in advertising, it is 'factual' and 'informative'. Yet the discourse of cutting-edge technological innovation is interesting in itself. Even in this brief example, we find elements containing the type of 'objectification' typical of scientific discourse (Potter, 1996; Hyland, 2009). By using passives, as in 'traction is maintained', the copywriter makes the text seem less personal, more 'scientific' and 'objective', and therefore more trustworthy as far as the technology goes. Moreover, in this text, 'intelligent all-wheel drive' actually operates as the subject of the sentence, so that the car's mechanism figures as an animate agent. At the same time, the spicing of the text with terminology that is unfamiliar to the layperson offers other potential readings. If the reader is an engineer or car enthusiast who is totally au fait with automotive technology, then the text will provide the 'argumentum ad hominem'. Techies will understand it at once. For the non-technical reader, the potential meaning is perhaps more interesting: as in the case of other scientific or technical uses of language in texts aimed at non-specialist readers, the effect is likely to be one of establishing the product's credibility by using important, scientific-sounding words. The discourses of science are arguably as effective when used with non-scientists as they are when used with scientists, but the way the effect operates is slightly different.

The non-technical car advertisement is conceptualized in a different way from the outset. The idea here is often to establish an image – a lifestyle that the buyer can identify with, or a value that the buyer shares – that will appeal to potential purchasers. In fact, most car advertisements adopt this approach in one way or another. It has been shown that the main tendency in car advertising over the last 80 years has been away from providing information towards building associations with human emotions (Stokes and Hallett, 1992).

To take a simple example, picture this: as the dusk gathers, an elegant silver Citroën C5 is parked facing us at an angle, in the middle of an elegant seventeenth-century square. The sky is pure royal blue, the buildings are cream with white columns and balustrades, subtly lit to bring out the finer details. The square, which is deserted, is paved with regular grey-brown cobblestones and creamy marble. The gleaming curves of the car perfectly complement the setting. The caption, headed by a fleur de lis, reads 'The beautifully engineered Citroën C5. Drive a piece of Europe.' This advertisement, published in the *Sydney Morning Herald*, taps into the rich metaphoricity of France, or perhaps for this audience, of Europe as a whole, with its associations of elegance and culture, of classical style and of time-tested achievement. On the other hand, we may compare the controversial TV commercial for the same car, intended mainly for European audiences, in which the Citroën sweeps through an array of images of German culture that can be described at best as outdated, at worst as an insulting caricature. This commercial evokes the Germany of a century ago: as a gaunt but dashing Teutonic hero fights a duel then speeds across a snow-bound landscape to the sound of the Ride of the Valkyries, until he finally alights in front of the Brandenburg Gate. The tagline 'Unmistakeably German' combines with the caption 'Made in France'. The humour, or at least interest, for the European audience lies in the interplay between our expectations (Citroën is strongly associated with France and has traditionally appealed to a Francophile customer base) and the heavily Teutonic symbolism that pervades the commercial on all levels from the spread eagle and Gothic lettering to the buxom dirndl-clad barmaid who serves the protagonist with outsize portions of beer and sausage. Here, cultural symbols are exploited in a way that is sophisticated, controversial and highly memorable.

We may contrast these approaches with another advertisement, this time for a Renault Kangoo as 'the ultimate family car'. Who would be better for advertising the ultimate family car than the ultimate family? This advertisement is one of a series in which the Simpsons are shown interacting with the vehicle: in this case, Homer has cut down the giant, ready-decorated Christmas tree set up in front of the City Hall, and is trying to stuff it into the back of the Kangoo as Bart and Lisa look on and Maggie perches high up in the branches. The caption is: 'New Renault Kangoo. More practical with its fully retractable backseats.' The associations of family fun, humour, warmth, togetherness and love, and the in-joke about the Simpsons and the hazards of family life, are all brought together in the slogan 'New Kangoo. Family proof.'

Last of all, another common trend in car advertising is to build up a set of vague futuristic associations relating to state-of-the-art engineering and ultra-modern design, often through the use of slogans or taglines that exploit the conceptual metaphor of the journey, which is peculiarly relevant in this context. Since the image of the car itself suggests motion, and car adverts often have a spectacular landscape or futuristic skyline as a backdrop, the general impression transmitted by these advertisements is one of movement, improvement, excitement and stylish modernity. Consider the following slogans and taglines:

2. If we never venture into the unknown, how do we get anywhere new? (Honda Civic)
3. Go further. (Ford)
4. Today, Tomorrow, Toyota. (Toyota)
5. Vorsprung durch Technik. (Volkswagen)
6. Nissan. Innovation that excites. (Nissan)

In their different ways, such slogans and taglines manage to combine a restless sense of future with a feeling of speed and excitement. The metaphor of forward movement generates a positive resonance with our image of the product (the car) and our concept of technological improvement (cutting-edge technology, futuristic designs), while also triggering a mental representation of what we would do if we owned the car (speed stylishly and comfortably across the dream landscape of the advertisement into a bright future). Such loose associations of this kind are the stuff of which advertising is made.

Metaphoricity and indeterminacy

One of the ultimate products that is hard to define in words, and hard to distinguish from its rivals on the shop shelf, is perfume. Like wine, perfume has been a feature of human life for a very long time – one need think only of the gospel references to the pouring of ointment of nard, or of the 4,000-year-old perfume factory, complete with stills, bowls and bottles, found in the Pyrgos excavations in Cyprus. However, unlike wine, perfume has always been defined as a luxury, if not *the* quintessential luxury item, sold in tiny quantities for huge sums of money. Perfume presents the ultimate challenge to the advertiser, since its effect can only be perceived by the sense of smell, and this is one of the senses that is least at the advertiser's disposal. After all, it is easy to reproduce images or sounds, and aspects of touch and taste can be communicated relatively easily through words and images, but smell is particularly inaccessible. In fact, the main approach to advertising perfume is to ignore the smell altogether, and instead to focus on the associations which the manufacturer believes will make the perfume attractive to its target purchasers. In this, they seek to evoke positive associations through metaphor and analogy, with the idea that the purchaser will want the glamour or other qualities with which the advertisement endows it. The richer the source domain of the metaphor, the more associations it will generate, and the more effective the advertisement will be (Ungerer, 2003). So images that evoke oriental culture are potentially capable of awakening associations of exotic beauty, dark mystery, ancient wisdom, mysticism and so on, which will create an aura of glamour around the product itself.

Using a different tactic, advertisers may instead consider the effect that the perfume will have on other people, showing how other people react to the wearer. The name of the perfume itself is an important part of the way it is marketed and advertised. We are all familiar with erotic names like 'Allure' and 'J'adore', and with the darker approach in the form of 'Opium' or 'Poison', redolent of danger and mystery. The relatively recent perfume by DKNY called 'Be delicious' exploits the web of associations generated around the symbol of the apple. The perfume bottle is apple-shaped, available in green or red, and the scent is slightly acid, with a whiff of fresh apple. The age-old links between the apple and seduction are balanced against the perfume's modern image, with photographs of New York street scenes prominent in most of the advertising.

To illustrate more clearly the way these different strategies work, let us look at two recent advertising campaigns. The first is for Miss Dior Chérie. A range of very similar versions of one particular image are to be found as full-page adverts in upmarket magazines. It shows a fair girl in a pale floaty chiffon dress drifting above Paris, held up only by some small balloons which she holds in her hand. The colours are pastel, the focus hazy, the image curiously timeless. In some versions, the only word is 'Dior', the letters – formed of pink satin ribbon – floating across the sky. The general sensation evoked in the person who sees the advertisement is one of lightness, airiness, youth, glamour, beauty. If we were to confine our analysis to actual words, there would be hardly any discourse to be analysed here, just the word 'Dior', with its connotations of fashion, glamour and expense.

A multimodal approach considerably extends the possibility of what we can say about the discourse of this advertisement. Faced with such examples, we might recall McLuhan's 50-year-old generalization that the text in advertisements is usually irrelevant, inserted as a distraction while the picture 'goes to work on the hypnotized viewer' (1964, p. 246). Here, the text is practically non-existent, but the imagery gives considerable material for the analyst to ponder on. If we start with the colour scheme, we are obviously looking at a highly gendered image: pastel and pink are inevitably associated with the feminine in our culture (Kress and van Leeuwen, 1996). Moving on to the (extremely hypnotic) image itself, we might be puzzled to say what it is supposed to signify unless we accept that advertising images have to be accessed mainly on the level of metaphor and analogy (Stöckl, 2004). Any analysis of images in terms of rational categories is likely to be insufficient, because images are dense in meaning and immediate in their cognitive and relational effect, but semantically vague and open-ended (Stöckl, 2010, pp. 48–9). In this case, we might interpret the image by saying that balloons are associated with lightness, and we know that the image of someone floating through the air might be analogous to the conceptual metaphor of 'walking on air' to express elation. The girl herself is both an iconic image of youthful beauty and an idealized image of the wearer of the perfume, but also functions as a metaphor for the scent itself, which is light, fresh and lovely. This is actually more complex than it might seem at first sight, because it seems that the advertiser is referring to one sense (smell) in terms of another (sensation of lightness, that is, touch) through a visual image (sight) evoking that sensation. The conventional concept of synaesthesia is often said to apply in these cases, when we refer to one sense in terms of another, such as when we describe a smell as 'sharp' or a colour as 'loud'. However, this case is not unusual in advertising, and we have seen that it actually performs a more complex mental operation, referring to one sense in terms of another, by means of a third. This mixing or blurring of senses is highly effective in conveying the kind of agreeable but undefinable sensation that might be produced by a perfume, but it is very hard to pin down exactly, or to analyse in terms of a conventional theory of signs by which one thing is clearly understood to stand for another.

Moreover, another type of metonymy is also at work which is very frequently found in advertising. We know that the pastel-shaded rooftops over which the girl floats are in Paris, because of the image of the Eiffel Tower in the distance. The Eiffel Tower, that symbol so beloved of film and literature, is a part of Paris, but here it stands metonymously for the whole, and most particularly, for the world of haute couture and expensive elegance with which this perfume is supposed to be associated. The ornate curvy lettering, too, points to a French origin. This relationship could be said to be indexical, in that the letter (which has nothing particular to do with France in a material sense) signifies that country and its culture. Peirce's concept of the 'index' (Ponzio, 2006) is often used in the interpretation of advertising, when an object or person is understood to represent another thing, or a relationship, or some abstract quality. Thus a ring can be used to signify marriage, or smoke to signify a fire. In advertising, a foreign word is often simply indexical of the foreign or exotic. In this advertisement, although we recognize Dior as a fashion house, the name 'Dior Chérie' is also indexical of Frenchness, with connotations of sophistication, glamour and romance.

The multimodal discourse established through advertising operates on many levels at the same time, mainly through association and connotation rather than through a straightforward process of representation. It would be quite misleading to 'interpret' advertising in terms of translating messages from one discourse (perhaps a visual one) to another (perhaps words). For one thing, the messages that advertising produces are not necessarily accessible to rational analysis, except on the level of the logic of the marketplace. Furthermore, when such messages are 'dissected' in this way, what is important about them often eludes us, since it is precisely the diffuse combinations of modes, messages and associations that create the powerful effect that advertisements undoubtedly have.

Precisely this indeterminacy is what makes advertising so entertaining for the general public and so stimulating – or perhaps irritating – for critics. One simple combination of a product and an image, perhaps even without text, can give rise to an inordinate number of interpretations, depending on the framework that is applied. Berger (2004) provides an amusing and illustrative example of how one perfume advertisement (an image of a Polynesian woman with a snake around her neck, holding a perfume named Fidgi) can be given six different interpretations, according to the framework we apply. A semiotic interpretation ascribes meanings to the different elements of the image as icons, indices and symbols: for example, the woman is an iconic representation of beauty, while the snake symbolizes danger, or rather, 'playing with fire'. A psychoanalytic interpretation shows how the advertisement appeals to primitive instincts under the sway of the Id. A sociological analysis posits that the advertisement builds an association between the perfume and an elite lifestyle. Marxist interpretation highlights the impulse to consume in order to assuage one's own alienation, and the way in which this feeds back into the capitalist system by boosting the producer's profits. Feminist analysis centres on how women are induced – through flattery and allure – to collude in their own subjugation. Finally, an analysis centring on the power of myth shows how the advertisement activates Medusa and Cleopatra myths associated with snakes, and even draws associative power from the story of the temptation of Eve in the Book of Genesis.

While we are concluding this section on product advertising, this might be the place to consider whether all of these manifestations have anything in common – whether there is a common 'advertising discourse' of some kind, or how we might refine our definition by purpose, that is, our definition of advertising as a genre that is intended to bring about a change in behaviour.

According to some experts, advertising can be defined genre-internally by three features that are almost always present (Galliot, 1955). First, in advertising, nothing is superfluous: the aim is to make the maximum impact in the shortest space or time, so advertising is characterized by a specific form of efficacy. A second common feature is its primordial desire to draw attention to itself, usually in a way that is positive, but sometimes by shocking the audience or appealing to their curiosity. This means that there is often a premium on the unexpected: like poetry (Coseriu, 1980), advertising sometimes deliberately violates our expectations. Thirdly, advertising characteristically makes use of the whole panoply of rhetorical figures, such as the various forms of repetition (alliteration, assonance, rhyme, doubling, tripling, straightforward repetition), as well as looser forms of emphasis such as synonymy or gradation; figures of position (changes in word order, parenthesis, etc.); figures of amplification (oxymoron, comparisons, superlatives etc.); figures of omission (ellipsis, zeugma); appellation (direct address, rhetorical questions, exclamations); and tropes (euphemism, allegory, metonymy and so on) (for a detailed list, see Spang, 2005, p. 208). In fact, I would argue that of all these features, by far the most important is the issue of metaphoricity, since it is the chief means by which associations are built up between some positive attribute of the product or service, and the images, words or sounds that form the substance of the advertisement. Everything about the advertisement, from the colours and images, to the soundtrack or background noise, to the text or dialogue, has the function of sending the audience a culturally encoded message about the merits of the product. The use of cultural associations, the application of motifs and images, all of these are in some sense metaphors, because they map between the positive associations of what is already known, and the positive attributes of the product that is being made known. Even the corny TV commercial for breakfast cereals showing a happy family around the table is in some sense projecting an iconic image of family life, which functions metonymically to take in the viewer's families, however different they may be, and provides a visual metaphor of the domestic happiness that results from purchasing the right brand of cereals.

5.3 Advertising discourse across cultures

One question that underlies some of the professional debate about advertising is whether it is possible to persuade consumers in different geographical and cultural areas using the same advertising message. The aim of 'global advertising' is expressly to connect with an audience or market that is as broad as possible, in order to save money and maximize the benefits from a single advertising campaign. However, the huge efforts that have to be made to devise such a campaign, and the sheer number of problems encountered along the route, are in themselves proof that a global audience is a fragile construct. In fact, there is a consensus among many professionals that most advertising works best if it is customized to reflect local culture (Dahl, 2000; de Mooij, 2010). Although people's basic needs may be the same around the world, the way in which these needs are met and satisfied differs from culture to culture, and the discourses used to promote the product in question are inevitably also different. Any marketing (or advertising) campaign should therefore reflect local habits, lifestyles and economic conditions in order to be effective.

This goes against the feeling that many people have that the world is becoming more uniform, so it is worth looking at the question in more detail. Some years ago, it was often suggested that the habits, lifestyles and values of people all over the world are converging: according to Levitt (1983, p. 92) 'a powerful force drives the world towards a converging commonality'. But there is plenty of evidence that points to a much more complex panorama. In some ways, people are becoming more similar: there is a global trend towards an ageing population, people everywhere expect colour televisions and dishwashers. But at the microlevel there are fewer resemblances: car owning and television watching habits vary greatly from one country to another, even in Europe. Eating habits are still mainly localized, and although fast food is gaining ground, the role that fast food restaurants play in social life varies enormously from one culture to another. Although young people around the world wear Nike and use mobile phones, the much vaunted homogeneous universal 'youth culture' does not exist: Dutch young people use their phones for entertainment, while Italians use them to socialize; Western youths wear sports shoes for comfort, while Asians do so as an indicator of social status (de Mooij, 2010). Moreover, experience has shown that it is not just a matter of waiting until the world's income has caught up with the United States. The effects of having greater wealth are likely to be different in different places. As de Mooij puts it (2010, p. 10), 'the wealthier countries become, the more manifest is the influence of culture on consumption and consumer behaviour'. Advertisers who work in international contexts often find that attempts to use the same advertisement across borders run into the sand, and major adaptations have to be made because even seemingly similar elements have a different significance to different groups of people.

Crossing cultural borders

The point about advertising is that it functions as it does because each element in it has a particular significance in a particular culture. If a positive resonance is established between the product and its associations, in one culture, and the advertisement and its associations, in the same culture, then the advertisement will do its job effectively. As Dahl explains (2000), an advertising message can most easily be decoded in the culture in which it was coded. If an advertisement is used in a different culture, its recipients will probably try to decode it using the schemata of their own culture, and the message may be severely distorted. One needs think only of the role that different drinks have in different countries, to see that tea would have to be advertised differently in, say, Germany or Italy, from the way it is promoted in Britain or Australia. One commonly used example along these lines is that of wine, which tends to be regarded as a luxury product in northern Europe, but which may be an everyday drink in Mediterranean countries. An advertisement stating that a medium-range wine 'adds a touch of luxury to everyday life' might be effective in Norway, but seem meaningless in Italy.

One interesting study that illustrates this point in more detail focuses on another popular drink that has different connotations in different countries: beer. Dahl (2000) looked at television commercials for beer in the United Kingdom, the Netherlands and Germany. At the time of his research, beer was the most popular alcoholic drink in all of these countries, but was in decline. All three countries also had fairly stringent restrictions on alcohol advertising at the time. Dahl analysed the content of the commercials in terms of the main message used to sell the product, and drew up a comparison between the commercials from the different countries. He found that humour was an important factor in British beer advertising, while Dutch and German commercials emphasized friendship. Most interestingly, however, British commercials were the only ones that associated beer with sex appeal, while German advertisements were unique in framing beer within discourses that evoked history and tradition.

Moreover, it is not just the product that is culturally defined. Almost any of the resources used to create the advertisement will also be culturally embedded, which means that if we transfer them to another culture, they may lose their meaning or acquire other meanings that were not intended. This applies to almost everything: images, sounds, words and phrases, or even seemingly instrumental factors like colours themselves (Aslam, 2006). To illustrate this, we need only to look at experimental studies of the kind conducted by Hynes and Janson (2007), in which subjects from different cultural backgrounds were interviewed about their reactions to two advertisements for mobile phones. Even basic aspects such as the choice of colours seemed to provoke contrasting reactions among the interviewees. For example, an advertisement for a Nokia telephone which made use of the Finnish national colours, blue and white, was evaluated positively by Finnish respondents, who felt that these colours were 'reliable', 'trustworthy' and 'comfortable'. However, Swedish people rejected the same colours as being 'boring' and 'cold'. The reaction from Chinese and Taiwanese subjects was even more negative, since they appeared to associate the colour white with funerals. A second advertisement, this time for an Eriksson mobile phone, was also rated by the same groups of people. This advertisement was predominantly red and yellow, which was generally appreciated by the different groups as giving a warm, familiar image to the product. However, the Chinese respondents disliked the use of these colours in this particular context, feeling that they were 'too personal' and therefore not appropriate to the product, which ought to have a more serious, business-like image.

Advertising and values

Advertising engages values, and to be successful, it must seek to connect positively with the values of the target market. 'Values' is a word that we all understand, but it is still important to define it, because this will help us to see why something that is a value in one culture might not be a value, or might be understood differently, in another culture. Many definitions of values are available, so let us return to the one we used previously by Rokeach (1973, p. 5): a value is 'an enduring belief that one mode of conduct or end-state of existence is preferable to an opposing mode of conduct or end-state of existence'. In cultures, values are not entirely independent, tending to link up together in systems: a value system is 'a learned organization of principles and rules to help one choose between alternatives, resolve conflicts, and make decisions' (Rokeach, 1973, p. 5). But of course, the values themselves and the value system that operates may be very different from one country to another. One needs only to think of stereotypical differences on matters such as punctuality or hospitality in different countries to see that different values are operative.

The issue of cultural values has been studied in some depth by scholars such as Hofstede (2001), who developed a set of categories for 'measuring' the unwritten rules of different cultures. In extensive empirical studies carried out in the 1970s with employees in subsidiaries of IBM all over the world, he found that people in different cultures responded in characteristic ways to the same types of question. This enabled him to identify five factors for logging the way in which people's attitudes and assumptions differ across cultures: uncertainty avoidance; masculinity/femininity; power distance; individualism/collectivism; and short-term/long-term orientation. Once a particular culture has been classified as having, say, high power distance, it is usually the case that various seemingly unconnected aspects of that culture can be seen to form part of a greater pattern. Thus high power distance often goes with a more rigid hierarchy at work, greater distance between teachers and students and more marked differences between formal and informal register – but also with a greater tendency to purchase luxury brands in order to assert one's social status. It is thus the case that two countries as seemingly dissimilar as Japan and Mexico share a high score on the power distance index, and both also show strong sales in luxury brands like Rolex, which are felt to denote wealth and high status.

Hofstede's framework is used by advertisers trying to communicate with markets, and it is also useful for analysts who are interested in the way that advertising discourses function. Since advertising is usually developed with one target culture in mind, the advertising discourses surrounding different products are likely to vary enormously from one country to another, according to the way that the product itself is understood in that country, and according to the connotations of any other symbol or device that might be used in association with the product or its target market. For example, we may see that advertisements in the United Kingdom or Hungary often stress competition, uniqueness and self-enhancement. This tallies with these countries' high scores on the individualism and masculinity indexes. In Mediterranean or Latin American countries which are rated as collectivist rather than individualist, however, advertising places a heavy emphasis on belonging to the group, and there is an emphasis on brands as symbols of collective identity, being 'in', being 'one of the gang'. It has been shown that car advertisements in Portugal and Spain tend to stress style and design, for example, to fit into cultures with high uncertainty avoidance and low individualism, whereas German car advertisements reflect a need for speed and high technology characteristic of high uncertainty avoidance and high individualism. In both cases, the avoidance of uncertainty is achieved: in the one, by discursive appeal to fashion and the safety of the group, and in the other, by discourses of technological expertise (de Mooij, 2010, p. 108).

As we might expect, Hofstede's framework has been accused of oversimplification and of encouraging stereotypes, and particular facets of it, such as his 'masculinity' index, have proved extremely controversial. He himself has emphasized that his criteria simply represent general trends across large numbers: there may well be a sharper difference between two members of one culture than between two representatives of two different cultures, in any given case. Moreover, we are all aware that cultures are dynamic: they change and develop constantly. None the less, Hofstede's framework adds an important dimension to the analysis of advertising by bringing values into focus in a systematic way.

Exploiting the local

Diametrically opposed to globalizing tendencies in advertising, we find the kind of advertising whose chief appeal lies in its strong local connotations. To take just one case, in Scotland it is common for advertising on television, on radio and in the press to make use of various linguistic features that denote Scottishness, in order to appeal to local consumers. This may consist of simply using regional accents or music on television and radio, in order to tap into local identities and loyalties. But it also extends to the calculated use of dialect words or even to wholly dialectal text or speech in some cases, when the advertiser predicts that this will have a positive effect. Some examples from Scotland are provided by Smith (1999, 2004). She describes a series of billboard advertisements for *The Glaswegian* newspaper in the late 1990s which contained slogans like 'Gonnygeezakeek. Ah've gone an' left ma Glaswegian at hame', followed by a final punchline 'The Glaswegian – talks your language' (Smith, 1999). Such indexes of 'Scottishness' are evidently often intended to be humorous, particularly when taken to an extreme. An instance that is quite obviously over the top is a magazine advertisement for conservatories and windows which promises a free haggis with every appointment, stating that:

7. Aye . . . yon's oor 'richt braw' offer tae all Scots Magazine readers. Imagine sittin in yet muckle conservatory wi a steamin plate o haggis, neeps and champit tatties. Braw eh!

Of course, as in the case of other aspects of advertising, it is not easy to generalize about the effect which is desired through the use of strongly local semiotic features, and the actual effect made on members of the audience may vary enormously. In the most basic sense, it is assumed that use of local language, like the use of other culture-bound semiotic aspects (local customs, dress, landscape, music, food and so on), is supposed to appeal to local people by evoking local or regional loyalties and identities, drawing on tradition and nostalgia as strongly emotive factors, as well as appealing to local humour. In a sense, this runs in parallel with the use of recognizable cultural symbols from elsewhere, such as the recurrent references to Paris in perfume advertising, except that local advertising is driven by the appeal of the known, rather than that of the exotic. None the less, in an increasingly globalized scenario, it is now also common for the local to be blended with the exotic. Since advertising is fuelled by novelty, advertisers have been quick to tune into the multicultural ambiance of twenty-first-century Britain, with commercials that humorously blend Glaswegian with Indian accents to proclaim that Homepride Sauces are 'so simple – even a Sassenach could make it' (Smith, 1999, p. 59). It seems likely that we shall see more of this cultural mixing in the future.

Towards global advertising?

Since advertising relies on the cultural resonance of particular signs and symbols, it is difficult to conceptualize the kind of advertisement that can cross cultural borders without losing some of its meaning, or gaining new meanings that were not originally intended. However, there has recently been a move to try to create advertising campaigns that can cross cultural borders and speak to people all over the world. For the company, such a campaign would represent a major saving, and would also help to create a cohesive global image.

Two companies that have had some success with global advertising campaigns are Coca Cola and Shell. Coca Cola is one of the world's best established brands, with a long tradition of high-profile advertising. Its advertisements are simple, based around associations with fun and happiness, which are valued in all cultures. Shell has also run very positive global advertising campaigns, all based on images of the sea which draw on associations with nature. Since nature is regarded as important everywhere, the same advertisement can be used in different cultures with positive effects. What these two companies have in common is that their global advertising is generally quite simple, focusing on one positive attribute (fun, nature) rather than engaging a range of values and associations. However, experts seem to be agreed that successful global advertising campaigns are the exception rather than the rule. If the same campaign does work well in different cultures, this is often the chance result of different underlying preferences.

Because of the complications that we have discussed above, many companies have opted for a compromise, preferring to launch quasi-global campaigns in which one simple idea is given a local manifestation in each country. One example of this is an upmarket advertisement for Omega watches, which uses George Clooney in its Western version, but features Bollywood actor Shah

Rukh Khan in the version for the Indian market (Gotti, 2011). Another is the series of advertisements for Actimel, in which the same abstract idea (Actimel regenerates people who are tired) is illustrated by examples that fit into each culture. The actors and backgrounds vary, but the idea is the same. Essentially, one discourse, one simple message, is devised and then inculturated in different concrete forms. At least for the moment, this is the direction that much 'global' advertising is taking.

5.4 Advocacy advertising

Advocacy advertising can be defined as the use of advertising to promote a particular message or cause. In other words, it is not designed to sell a product or service, but rather to change people's ideas. NGOs and pressure groups have long realized the power of advertising, and some of the most memorable campaigns have been those which shook the public consciousness, bringing floods and famines into the suburban living room. In a recent example, the World Wildlife Fund adopted a variety of direct and shocking strategies to bring home its message to the public. One advertisement has a close-up image of a tiger looking the reader in the eye, with the slogan 'What will you do when I'm gone?', followed by the text:

8. My home is vanishing. The forests I once ruled are being cut down.
   When they are gone, so am I.
   It's not too late. But soon it will be.
   Don't let me go.

At the foot of the page, the advertisement explains in smaller type how tigers are on the brink of extinction, and encourages people to adopt tigers by donating money to the Fund. This type of direct appeal appears to be common in advocacy advertising carried out by NGOs. Phrased as direct speech, with a photograph that looks the reader in the eye in a way that constitutes a direct appeal (Kress and van Leeuwen, 1996), these advertisements are the media equivalent of a person who stops you in the street and asks you for money. However, other forms of advocacy advertising also exist which are more subtle in their aims and claims. We need to remember that advertising is not just about selling soap powder or rattling a tin for money. It can be used to attempt to change the way people understand the world. Amnesty International has been running visually effective campaigns for human rights issues, which appear to be designed to bring particular abuses to the public attention for sociopolitical reasons, rather than to obtain money. Such advertising is a conscious-raising exercise designed to alter people's perceptions.

Discourses of corporate legitimation

Advocacy advertising is not just used by conventional 'good causes'. Large companies also produce certain types of advertising which are intended less to sell than to change the way people think, by bringing particular aspects of their company and its activities to the public notice. Companies use general advertising campaigns to present a brighter, cleaner public image, or to bring information liable to benefit the company to a wider audience.

One recent example of this type of advertising dates from summer 2010. The oil industry has had a tarnished record as far as ecology and human rights are concerned, and the year 2010 was marked by the Deepwater Horizon disaster, when a BP oil well broke and sent thousands of gallons of crude oil into the Gulf of Mexico sea. Three months after this catastrophe, when the oil spill was still being cleaned up, Shell published a double-page advertisement consisting mainly of a photograph of two young boys flying brightly coloured kites on a beach in Brazil. The sea is a deep blue colour, as is the sky, which occupies around three-quarters of the image. There are two areas of text set into the sky in a lighter shade of blue. The one on the left states: 'Let's help to keep the skies blue. Let's go.' The one on the right contains the following words, printed in a smaller font size:

9. We all need clean air. Not just for today's kite flying trip, but for future generations who want to live and play under cleaner blue skies. That's why, for example, at Shell Brazil we've created a fuel oil for factories that can cut soot emissions by up to 75%. It should help Raul and his friends breathe a little easier. Just one of the many things we're doing to help build a better energy future. Let's go. www.shell.com/letsgo

This type of advertising is corporate advocacy: the aim is to bring a better image of the company to the wider audience, and to create positive associations that will offset the negative impressions often generated around this industry by the media. Both the text and the image are upbeat and familiar, roping the reader in through a variety of strategies. The photograph is taken in such a way that the reader could be standing next to the first boy, thus inviting a participant stance. The text continues this theme by first-person generalizations such as 'we all need clean air', a reader-inclusive 'we' identity which is then absorbed into a company 'we' that speaks on behalf of Shell Brazil. At the same time, the text uses a combination of power words – 'created', 'build' – with a sustainability motif – 'future generations', 'a better future'. The use of comparatives – 'cleaner', 'easier', 'better' – reinforces the positive message, with the subtext that even if things have not been perfect in the past, the company is heading that way in the future. In fact, this advertisement is one of a series, showing children in different parts of the world and explaining how Shell is benefiting them. The potent image of the child, as the embodiment of our hopes for the future, becomes allied in readers' minds with the company and its aspirations to 'build a better energy future'.

This type of advertising is by no means limited to one campaign. Livesey (2002b) documents how the oil industry has been pushed into a defensive position over the last 30 years, as a series of ecological disasters have been taken up by environmental pressure groups as evidence of their malpractice, and public opinion in developed countries has increasingly come to take green issues seriously. The reaction among leading oil companies has been diverse: some, such as Shell and BP, have opted to embrace renewable energy technologies and impose voluntary restrictions along the lines proposed in the Kyoto Protocol (1997). The example quoted above, from Shell's 2010 advertising campaign, suffices to illustrate the type of advertising being carried out by these companies to bring a cleaner corporate image into the public consciousness.

However, other oil corporations, particularly those based in the United States, embarked on public relations campaigns designed to defend continued use of fossil fuels, attack attempts at regulatory legislation and encourage the notion of a 'balanced' environmental policy which would allow considerable scope for oil producers. Livesey (2002b) describes an extensive public relations campaign carried out by ExxonMobil in 2000, consisting of a large number of advertorials (see below), booklets and web-based material. The main rhetorical task of these advertorials was to undermine the environmental discourses current in the wake of the Kyoto Protocol, and establish businesses and technology as the true heroes who would solve the world's energy problems. The advertisements credit corporations and scientists with attributes such as 'prudence' and 'responsibility', and convey the message that it is companies like ExxonMobil which represent best the public interest, because they identify with their needs and concerns. Climate change forecasts are likened to weather forecasts, so that their credibility is severely undermined. At the same time, changes in business practices are identified with high costs to little purpose, which will 'harm the health of the economy' (Livesey, 2002b, p. 128). 'Hysterical' reactions to matters of climate change, resulting in sudden changes in policy, are likely only to cause damage. By usurping the discourses of the environmentalists themselves, the corporation manages to 'show' that it is responsible to act as oil corporations do, and irresponsible to make changes (Exxonmobil, quoted in Livesey, 2002b, p. 129):

10. A prudent approach to the climate issue must recognize that there is not enough information to justify harming economies and forcing the world's population to endure unwarranted lifestyle changes by dramatically reducing the use of energy now.

By skilled use of discursive resources, the American public and their 'lifestyle' are constructed as the most important player, the one to be protected at all cost, while restrictions and regulations, such as the Kyoto Protocol, are positioned as a 'threat', and an 'unfair' one at that. By putting economic development at risk, we are told, the Kyoto proposals threaten progress itself. By the end of the advertisement, ExxonMobil has managed to prove that the proposed reforms, 'unless properly formulated' will 'restrict life itself' (Livesey, 2002b, p. 130): that is, by means of a trick of rhetoric, the American fuel-burning 'lifestyle' has become 'life itself', and the uncertainties of science concerning climate change predictions have been overruled by the 'certainties' of economic science concerning the economy built on fossil fuels. 'Social well-being' is allied with high oil consumption, 'the public interest' is merged with the profit-making interests of oil companies, and the company itself assumes the mantle of 'responsibility' which might otherwise be thought to belong to the international bodies that signed the Kyoto Protocol.

As Livesey points out, in a Foucauldian analysis of the metaphors around which the main arguments are constructed, the entire text problematizes and completely redirects the 'health/harm' metaphor that is conventionally used to explain environmental issues. It reconstitutes the economy as the entity in need of nurturing and protection. Moreover, it appropriates and subtly twists the discourse of sustainable development that characterizes public policy in documents such as the Kyoto Protocol and its predecessors, by equating the American 'lifestyle' with 'life itself', and representing government restrictions as 'extreme' or 'irresponsible', and a threat to 'balanced development' (Livesey, 2002b, p. 135). Scientific research about climate change is constructed sceptically as 'debate', while economic predictions are presented as uncontrovertible fact. As Livesey states (2002b, p. 139), the ExxonMobil texts reactualize other texts, specifically discourses of environment and economic development taken from international agreements. In the sense developed by Fairclough (1989), these texts are a 'site of struggle' in which a battle to reconcile different discourses is perceptible. The ExxonMobil advertisements create a new hybrid discourse of 'eco-efficiency' and 'responsible capitalism' which makes strong claims to rationality while downplaying environmental concerns. They thus embody 'the dynamic interplay of discourses' and show the political role of language in wider processes of ongoing social change.

5.5 Hybrid genres

Since advertising continually borrows features from other genres, it might seem strange to devote a section of this particular chapter to hybrid genres. However, the type of advertisement that we are going to examine here is special because it is an advertisement that is in some sense presented as though it were something else. Normally, advertisements occupy particular spaces that are customarily reserved for them, and readers easily identify them for what they are. Moreover, advertisements generally stand out from their surroundings because they are different in terms of visual presentation, content and style. Even if an advertisement pops up in the middle of a newspaper webpage, it is generally quite clear to the reader that this is an advertisement and not a news flash. But there are some types of advertisement that appear to invade the space and usurp the features that we more normally associate with informative genres. These are commonly known as 'advertorials', although a variety of other names exist, such as 'infomercials' for the television equivalent. It may thus happen that someone is reading a magazine, and actually reads to the end of an advertorial without realizing that it is not just another article, because the presentation, format, content and style are those that are characteristically associated with journalism.

The use of advertorials is probably a strategy by which advertisers hope to avoid some of the disadvantages of traditional advertising. Advertising tends to be received sceptically by media users, because the communicative purpose is all too obvious. On the other hand, other means of obtaining publicity, such as use of press releases, leaves too much freedom to the newspapers or television channels, and there is no guarantee that the intended message will be conveyed. Advertorials are felt to provide the 'benefit mix' whereby the sponsor keeps control over the message, and yet the audience still perceives the message to be credible (Balasubramanian, 1994, p. 29; Twitchell, 1996, pp. 16–18). Advertorials can thus be regarded as essentially an innocuous hybrid genre that combines information with a marketing message, or, in a more sinister sense, as a 'bent genre' (Bhatia, 2004), that is, a kind of discursive wolf in sheep's clothing. Some critics have been vociferous on this point: Angus (2000) described advertorials as 'an unholy marriage' which may undermine the credibility of editorial content in general, while Eckman and Lindlof (2003, p. 65) decry the existence of an expanding 'grey area' in the newspaper industry which threatens social confidence in the media. One of the key issues here is, of course, whether or not readers are taken in by the advertorial. Some research has been carried out to find out the answer to this question. For example, Cameron and Ju-Pak (2000) analysed 430 such texts in US magazines and newspapers, and found that many of them looked exactly like news articles. Moreover, they were often found in combination with a traditional advertisement for the same product, a stratagem which is likely to confuse readers even more, since it seems odd to find two advertisements for the same product on the same page. In another empirical study, Cameron (1994) found that readers remembered more of the content of advertorials than of advertisements, presumably because they mentally classified the contents as news rather than promotion.

All of this varies somewhat from place to place. In some countries, self-regulatory measures exist whereby the media themselves agree to stipulate that advertisements of any kind must be identified as such. In this case, the reader may well be led to believe that the advertorial is a normal article. However, when the reader reaches the end, he or she will usually become aware that the text is not entirely what it seems, because the page may well inform the reader somewhere – perhaps rather unobtrusively – that this is in fact an advertisement. None the less, this is not true everywhere, and even in countries with self-regulatory codes, some research indicates that the media are reluctant to observe the guidelines (Salsnik, 2010).

Bhatia (2004, pp. 133–6) discusses advertorials and the way in which they generally differ from 'normal' advertisements. In his view, the main contrast lies in the absence of any direct attempt to establish the credentials of the company in question, and in the lack of a direct appeal to the reader. In other words, the stance of the advertorial writer mimics that of the news reporter, claiming a degree of objectivity and an 'independent' voice. At the same time, Bhatia feels that this independence only goes so far: unlike most editorials or feature articles, the advertorial stresses the positive aspects of the product in question, since any negative elements would create a conflict of purpose.

To examine these claims, let us take a look at a rather typical example of an advertorial on a familiar subject: a face cream that eliminates wrinkles. Placed in a magazine containing articles on health, beauty and diet, the subject of the advertorial is not dissimilar from that of the articles around it. For the advertorial to have any credibility, this has to be the case.

The advertorial is also presented visually in such a way that it appears to be a normal magazine page. It has typical headlines and subheadings, graphics, photo inserts, and even a 'real' advertisement for the product, in the bottom right-hand corner space normally reserved for advertising. The page is headed 'Health news', and there is a large headline followed by a subheading, followed by a summarizing statement of the type found at the beginning of many news articles:

11. Erase wrinkles without Botox

     Breakthrough anti-aging cream combines three scientifically advanced wrinkle-reducing ingredients to rival the results of Botox.

     In recent years Botox has been promoted as the leader of anti-wrinkle treatments. Although it can be very successful, it is very expensive, painful, must be administered by a physician, and, in many cases, two to three treatments are needed for the desired corrections. After years of research and testing, a new safe, more affordable product offering comparable results is now available.

The advertorial mimics the visual appearance of the magazine page perfectly. However, as Bhatia observed in his analysis, the discourse of the advertorial is subtly different from that of the usual feature article. In the second extract below, the writer's stance seems at first to waver between a 'journalist' position, in which he/she feigns scepticism to claim objectivity, in the first sentence, and a more confident 'advertiser' position in the second sentence. The writer then consolidates the 'advertiser' voice by ending with a hard sell:

12. Unless you've actually tried Hydroxatone, it's hard to imagine it can work the miracles users claim it does. But women and men of all ages are using Hydroxatone and seeing real and noticeable results every day (. . .) Forget Botox or any other radical treatments. Throw out other creams that simply don't work (. . .) Within two weeks, Hydroxatone users will start to see results. With continued use, their skin will become softer, smoother, more radiant, and younger-looking, and that's GUARANTEED.

Although this may not always be the case, it seems to be most usual for advertorials to usurp the visual features of the magazine or news article or page, to the extent of including a 'real' advertisement for the product itself in the advertising space. On a discursive level, however, it is easier to distinguish between advertorials and genuine journalism, because the type of claims made, the absence of divergent voices and the general tone of the text tend to reflect some of the characteristics of advertising. At least at the present time, this is the kind of advertorial that is to be found in magazines and newspapers of all kinds, and there is no sign that this trend is likely to peter out.

None the less, as Izquierdo points out (2010a, 2010b), since the entire advertorial enterprise is fuelled by the hope that readers will believe that what they are reading is on the level of a news or feature article, or at least, has more credibility than a normal advertisement, it is likely that the advertorial genre will undergo a process of constant renewal, with new names and new genre features intended to convince readers in new ways. One current trend is that of the sponsored television documentary, such as that launched by McDonalds in Australia in 2012 (*Sydney Morning Herald*, 2012). The film 'McDonalds gets grilled', though paid for by the company, was made by an independent production company which ostensibly 'investigated' the company's performance and procedures, and billed as an 'objective' assessment of the company's quality. Critics within the Australian media expressed the view that films of this kind are likely to undermine public confidence in the media. However, in a commercial climate in which television channels are hungry for programmes but lack funding to make their own, initiatives such as sponsored programmes, which sprawl uncomfortably across the borders between advertising, sponsorship and objective reporting, are likely to become ever more frequent.

5.6 Discourses of branding

As the corporate world learns more about why people choose to buy one product rather than another, companies' overall promotional strategies increasingly centre on the brand as a a whole, rather than on specific items. Brands are understood as a network of associations in the mind of the consumer, a map of positive or negative associations or a symbolic language (de Mooij, 2010, p. 24). Particular groups of consumers have a common way of perceiving certain things. With persuasion, they may be induced to share certain associations, and the sharing of those associations will give them greater strength and meaning.

Thus brands are built of associations (between specific products and makes and their features and qualities) and of communities (of people who use particular brands).

Communities of consumption

Let us look at this in more detail. The importance of the community – whatever its definition – is undeniable. A community is a group of people who identify themselves as a group on the basis of some shared characteristic, whether in terms of ethnicity, geographical location, occupation, leisure interest, political convictions or religious beliefs and practices. It is clear that communities are instrumental to human well-being. Through communities, people share essential resources and build meanings that help them to sustain their lives. However, the close-knit, tightly defined communities of the past, identified by location, social class, religious affiliation, profession and so on, are disappearing everywhere, with greater social and physical mobility, erosion of barriers, changes in kinship groups and so on. This has led sociologists and others to talk of the disintegration of traditional communities and the rise of other forms of social association in their place (Giddens, 1984; Baudrillard, 1998). In the words of McAlexander et al. (2002, p. 38):

> With no more than a cursory look at contemporary society, we can identify communities whose primary bases of identification are either brands or consumption activities, that is, whose meaningfulness is negotiated through the symbolism of the marketplace.

Boorstin (1974, p. 89) already talked of consumption communities, which he characterized as 'invisible new communities (. . .) created and preserved by how and what men (*sic*) consume'. He traces this tendency to the United States after the industrial revolution, when people's sense of community shifted away from tightly bound geographical collectives towards tenuous bonds of consumer habits and brand affiliation (Boorstin, 1974, p. 148):

> The modern American, then, was tied, if only by the thinnest of threads and by the most volatile, switchable loyalties, to thousands of other Americans in nearly everything he ate or drank or drove or read or used. Old-fashioned political and religious communities now became only two among many new, once unimagined fellowships. Americans were increasingly held to others not

by a few iron bonds, but by countless gossamer webs knitting together the trivia of their lives.

McAlexander et al. (2002) dispute the nature of the 'gossamer webs' to which Boorstin alludes, and develop a more sophisticated model to describe the nature of the brand community. They show how relationships between customers play a leading role in those customers' loyalty to a particular brand, but surmise that this is not the whole story. Other relationships are also important, such as the relationship between the customer and the branded object itself, between the customer and the marketing agent and between the customer and the institution that owns the brand. In their analysis, the brand community centring on the customer is a dynamic entity influenced by many factors. A brand community may be geographically bounded, it may be rich in social context or completely devoid of it, it may be stable or transient, it may intermesh with other brand communities or stand alone.

In their study of brand communities, McAlexander et al. (2002) used ethnographic methodology to investigate Jeep and Harley Davidson communities through fieldwork conducted at 'brandfests' (i.e. Jeep Jamborees) as well as self-report data from members. At the 'brandfests', shared consciousness, rituals and traditions were observed, along with a shared moral responsibility, all of which were heightened at the event, probably boosted by a desire to experience a sense of 'belonging' and a fear of rejection. Moreover, in these events, veterans charactistically took a leading role and offered support to newcomers, helping to build the brand community through talk and action. Event organizers and marketers also deliberately carried out community-building activities, including road safety programmes, brand-related story-telling, exaltation of related lifestyle patterns and so on. By the end of such events, the brand community had been further strengthened by the friendships forged among members, which might be maintained throughout the year, or renewed at the next event. McAlexander et al. (2002) triangulated their fieldwork with quantitative data, finding that brand users were generally more positive about the brand after they had participated in an event. One participant said that she now felt that she belonged to a 'benevolent family of Jeep owners that includes both owners and marketers' (2002, p. 47). The discursive construction of community had coalesced around the brand in her mind.

Of course, these results come with the proviso that such strong brand communities might be more typical in the case of brands for large, expensive and noticeable products (like cars), and that the findings of studies like these might well be less applicable in the case of smaller, cheaper products. None the less, it seems that the brand community is the ultimate form of 'buy-in'. This goes beyond the persuasive metaphors of advertising, which are supposed to evoke positive associations in people's minds. In the brand community, the consumers themselves live out the metaphor and define themselves by the product. But perhaps, as Baudrillard says, all advertising is ultimately about brand and image. These are the only meaningful sign. In his view, the juxtaposed signs of any advertisement 'culminate in the super-sign that is the brand name, which is the only real message' (1998, p. 148) in the order of signification organized around consumption that underpins the consumer society. All advertising, all brands, tend towards this type of 'brand community', as people increasingly seek their own identity in consumption.

5.7 Assessing advertising

Deceitful or ludic?

Advertising is ubiquitous, but it is also curiously indeterminate. Discourse analysts have considerable difficulty explaining exactly what advertising is, or drawing up reliable guidelines as to how advertising works. Moreover, observers and critics are divided as to what value should be attached to the advertising phenomenon. Is advertising the most powerful modern art form, or is it the ultimate expression of an empty, materialistic society? Does it set off the cycle of insatiability and dissatisfaction that constitutes one of the underlying mechanisms of the consumer society? Is it an evil deception, which tricks consumers into spending money by appealing to their greed, vanity or lust? Is it a shocking indictment of human weakness, indicative not so much of the advertisers' desire to seduce as of 'our desire to be seduced' (Baudrillard, 1998, p. 127)? Does it exert an unhealthy power over people by undermining their self-esteem and preying on their insecurities? Or is it simply a kind of game, a sort of pleasant joke that can be shared with other members of our peer group to promote social bonding?

   On an anthropological level, Goffman (1979) draws on studies in ethnography of communication (Malinowski, 1923) to explain how advertising often makes use of communicative behaviour that could be classed as 'ritual boasting' or 'display'. Such activity is not designed primarily to convey information, nor is it entirely phatic, but it seems rather to be a fundamental aspect of human behaviour which could be linked to some basic competitive instinct. In Cook's view (1992), advertising seems to reflect such a purpose. The very repetitiveness and predictability of advertisements both undermine their informational content and bolster the idea that they belong to the category of social display. There is even a suggestion that the kind of repetitive function offered by advertisements has taken the place of other socially accepted forms of repetition, such as folksong, poetry and prayer. In Cook's words (1992, p. 228):

> One might speculate that repetition induces a sense of security, community, and is a means of establishing or confirming (if only to oneself) identity within the society to which the text belongs (because everyone within the society knows the same text).

A second way in which advertising challenges the analyst is in its aesthetic dimension, and the extent to which this is undermined by its commercial purpose. As Cook points out, advertising is generally thought to have little value, because it is funded by companies wishing to sell, while art (music, painting, poetry) is felt to be intrinsically valuable, even though many great works of art were 'sponsored' by wealthy patrons and would never have been executed without them. Art, some people feel, is intrinsically 'rebellious' and 'honest', whereas advertising is tainted with commercialism. Yet the concept of the artist implicit in this view is essentially a product of Romanticism: it projects an image of the creative artist who is radically at odds with the society around. Earlier eras would have recognized no such criterion.

Many critics of advertising place the 'real world' in counterposition to the 'dream world' of advertising, arguing that it is fundamentally mendacious and conducive to a condition of permanent dissatisfaction in its receivers. Advertising, they argue, leads people on to purchase things that they do not need. It is deceitful in its claims. It takes no responsibility for its effects, caring only for profit (Cook, 1992). Some critics would push the argument further: the consumer society is itself a symbolic system based on the exchange of signs. Consumption is an order of significations, a system of signs, which functions as an ideological structure that exerts pressure on the individuals who participate in that system. In this, the system of consumption runs parallel to and interacts with the system of production. In Baudrillard's words, 'the system of needs is the product of the system of production' (1998, p. 74). In such a system, Baudrillard tends to adopt the view that advertising is merely a set of signs standing for other signs (the products), which forms part of the structure that leads people to consume more and different signs, in an endless cycle of unsatisfied needs: 'this forever unquenchable desire which signifies itself locally in successive objects and needs' (p. 77). However, his analysis of advertising is somewhat contradictory – like many of his ideas, which tend to the visionary rather than the systematic. On the one hand, he attributes some special power to the signs projected by advertising, since they conjure up a 'magical, miraculous, fantasic world' (p. 17) which fuels the impulse to consume and endows people's imagined 'needs' with a compulsive quality. Yet although advertising is the ultimate 'pseudo-event' (1998, p. 126), we cannot dismiss it as lies. Baudrillard sets out the issue in the following way (1998, pp. 127–8):

> The problem of the 'veracity' of advertising should be posed as follows: if advertising men really 'lied', they would be easy to unmask. But they do not. (. . .) For the good reason that there is no longer either any original or any real referential dimension and, like all myths and magic formulas, advertising is based on a different kind of verification, that of the self-fulfilling prophecy. (. . .) Advertising is prophetic language, in so far as it promotes not learning or understanding, but hope. What it says presupposes no anterior truth (that of the object's use value), but an ulterior confirmation by the reality of the prophetic sign it sends out. (. . .) The consumer, by his purchase, will merely ratify the coming to pass of the myth.

In a still more sinister sense, Baudrillard sees advertising as part of a system of social control and regulation which plays an ideological role, integrating people into ways of behaving and thinking that underpin society. Individuals are constructed as compliant members of society precisely through being constructed as consumers and producers. His view of integration through consumption is expressed as follows (1998, p. 94):

> It is by training them in the unconscious discipline of a code, and competitive cooperation at the level of that code; it is not by creating more creature comforts, but by getting them to play by the rules of the game. This is how consumption can on its own substitute for all ideologies, and, in the long run take over the role of integrating the whole of society, as hierarchical or religious rituals did in primitive societies.

Assessments of advertising that are less visionary, more balanced, yet still critical, are to be found in a variety of sources. On the one hand, advertisers themselves argue that they are essential in the modern economy, and that the discourses they use are simply a reflection of the society in which they operate.

On the other hand, some mainstream religious bodies have shown themselves to be sensitive to the potentially manipulative powers of the advertising campaign. In its statement on ethics in advertising, the Pontifical Council for Social Communications acknowledges the informative and creative functions of advertising, but states (1997, I, 3):

> We disagree with the assertion that advertising simply mirrors the attitudes and values of the surrounding culture. No doubt advertising, like the media of social communications in general, does act as a mirror. But, also like media in general, it is a mirror that helps shape the reality it reflects, and sometimes it presents a distorted image of reality. Advertisers are selective about the values and attitudes to be fostered and encouraged, promoting some while ignoring others.

This distorting effect, the authors argue, is particularly obvious where advertising celebrates materialism and propagates the myth that 'abundance of possessions leads to happiness and fulfillment', creating 'needs' where there are none. Advertisers are reminded that they have 'a serious duty to express and foster an authentic vision of human development in its material, cultural and spiritual dimensions' (1997, IV, 17) which should not be overridden by the pressing need for constant novelty which characterizes the work of the copywriter.

One very interesting idea about advertising, which goes some way towards addressing some of the above points, is that it now enjoys such a huge presence in our lives that it has become an inseparable part of popular culture. In this view, advertising is essentially light-weight, tossing up patterns of code-play that build connections across different areas of life. It fuses the private domain with public discourses, but does so in a way that is trivial rather than profound. Advertising contributes to the 'fun' element of our shared culture, adds colour, and allows us to 'play' with words and concepts, or to laugh at ourselves. Rather than being deeply deceitful or immoral, advertising may be simply a form of cultural communication that is largely trivial or ludic.

But although advertising might be light-weight in its individual manifestations, it may be more sinister in the overall distortion caused by its ubiquitous presence and the shallowness of its promises. Advertising is on the edge of our consciousness, likely to pass unnoticed. Yet it is one of the threads that holds together the fabric of social existence today. The values that it propagates will influence us unless we have an educated critical consciousness and the will-power to resist. Educators have a vital role to play in teaching young people how to deconstruct the discourses of advertising, and how to recognize the distortions that advertising perpetrates in our value system.

Challenges for the analyst

Of all the discourses associated with corporations, advertising must be the most complex and the most challenging to the analyst. It is not just that advertising is a kind of secondary genre which takes its concrete form from a multitude of other genres. Even once we have accepted that advertising could, potentially, borrow from almost any other visual or textual genre, we are faced with the problem of explaining what the essence might be that unites all of these different realizations. Do they share the communicative purpose of selling or promoting something? Most do, but some actually do the opposite. So is the purpose simply to bring about a change in behaviour, either one way or the other? If so, what makes advertising different from other genres intended to change people's behaviour, such as health information leaflets, educational literature or religious tracts? Where can we draw the dividing line between advertising discourse as such, and the type of promotional discourse that pervades other corporate genres?

Perhaps it would be wrong to take the straightforward view that a boundary has to exist. In reality, genres seep into each other at the edges, or merge together to form hybrids, and discourses may run across many genres without threatening their integrity. Corporate discourse almost always seems to contain a promotional element, which is most obvious in advertising, but which is very prominent in other aspects of corporate communications. Moreover, as public relations strategies become increasingly sophisticated, and our knowledge of audience reactions grows, we can expect that the trend towards blending promotional discourses with information will continue, and that the corporate image will increasingly be presented in the most positive light possible at all times, by the controlled use of a broad repertoire of discursive resources. In other words, the phenomena we have seen operating in advertising will gradually come to pervade all the other discourses that are within the company's control.

6

Communicating with the World: Websites, Reviews, Sponsorship

A large proportion of the communicative output of companies is not directed towards one specific audience, but rather to the world at large, to anyone who might be interested in finding out about the company and its activities. This would include stakeholders of all kinds, such as the ones we have talked about in the previous chapters, but also people who have perhaps a more general – or a more particular – interest in what the company is doing. This might include people who just want to know where the nearest furniture store is, or what oil companies are doing about the environment, for example, but it might also take in people who really want to know precisely what profit a company made in 2008, or where they can buy bulk supplies of their favourite energy drink. Of course, the first place where most people will begin their enquiry is now the internet. Company websites almost always include an 'about us' section explaining salient aspects of the company's identity. If people have a more specific query about some aspect of the company's activities, they may go to one of the other documents freely available on the website. These could include an illustrated Annual Review, which some companies produce as a shorter, less technical alternative to the Annual Report, or a range of more specialized corporate publications, with titles like 'Corporate Social Responsibility Report' or 'Sustainability Report'. At the same time, the general public will also be made aware of the company's actions through the media in general. The media often centre on negative events – and the company's actions may often be directed towards 'crisis management' activities of various kinds, all of which have a discursive dimension. At the same time, companies also attract media attention in a more predictable way, as sponsors of sports events, development programmes and so on. In this chapter, we shall look at the discourses employed when companies communicate with the world at large.

6.1 Corporate websites

The company webpage is hugely important in the company's public relations enterprise as a whole. Just as firms use shop windows and store design to influence the impressions of their visitors and differentiate themselves from the competition, so in cyberspace, the corporate website is used to present the company visually to anyone who drops in. It is important to note that this is a direct form of contact, like the shop window, and is quite unlike the mediated contact that consumers might have with a company through the press or television, for example. Moreover, just as consumers who try to make a purchase in a retail store receive a positive or negative impression of the company, so website visitors also form their impression of the company on the basis of the design and organization of the website (Winter et al., 2003; Pollach, 2005). In this, sites have to be user-friendly, the information must be credible and well organized, and the presentation must be attractive (Pollach, 2005). Although this is something we all know intuitively, it is a subject of particularly intense interest to public relations professionals, who understand that the task of global 'impression management' carried out by the company's communication department is conducted more and more through online media (Heinze and Hu, 2006). Increasingly, companies are turning their attention to managing the public impressions of entire organizations, by a coordinated approach to the different branches of corporate communication, and the website, which is arguably the most visible and accessible manifestation of the company, is a prime site for putting this aim into practice.

Information and interaction

In an increasingly competitive global scenario, it is not enough for companies just to provide information or offer a good image. People must be induced to use the website and preferably also to make purchases through it. The website must be appropriately tagged and indexed, so that people looking for a particular product or service are quickly directed to it from the search engines. But once they are there, the site itself must be attractive enough to encourage the user to stay and buy, or at least stay and read. To this end, the website must be visually satisfying and easy to navigate. If possible, it should also offer some concrete uses, such as e-commerce or problem-solving facilities. Heinze and Hu (2006) conducted a major study of the websites of all the Standard and Poors 500 companies (the largest firms in the US economy), and measured eight different features that were included. These were: product advertisement, product information, career opportunities, investor information, online sales, online account access, support contact and customer support. They found that in the six years from 1997 to 2003, there had been a spectacular increase in all of these features across almost all sectors of the economy. Online sales had become particularly important in the retail trade, and online account management had taken on an important role in the financial sector. In a word, these websites had developed to let customers actually do things with them. They had become interactive in a meaningful sense.

But what is interactivity? People often use the word to mean all kinds of 'new' features that imply some kind of interaction between a user and a site. However, some critics have suggested that the word 'interactivity' is used to serve so many different meanings that it tends to cause confusion with other concepts, such as user-friendliness (Heeter, 2000). Interactivity basically has to imply some kind of reciprocity experienced by the user of a site. However, full interactivity sometimes means more than this. For example, Rafaeli (1988) makes a distinction between three different levels of communication: (1) two-way (non-interactive), (2) reactive (quasi-interactive) and (3) fully interactive (Rafaeli, 1988, p. 120). Complete interactivity demands both sides react to each other, permitting both sides to participate in the conversation flow, with both partners producing their own information and understanding the information offered by the other. Such 'interactivity' is obviously something more than the kind of interaction familiar to website users which involves clicking on a link to obtain information or register a choice.

It makes it slightly clearer if we try to break down the concept of interactivity into the different types of feature that may embody this on the web. One suggestion is that interactivity in websites can usefully be understood as existing in six aspects of internet: user control, responsiveness, real-time interaction, connectedness, personalization and playfulness (Dhokalia et al., 2000; Gustavsen and Tilley, 2003). These authors explain these six aspects as follows (based on Dhokalia et al., 2000, pp. 6–8):

- User control: the extent to which the user can choose the timing, content and sequence. Most websites allow people to navigate them at their own pace, select what to visit and choose their own path through the contents. Some offer choice of language, search engines and print or text only options.
- Personalization: information is tailored to meet the needs of the user (i.e. through systems of user registration and tracking, or by offering different sections for different groups of people).

- Responsiveness: the degree to which users can influence the content of the page, such as by completing feedback questionnaires, adding questions to FAQ sections or sending an email in the 'contact' box.
- Connectedness: the feeling of being linked to the world outside the site, by communicating asynchronously with other users in forums, message boards and online user communities.
- Real-time interaction: the option to communicate with other users or with representatives of the company in real time, as in chat rooms or online interactive question-and-answer sessions.
- Playfulness: the combination of information and entertainment, including animation and interactive games.

Which of these features are included is a matter for the site design. Gustavsen and Tilley surveyed the corporate websites of 16 major American companies in 2003, and found that at that time only one – Microsoft – incorporated elements of all six kinds. Three other companies had four kinds of element, and the rest all contained fewer. User control and responsiveness were features of most of the sites, though not all, while personalization features were found in seven, real-time interactions and playfulness in four, and connectedness in only one.

Since the time of this study, the situation has developed considerably, particularly in the area of personalization. One of the variables that can be determined from the outset is the location. For example, the financial management company, Aberdeen Asset Management, places the geographical option at the start, opening its group home page with the words 'Welcome to the global investment world of Aberdeen Asset Management. Please choose your location. Americas. Europe. Asia and Australia' blazoned across an image of the world. However, this is not the only variable. Corporate sites today usually include a menu of 'user roles' so that the person who enters the site can immediately identify him/herself as an 'investor' or a 'client', and click through to a new page containing options appropriate for people acting in this role. The possible 'roles' vary, according to the sector and the uses for which the company has designed the website. Unilever provides a general home page with informative-promotional sections such as 'brands in action' and 'sustainable living', but discreetly includes icons that point investors towards the 'investor centre', those interested in media coverage to the 'media centre', and job hunters to the 'careers' section. Home pages offering specific user tracks doubtless serve to order information in a way that is useful. However, they also delineate the kind of roles that a user may take on.

The personalized approach is taken further on the pages of companies that sell directly to the public. For companies that sell to the public, personalization facilities are not just intended for consumer convenience. Since user registration is a requisite if orders are going to be placed, companies have learnt to put the information that they obtain through this to good use. The more sophisticated e-commerce websites such as Amazon now include consumer tracking devices which enable them to record what a particular user has bought and recommend new purchases along similar lines.

Despite the increasing personalization, other dimensions of interactivity seem to be less frequent. In the ten years that have passed since Gustavsen and Tilley's sample was collected, major US and UK company websites have not greatly expanded their affordances in the areas of real-time interaction or connectedness. Obviously, the technical facilities are there, so it could be that other factors influence the kind of interactivity found on corporate websites. Research into interactive resources has suggested that different types of resource appear to be more popular in different kinds of culture. If we try to analyse these phenomena in terms of Hofstede's indices (2001, see chapter 5), we see that countries with a high score on collectivism tend to prefer customer–customer communication, in the form of forums and chatrooms. Individualistic cultures offer more opportunities for the consumer to interact with the company. A comparison between corporate websites in China and the United States (Pan and Xu, 2009) found that US corporations provided more direct online marketing, often with direct communication with consumers, including facilities such as the 'personal choice helper', as well as a wider choice with more search functions. However, Chinese corporations were more likely to offer online space for customer interaction (found in 15% of the Chinese sites investigated as opposed to only 5% of those from the United States). We could also speculate that the sudden rise of social networks like Facebook has helped to define the role of the webpage more clearly. Such networks are easily updated and offer an ideal platform for news and photographs, user comments and so on. The webpage, by contrast, is something more solid and monumental, relatively permanent over time, with a rather 'official' character.

Another type of analysis that has been carried out in this area relates to the degree of interactivity found in particular areas of corporate websites. The more interactive a particular section of the website is, the more it helps to build a relationship with the public. A section that only provides information in a 'flat' format is essentially unidirectional: the company explains itself to its audience. But a section that is interactive or allows users to give feedback facilitates two-way communication and makes it possible for the company to build relationships with the audience. Capriotti and Moreno (2007) looked at the sites of all the companies quoted in the selective index of the Spanish stock exchange, the IBEX-35, to find out how interactive the sections devoted to corporate social responsibility were. Although most of the companies had a specific section about CSR, these sections were predominantly expository rather than interactive. All the companies that had CSR sections used graphic resources on them, but only 57 per cent used interactive elements. None had interactive opinion polls, forums or chatrooms that would allow visitors to interact with each other, or with the company, about these issues. In this particular context, it seems that CSR is understood as part of the company's role to inform the public and legitimize itself in their eyes. These companies do not understand this as a dialogic process, or one in which the audience has a voice. Thus the 'interactiveness' of particular parts of the website can help analysts to interpret how the company might intend us to read and react to those sections.

Organizing information, building conceptual models

Professionals who work in the field of internet design and hypermedia in general have paid considerable attention to the way in which users navigate through websites, and the conceptual model of the information in that site that users are able to construct. Because people explore websites by traversing hyperlinks from one webpage to another, their ability to build a model in their mind of what the website has to tell them is influenced by the interplay between the site's content organization, its design and its navigability features, such as hyperlinks and search facilities. For the designers who create corporate webpages, it is vital to facilitate user orientation. This means that they need to understand how the organization of information in websites reflects the interplay between design and information, and predict the way that users will negotiate different features.

This aspect of websites is obviously of interest to the discourse analyst, as well as to the designer, but the complexity involved in researching multimedia material makes it particularly challenging. The research that exists tends to fall into one of two categories. It may be focused on individual pages, taking into account their 'depth' in the sense of the number of clicks required to reach them from the home page, and their 'width' in the sense of the number of pages accessible from that page. Studies of this kind often centre on how easy the page is to use, or on the hierarchy of information established by the varying 'depths' of different aspects. The other approach takes a holistic view of the webpage, understanding it as having a horizontal dimension in terms of the number of sections it is divided into, and a vertical dimension which covers the number of subdivisions within the sections. The 'holistic' approach pays greater attention to the meaningful grouping of pages, and tends to see the homepage itself as the highest level of hierarchy.

Djonov (2007) developed a framework for understanding webpages based on systemic functional linguistics (Halliday and Hasan, 1976; Halliday and Matthiesen, 2004). She takes the three fundamental areas of meaning-making familiar within the field of systemic functional linguistics, namely ideational, interpersonal and textual, and extends her analysis to include images, sound and the interaction of other multimedia resources (Kress and van Leeuwen, 2001). She starts from the Hallidayan notion (derived from the Prague school of lingistics) of the 'theme'. Within the clause, the 'theme' is 'the element which serves as the point of departure for the message; it is that with which the clause is concerned' (Halliday, 1994, p. 37); it is what the rest of the clause, the 'rheme', is about. Martin (1992) extends this to create the notion of the 'hyper-theme', which is an introductory group of sentences that can be used to predict a particular pattern in what follows. Djonov (2007) applies this idea to the home page of the website, with its icons and titles that enable users to predict what the rest of the page will contain. In other words, they have a 'cataphoric' textual function, pointing forwards to the contents of the site. In another sense, these icons and titles also establish an interpersonal relationship with the users: in the case of corporate websites, for example, this can be seen in the way some companies offer specific sections or 'tracks' for different categories of user, such as investors or clients. Moreover, the main page of each section functions as a 'theme' page that sets the tone for the sections indexed from it. Visual elements such as titles or images may also function as 'themes' within a multi-modal unit (Thibault, 2001). In Djonov's framework (2007, p. 152), the relationship between a home page and the main pages of the sections, the subsections of these sections and so on, can be understood in systemic functional terms as a hierarchy of themes.

The visual identity of the site as a whole, and of sections within themselves, is usually established through common design features, frames, navigation bars, colour schemes and so on. Elements such as the navigation bar often reinforce the hierarchy of themes by showing the user exactly 'where' he or she is in the scheme of things at this particular time. This imposes a certain macrostructure on the information that is otherwise freely available, and may suggest a particular conceptual structure to the user. On the other hand, a kind of linearity is also enforced, in cases where one element can only be visualized after another, that is, a specific sequence is imposed, as in the case of certain educational platforms. Moreover, some elements in the site, such as the home page, have a 'core' status, whereas other parts are 'optional', which again affects the way in which the user relates to the content. But there again, the different subsections may also be linked to each other in an intricate network of internal hyperlinks, which makes it very difficult to establish a clear order, path or hierarchy. Sites with dense internal hypertext links offer an abundance of alternative orders and paths to the user. Some websites are very hierarchical or linear in their structure, tending to enforce a particular concept of how the contents should be understood. Others leave more freedom to the user and encourage exploration. Since company sites tend towards the first of these, we can suppose their designers wish to impose a particular conceptual model of the firm and its activities: this is a top-down textual organization of a somewhat monologic kind.

Of course, there is also the question of how one website relates to other sites out there in cyberspace, in the form of outward-pointing hyperlinks. These tend not to be analysed in depth by researchers who study the semiotics of webpages, because such links are not 'contained' within the architecture of the page itself, but relate to it in a tangential sort of way, rather as a landscape does to a building. This dimension is 'horizontal', in the sense that it is similar to the 'spread' of sections that are interlinked on the same level within a page, but is much wider in its potential scope. In fact, company websites rarely contain outward-pointing links, tending to be self-contained universes holding within them everything that it is desirable for stakeholders to know.

A discourse analytical approach to corporate websites could proceed by taking into account the 'vertical' and 'horizontal' planes on which webpages operate, but also by considering what is thematized, what hierarchies are established and how these are reinforced or complicated by hyperlinking patterns.

6.2 'About us' sections

Since it is a very complex undertaking to research the whole of a corporate website, because of the sheer volume of information, and the intricate nature of the way the different types of content are connected to each other, we shall now focus on one extremely significant section found in most corporate websites: the section in which the company presents itself to the general public, often known as the 'about us' section. An overview of the 'about us' pages from FTSE top-100 companies will be used to illustrate an interesting range of strategies that companies appear to be deploying in this section.

As we have seen, there are many possible ways of analysing webpages in terms of size and complexity, yet studies that combine design issues with language issues are less frequent. Few studies of corporate websites take in the discursive level. However, some analysts have returned to Halliday's threefold structure (ideational, textual, interpersonal) to make sense of the type of communication that is established through webpages (Pollach, 2005; Djonov, 2007). As we saw in Chapter 2, in Hyland's framework (1998, 2005), the textual and the interpersonal aspects of the text are reorganized under the heading of 'interactional resources', that is, ways in which the writers try to involve readers in the text, in terms of 'stance' and 'engagement'. In the context of multimodal phenomena, however, this analysis needs to be opened up to include other aspects. In what follows, the 'about us' sections of the corporate webpages will be analysed in terms of their most striking features.

Presenting the positive points

If we take a look at the 'about us' sections from the websites of companies, we will find that the contents of these sections have many common themes, even though they also vary across sectors. Most will contain some company history and an outline of the company's current status, mission statements, information about senior management and allusions to corporate social responsibility issues. Although they have a lot in common with certain sections of the Annual Report (see Chapter 4), it is worth reviewing some of their main discursive features quickly, to complement our understanding of the corporate website and its contents.

Many of these companies include numerical data to convey a sense of importance. These may be highlighted by using colours, graphs or a striking visual format, as in the following 'information box' from Royal Dutch Shell's 'Shell at a glance' section:

1. Shell by numbers

   + 80 countries where we operate
   ~90,000 number of employees
   48% of our production is natural gas
   18.8 million tonnes of LNG sold during the year
   3.2 million barrels of gas and oil we produce every day
   43,000 Shell service stations worldwide (Royal Dutch Shell)

Another frequent method of reinforcing the company's positive self-description is by mentioning external validation, such as awards or positions in company rankings. For example, pharmaceutical company GlaxoSmithKline has an entire section of the webpage dedicated to 'our awards'; which is indexed from the 'about us' landing page. Here, we can click on links such as:

2. Our world-class health and safety excellent awards.

   Find out why we are a respected leader in recruitment.

   We have awards for diversity and our community work. (GlaxoSmithKline)

The presence of links of this kind help to structure our perception of the company in a positive manner.

Heading off criticism

Various aspects of the 'about us' sections can also be understood as being dialogic in the sense that they fulfil the function of warding off potential criticisms. This 'legitimatory' function (see Chapter 4) may be aimed at dispelling the idea that a company is suffering from the economic downturn, or may be directed at possible criticisms of its business practices, products or social and environmental record. Classic examples of this are found on the webpages of oil and mining companies, since they belong to a sector which has not had an unblemished record in these respects:

3. Rio Tinto is a leading international mining group (. . .) To deliver superior returns to shareholders over time, Rio Tinto takes a long term and responsible approach to the Group's business (. . .) Our products help fulfil vital consumer needs and improve living standards. We operate, and eventually close, our operations safely, responsibly and sustainably. (Rio Tinto)

The 'about us' sections found on the company webpages in 2012 – an era of crisis – contain many allusions to efficiency and value for money. The following example about a drugs company's scientific research is strongly agentive and saturated with economic discourse (externalization, investments, opportunity, sharing risk). Notably, it also positions the company's research scientists as economic resources (italics):

4. We have increased the level of externalization of our research, allowing us to access new areas of science and to share the risk of development with our

partners. We have also made decisions earlier around pipeline progressions, so that only those medicines that we believe will be significantly differentiated from existing therapies are progressed. We are ensuring our early stage research investments are made where the science suggests there is greatest opportunity. *We have created smaller, more agile groups of scientists* who are accountable for progressing their projects through discovery and development. (GlaxoSmithKline)

Social and environmental concerns are increasingly grouped together under the heading of 'sustainability'. The leitmotiv of sustainability pervades their webpages, usually being present in the 'about us' section, as well as having sizeable sections of its own. Indeed, some companies no longer produce a 'corporate social responsibility report', preferring to call its replacement the 'sustainability report' (Unilever).

5. To embed sustainability into every stage of the life cycle of our products, we're working with our suppliers to support responsible approaches to agriculture. We're also learning from NGOs and other organizations, recognising that building a truly sustainable business is not something we can do without expert advice. (Unilever)

Many of the aspects emphasized particularly in these sections vary from sector to sector. Oil companies try to ward off one kind of criticism, but other companies are engaged in dialogue with other critical voices. For example, British American Tobacco states that:

6. We believe that because our products pose risks to health, it is all the more important that our business is managed responsibly. (British American Tobacco)

Twenty-first-century corporations show a marked tendency to communicate in terms of 'good business practices', 'standards' and 'codes', which has the effect of enshrining their operations in a quasi-legal framework and thereby appearing to guarantee their quality:

7. We want to work with suppliers who have values similar to our own and work to the same standards we do. Our Business partner code, aligned to our own Code of business principles, comprises ten principles covering business integrity and responsibilities relating to employees, consumers and the environment. (Unilever)

We may also observe that while promotional language tends to be much the same in tone over the years, legitimatory discourses vary according to the sensibility of the moment. If the impact of oil companies on the environment is under the media spotlight, then oil companies make a more determined attempt to ward of criticism by stressing their ecological record. If recent attention has been drawn to corruption in the banking industry, then banks are more likely to draw attention to proper business practices. In this, local cultural issues are also important. Chinese corporations devoted considerable efforts to explaining the history of the company, and to demonstrating that they had quality certification such as ISO 9000, which was highlighted in 40 per cent of cases. US companies dedicated less space to company history, and only 13 per cent mentioned quality certification (Pan and Xu, 2009). On the other hand, US companies were much more concerned to explain that they acted in a way that was socially and environmentally responsible (77% of US corporations did this, compared with 44% of Chinese companies). This reflects the growing need for legitimatory activities in Western corporations, and seems to point to issues regarding the levels of development in these two countries.

Textual organization

The landing page of 'about us' may well contain the main information, or it may refer users on to an 'at a glance', 'overview' or 'introduction' in which the principal facts or ideas are expressed. In terms of textual organization, the 'about us' sections are usually further divided into subsections that can be accessed from an index that remains on the page. This index usually contains sections on company history, strategy or vision, management, and perhaps references to corporate social responsibility in the form of particular social or environmental initiatives, or to a 'foundation' established for this purpose. The role of this index is vital in establishing the conceptual organization of the page, and thereby shaping the model of the company that is offered to the user. Through these textual devices, the company is framed as an entity with a history ('past') and a strategy ('future'), guided by human agency, and acting benignly to benefit humankind.

Other textual features common in these sections are the use of visually attractive headings ('responsible business', 'innovation') within the page, which serve to order information, break up the visual monotony and set a positive tone; the organization of information into very short paragraphs, consisting of one or two bald assertions; the inclusion of interactive elements, particularly timelines and maps, to illustrate the company's history and the scope of its operations; and the inclusion of links in the margins, or hyperlinks in the text, that take the user 'out' into other areas of the corporate website that the company wants to emphasize.

Interpersonal elements

As Pollach (2005) found, company self-presentations contain interpersonal elements of various kinds. These classically include attitudinal lexis (positive adjectives and adverbs, for example), as well as grammatical features such as pronouns, direct questions, imperatives. However, in webpages, we might add other features to the list, such as interactive options, quizzes, user roles and contact facilities.

Personality and impersonality

As might be expected in an 'about us' section, a large number of the statements in these sections begin with 'we':

8. Our mission is to deliver strong fund performance across diverse asset classes in which we believe we have a sustainable competitive edge. (Aberdeen Asset Management)

As in the Annual Report, the omnipresence of 'we' tends to project a strong corporate identity, and engages the reader directly. Along similar lines, the 'about us' sections also often take trouble to provide a 'human face' for the organization, in the form of photographs of the CEO or the management team, which might be supposed to have a humanizing and personalizing function. Some sections even speak directly to the user, simulating a conversation with a client:

9. You told us you wanted simpler, more powerful communication tools for your business. And you asked for easy access to your network files, your emails, your staff, customers and suppliers. Our answer is the range of integrated (. . .) services that we call total communications. By bringing all of your communications together, we give your people the freedom to work how and where they want (. . .) (Vodafone)

However, on occasions agency is removed in order to lend an air of impersonality to the statements. Logically enough, this seems to be particularly frequent when there may be some negative consequences. The following example implies that the company has made cuts, and reduced the workforce:

10. The savings have been derived through improvements to our manufacturing operations, consolidation and streamlining of our support functions and increased efficiencies in R&D. (GlaxoSmithKline)

By manoeuvring in this way through the relational systems of discourse, companies step in and out of an agentive role as it suits their purposes.

Presenting a positive image

Another interpersonal aspect of these pages is the high proportion of evaluative vocabulary and the overwhelmingly positive framing of the information that is provided. In her study of similar pages, Pollach (2005) analyses the attitudinal aspects of corporate webpages as falling into four categories: size and scope, leadership, agents of change and corporate citizenship. The 'about us' sections in our sample follow the same pattern. In particular, they are peppered with words in the lexical range described in Chapter 4, which are sometimes known as 'power words', or which could be classified in terms of Appraisal analysis (Martin and White, 2004) as implying positive judgement (social esteem) and positive appreciation (reaction, composition and valuation):

11. *Millions* of businesses around the world use Vodafone to help them *grow*, reach new customers and *achieve extraordinary things*.

Some keywords recur, marking the tone of the message with particular force:

12. We are a *global* business with a *global* vision. We have *global* strategies and hard-won *global* scale. We must use and leverage these in order to win against *global* competition. To do so, requires *global* cohesion and discipline. (British American Tobacco)

It is also noticeable that claims about the future are often presented as categorical assertions expressed with 'will', and with use of verbs that imply positive action:

13. The Unilever Foundation's partnership with Oxfam *will improve* lives around the world through programmes designed *to empower* individuals. (Unilever)

Interactivity

The 'about us' sections of these pages generally contain an explicit 'contact' section, in which users can fill in a box or form to send a comment or enquiry to the company. The sections also refer users onwards to other contents, through hyperlinks that are phrased as direct imperatives or questions. Particularly in the case of manufacturing companies, these links often lead the user from an 'interested public' role projected in 'about us', to a 'consumer' role. For example, Unilever's 'about us' section consists mainly of a list of the company's achievements and aspirations phrased in the first-person plural, addressing the public in general, or a generic stakeholder who wants to know what the company is doing:

14. In 2010 we launched the Unilever Sustainable Living Plan – a set of targets designed to help us deliver our objective of growing our business while minimising our impact on the environment. (Unilever)

But as the reader goes down the same page, his or her eye will also move across into the right-hand margin where a different role is offered:

15. Home care

    Whether you want fresh, soft clothes or sparklingly clean bathrooms, our global home care brands can help. (Unilever)

The way that roles can be interchanged so quickly in an interactive environment is striking. However, as we shall see in section 6.5, the blurring of stakeholder roles is not only occurring on websites, but also extends to other aspects of corporate communication.

Multimodality

The 'about us' pages are made visually interesting by the use of colour and information boxes, but also by including images and videos. We may be struck by the abundance of attractive photographs that often have little direct connection with the text. Many of them show smiling people from many different ethnic backgrounds, or against backgrounds that suggest exotic locations. Videos also play an important part these pages, as do interactive graphics of different kinds (see above).

In general, we can see that the corporations opt to use multiple channels in order to put across their vision of what they are and what they do. Moreover, they structure this information textually to present a particular dynamic, forward-looking, human, responsible view of the company. In relational terms, these pages speak directly using the corporate 'we', to a user or users who may sometimes be constructed simply as an 'interested party', but sometimes offered a range of more specific roles ('investor', 'consumer'), or even presented with several at the same time. The relationality of the pages is heightened by inclusion of interactive sections which offer different choices to the user. But of course, the topoi of corporate communications are omnipresent – dynamism, size and scope, leadership and vision, quality and standards – and the discursive style remains within the range that we have already identified in the sections on employee and investor communications. The user seems to have a choice. But that choice is tightly constrained by the structure of the page, and by the predetermined options that have been prepared. Notably, the links on these pages are mainly internal, so that the website is a kind of 'closed system'. Even though external sources are often quoted, for example in the 'media' or 'awards' sections, it is rare to find links to external sources.

6.3 Corporate mission statements

Mission statements are a short encapsulation of the company's raison d'être, often including references to its achievements and aspirations, but also to more abstract entities such as its spirit and values. They are now regarded as a key instrument in the corporation, functioning both to anchor the corporation's identity within the company, and influence the image that it conveys to clients, investors and the general audience. They thus have a role in building team spirit among the employees and inculcating the values of the company among them. Yet they are also understood as being a statement to customers in which the company agenda is clearly expressed; and they are also intended as a message to investors, and to the media and general public.

Not only do companies dedicate considerable efforts to formulating their mission statements, but they also take care to communicate them to their employees. DeGenaro (2009, pp. 101–2) asserts that:

> Such statements act as mantras for organization members, reminding them what their objectives are (. . .) In a corporate environment, memorable missions foster loyalty and profitability (. . .) Customers likewise come to believe in the product based on repeatedly hearing a phrase (. . .) Regardless of length, a mission statement is a discursive articulation of an organization's purpose, crafted to build ethos.

If the word 'mantras' used here seems too strong, then we should consider the testimony by Rathbun (2007, p. 552), in which she explains that:

> In one experience with an organization, a ritual of reciting outloud the mission statement on a laminated card was performed at the monthly staff meetings. Before the meeting commenced, we were instructed to 'take out' our cards, which contained the vague metaphorical language (. . .) The mission statement's chant began: 'We are an elite team of inter-dependent professionals, who are experts at creating upscale living environments. We cultivate situational awareness and act with professionalism and integrity. We are proud. We are a team.'

In their ground-breaking discourse study of mission statements, Swales and Rogers (1995, p. 225) describe the statements as 'carriers of ideology' which rely heavily on abstractions to convey persuasive messages designed to bring stakeholders into line with the company's desired self-understanding. Mazza (1999) also explores corporate mission statements and points out the legitimatory functions that they exert, justifying the company's actions in the eyes of the world by showing that the company upholds certain norms or values that are socially recognized. In his words, these statements are 'the missing link between organizational action and social norms' (1999, p. 13). In what follows, we shall consider some representative examples of corporate mission statements from a sample of *Fortune* 500 companies (the 500 US companies with the highest revenues) in terms of their most typical features.

Concision, abstraction and metaphoricity

Since mission statements are by their very nature brief, their writers are concerned not to waste words. One manifestation of this could be described as a very concise use of language. Yet conciseness does not imply concreteness. In fact, the statements tend rather to abstraction. An overview of these mission statements shows the efforts made to encapsulate the company's past, present and future in the briefest of texts, which may only consist of one sentence. The following example illustrates the more concrete approach, where several points are packed into one sentence:

14. To combine aggressive strategic marketing with quality products and services at competitive prices to provide the best insurance value for consumers. (Aflac)

On the other hand, the opposite tendency, designed to achieve generalizability through abstraction, produces mission statements that verge on the mystical:

15. To unlock the potential of nature to improve the quality of life. (ADM)
16. Use our pioneering spirit to responsibly deliver energy to the world. (ConocoPhillips)

Such a level of abstraction is common in certain types of corporate mission statement, and may have various functions, including allowing a margin of versatility or manipulability for future applications. Such a tendency to abstraction may also be partly motivated by the need to achieve consensus: highly abstract statements admit of a variety of interpretations, since they are actually rather vague. In the context of legal discourse, it has often been commented that vagueness in normative texts serves a strategic purpose, since it allows for flexibility of interpretation and application (Engberg and Heller, 2008). In the very different context of mission statements, vagueness or generality may have a similar purpose.

Hyperbole is frequent in statements of both types:

17. We will be the easiest pharmacy retailer for customers to use. (CVS Corporation)

As Fox and Fox (2004) point out, mission statements abound in superlatives, sweeping generalizations and verbs marking processes, often expressed through the first-person singular plural 'we will'. The following example shows how all these tendencies come together to make a mission statement that encompasses present and future, draws in the employees as valued agents and the world as appreciative recipient and performs an ideological function of inclusive corporate self-affirmation:

18. People love our clothes and trust our company. We will market the most appealing and widely worn casual clothing in the world. We will clothe the world. (Laidlaw International Levi Strauss & Co)

It has also been pointed out that mission statements often embody a metaphorical framework to which employees, in particular, are expected to 'buy in', that is, to internalize the symbolic system that is supposed to inform the company's activities (Gergen, 1999). These metaphors are, of their essence, vague, which means that they can be applied to everything or nothing, as it suits those who control the official discourse. When ConocoPhillips talks of using 'our pioneering spirit', it is applying a metaphorical framework of 'being the first' and 'opening new territory', which can also be understood to mean leadership and technological innovation.

The actual uses and workings of such mission statements in real companies have received some critical attention. Rathbun (2007, p. 553) describes the effect of vague metaphorical terms such as 'inter-dependency' in her own professional experience. Though presumably intended to convey solidarity and a sense of team, in fact the repeated use of this metaphorical term made her feel alienated because she could not understand it. Her sense of isolation was particularly acute because any attempts at discussion of this rather abstract value were silenced. Her own confusion, which was compounded by the observation that prominent members of the organization did not appear to be committed to the values to which they paid lip service when reciting the mission statement, led her to observe that employees may often suffer considerable anxiety when they are asked to subscribe to ideas that they do not understand. In Choo's explanation (2006), when ambiguity is high, people are confused and anxious because they lack an understandable frame of reference to interpret their work. Returning to Swales and Rogers (1995, p. 237), we can observe that mission statements of the more visionary kind may be 'more poetry than product'. The degree to which they persuade employees to commune in symbolic union with the company is doubtful, particularly if no hermeneutic aids are on offer. Although highly metaphorical, even mystical mission statements have an ideological significance, in that they are intended to persuade employees and others of the existential value, importance and potency of the company and the superior qualities of its products, the high abilities and noble aspirations of all those who work in it and so on, it is not certain how far they actually succeed in indoctrinating their employees or convincing their customers. Perhaps now, more than ever, people are wary of 'hype' and promotional discourses of all kinds, and tend to regard blatant manifestations of hyperbole such as those found in many corporate mission statements with a fair degree of scepticism.

6.4 Corporate social responsibility reports

The notion of corporate social responsibility and the need for companies to show that they act responsibly are not new. At least since the beginning of the twentieth century, companies have been concerned to explain to the public that their actions are ethical, or even beneficial for society as a whole (Owen and

O'Dwyer, 2008). The roots of this trend probably go even further back, to the enlightened capitalists of the nineteenth century, who found that improving the lives of their workers was fully compatible with running a successful enterprise.

The trend towards reporting social and environmental activities has gathered momentum in the last 15 years, and most major corporations now publish reports about these issues every year. Of course, different companies have different levels of commitment to these issues. For some, a responsible attitude to the social and physical environment is an integral part of their corporate identity and business strategy, while others show only marginal interest. None the less, there is a growing consensus across the whole business world that it is important to say something about how the company handles social and environmental issues, even if 'saying something' amounts to little more than paying lip service. Interestingly, the nomenclature seems to be changing. Whereas ten years ago, many companies had an 'environmental report', now the term 'sustainability report' seems to be growing in popularity (Catenaccio, 2011).

Like the name, the contents of the Corporate Social Responsibility (CSR) report have also undergone some development over the decade. While the earliest CSR reports centred on the environment, particularly climate change and use of different energy sources, more recent reports also include social issues, including labour standards in developing countries, human rights, bioethical issues and questions of corporate accountability and transparency. It has been predicted that future CSR reports will also focus on issues such as diversity/inclusivity, democracy in the workplace and geopolitical questions related to globalization. Nike's highly developed online interactive CSR report is organized from the outset by means of bookmarks, into 'strategy', 'environment', 'communities', 'people and culture' and 'public policy and advocacy'. It is likely that other companies will move in this direction, envisioning 'corporate responsibility' across a very broad range of issues.

At present, most CSR reports tend to cluster around four main themes: care for the environment, social and community issues, efficiency and sustainability. The following example combines all of these issues in one message:

19. In a resource-constrained world, we must use innovation as a driver to conserve water, increase our energy efficiency, reuse and recycle our products. We hear about the promise and potential of a sustainable economy; one that balances people, planet and profit. That vision requires a shift in thinking and approach. (NIKE)

CSR reports are characterized visually by photographs of idyllic natural scenes and happy smiling people. Some companies use text or video narrative to tell heart-warming stories about ways in which the company has helped local people or invested in the environment. These examples from Patagonia's 'Environmental Essays' section are characteristic in tone:

20. Standing in front of the room in creased, pleated khakis and a collared shirt, Mark Capelli spoke first. It had been 35 years since he first knocked on Patagonia's door. With photos of steelhead in hand, the young graduate-student had asked for support in his lone campaign to prove that the Ventura River was still alive. Patagonia gave him office space and a mailbox, and the story of Mark's victory over water- and land-developers became company lore – and inspiration for Patagonia's future grassroots giving.

Such personal stories appeal to the audience through standard narrative techniques: these are tales about how the good guys have to struggle to win through, 'moral' tales about how we should look after our environment. Very often they begin with a 'hook', an original beginning that helps readers to identify with the protagonists, awakens our curiosity and engages our sympathy. This example is also from the Patagonia CSR site:

21. Matilija Coalition founder Paul Jenkin's quest to tear down a dam began not on a river, but on the beach at Surfer's Point in Ventura, California, where ocean waves threatened to devour a new bike path, and talk of building a half-mile seawall to protect it was growing louder.

However, like the Annual Report, CSR reports may contain information of different types, from different sources. Alongside appealing personal testimonies, we find declarations from audits by independent bodies, such as the 'Independent assurance statement' by Ernst and Young for British American Tobacco, which is fronted by the following statement that delimits responsibility in the manner of a disclaimer:

22. Our responsibility, in accordance with management's instructions, is to carry out a 'reasonable level' assurance engagement on the information presented in the Report regarding the stakeholder dialogue sessions and a 'limited level' assurance engagement on the rest of the Report. We do not accept or assume any responsibility for any other purpose or to any other

person or organization. Any reliance any such third party may place on the Report is entirely at its own risk. (British American Tobacco)

The legal language of such disclaimers jars somewhat with the warm, attractive surroundings and casts a small shadow of doubt on the credibility of the document as a whole. Just as the financial information in the Annual Report should be read carefully, and the copious text proclaiming the company's virtues and successes in the rest of the report needs to be weighed up carefully against the financial evidence, so the data from the independent assurance statement should be considered with care and used to counterbalance the claims made in other sections of the CSR report.

We may also note that as the CSR report gains importance throughout the world, its emphasis varies. Different issues gain prominence in different areas, and the legitimatory function of the CSR report is never far from the surface. We have seen that Chinese companies are often particularly concerned in their 'About us' section to show that they adhere to international quality standards (Pan and Xu, 2009). Along similar lines, researchers have found that Russian oil corporations use their CSR reports to emphasize how they obey the appropriate legislation (Goletiani, 2011). This legitimatory discourse evidently needs to be understood against the background of particular companies' reputations within the Russian federation and beyond. In the case of Russian and Chinese corporations, such reports are at least partly addressed to foreign investors and trading partners, sending the message that the companies are endeavouring to comply with international business standards.

6.5 Annual reviews, interactive reviews and reports

At the beginning of this chapter, we noted one important change in the legislation concerning the Annual Report. In the United Kingdom, legal requirements were modified in the Companies Act of 2006, allowing online reporting to be the default option for company reporting. In addition to permitting greater exploitation of online resources in corporate communications, this had the side-effect of giving companies greater freedom concerning the type of information provided for shareholders on a routine basis. These developments appear to have contributed to the destabilization of the genre of the Annual Report, which was formerly the principal means by which shareholders obtained information about the companies in which they had invested. Since it is no longer mandatory to send full reports to all shareholders, some companies have now opted to replace the Annual Report, with its complex factual and financial details, with an Annual Review, which may look similar, but which contains a much greater proportion of promotional content and may not contain detailed financial data. Although the Annual Report must still be available for shareholders to consult, companies may now use the Annual Review as the first line of communication with shareholders.

In addition to this, since Reports and Reviews may now be published in online formats, the multiple affordances of multimedia technology and the internet are increasingly being exploited for promotional purposes where this is permissible. While the Report is still bound by a specific legal framework, the Review is now being designed using more creative approaches, including sound, video and interactive displays involving pop-ups and peel-backs.

In the case of the major UK supermarket chain J. Sainsbury plc, 1999 marked the birth of the Annual Review as a spin-off from the Annual Report (Breeze, 2011a). In this year, the Annual Report and Review were both designed as paper brochures (PDF accessible online), and the Review was essentially an abbreviated version of the Review, with the same text, photographs and design as the first part of the Report, but lacking the more detailed financial analysis provided in the second section of the Report. The Review seems to have acquired the status of an independent genre (rather than a mere digest of the Annual Report) over the early 2000s. At the beginning of the decade, both are available as PDFs and as websites with downloadable documents. The Review was essentially an abbreviated version of the Report, but included an important disclaimer referring readers to the Report 'for a full understanding of the results of the Group'. By 2004, the Annual Review actually had a different format from the Report. In 2006, the Review was still available as a PDF, but could also be viewed as an interactive document in standard webpage format.

A significant turning point happened in 2008: the Review was re-named the 'Illustrated Review', and only made available in an interactive format, while the Report was still present as a PDF document. The separation between the Review and Report was complete. The interactive Review for 2008 mimics the traditional brochure in its initial presentation, online page-turning devices and general design. Yet it also emphasizes the innovative interactive format with the declaration 'I'm not a printed report', blazoned on the cover, which establishes a pseudo-dialogue with readers. This 'dialogue' is maintained throughout the Review's 24 pages via a range of interactive features that simulate communication while lacking many of the distinctive elements present in genuine communication.

In this, the Review takes on many of the characteristics of computer interactivity, which has been described as a 'process of pseudo-communication' (Nake and Grabowski, 2001, p. 441), and which lends itself for use as an instrument of symbolic control, since it confines and channels the possible responses while affording the illusion of free choice (Yoshida, 2008).

In the 2008 Review, the interactive structure of representation explicitly projects a reader who is concerned about quality and efficiency in food retailing, and about issues of social and environmental responsibility. This is established through a question–answer structure which purports to create an ongoing dialogue with readers. The inscribed reader is concerned about certain key issues, usually expressed in the questions on the main page ('Was the supplier treated fairly?'). The simulated dialogue is maintained in a variety of ways, using pop-up book devices to answer the question that has been set. This ludic approach, with its clean, attractive designs and primary colour schemes, projects an upbeat, youthful image for the company. However, it should be noted that the inscribed reader is primarily positioned as a consumer, and the subject of profitability, traditionally one of the shareholder's main preoccupations, plays only a secondary role in this dialogue.

Video appears at several points, notably as 'talking pictures' in which the chairman delivers a video 'message to shareholders' and 'conclusions', both against a busy supermarket background. The chairman's tone is markedly more sober than that of the middle pages of the Review: these sections set a tone of seriousness, against the slightly intrusive background video of the working store which reminds readers of the company's massive retail activity. The direct address by the chairman appears to function as a way of anchoring the predominantly visual impact of the pages that follow (Barthes, 1977) by stressing the key themes for the year.

In 2009, the brochure format was replaced by a computer game format, inviting readers to navigate the interactive store with a mouse, or select from a pop-up shopping list. The supermarket background with its lively moving figures and simulated store noise provides a subliminal promotional message, encouraging the reader/user to participate rather than evaluate. Indeed, the principal subject position offered to the user seems to be that of customer, since he/she is placed inside a virtual store and given a shopping list as navigational aid. The Review still appears to provide some information for shareholders – the first item on the shopping list is a video message from the CEO, and the in-store announcements delivered while the reader surfs the interactive site blend information for shareholders (proper to the Report), such as 'this is a shareholder announcement:

Sainsbury's is proud to celebrate its 140th anniversary', with information for customers of both a probable and a jocose nature 'there is a gorilla roaming around the store'. However, the situational positioning of the reader/user as customer, and the looser network of discursive positioning as stakeholder-customer–shareholder, generally serve to merge the company–shareholder relationship into a broader, more diffuse type of involvement. Hybridity of textual genre – informational elements combined with promotional elements – combines with hybridity of format – features of interactive simulation, video statements, TV commercials, information leaflets – to generate a new mode of corporate communication that is open to interpretation on many layers.

In general, if we look at all the features of the most recent Reviews as a whole, the communicative purpose of this emergent genre seems to be to encourage investors to 'buy in' to the firm's agenda of quality, efficiency and corporate responsibility (its 'key values'), rather than to assess its viability as an investment. This is very much in line with recent trends in corporate communications, which stress the importance of branding and the involvement of different stakeholders in the corporate mission (Solomon et al., 2006). Moreover, this tendency is reinforced by use of interactive media, which involve the reader as a consumer or loosely defined stakeholder rather than as an independent assessor. In conclusion, the changes described here indicate that an informational genre has largely been supplanted by a promotional one.

As we have seen, the change of medium can be seen to have contributed to the destabilization of the genre of the Annual Review, and there is now a considerable degree of hybridity and genre-bending (Bhatia, 2004). In the specific case of J. Sainsbury plc examined here, there seems to be a general move away from an informative genre towards an advertising genre, which is evident on various levels. The fact that the largely promotional Review now replaces the factual Annual Report as the chief means of communication with shareholders is highly significant in the light of critical theory and developments in late capitalism that have been widely documented in other contexts (Fairclough and Chouliaraki, 1999). The shareholder is positioned as a general stakeholder or even as a consumer, rather than as an impartial decision-maker. In a sense, the earlier shareholder role seems to have been erased, as the discourses which formerly characterized company communication with investors have been colonized by the discourses of consumer relations. Promotional discourse and consumer positioning are increasingly pervasive in our current socio-economic system, and phenomena such as the blurring of boundaries and bending of genres observed in the present study contribute significantly to the generation and reproduction of the dominant systems. The changes noted in the present chapter can be interpreted as further evidence of the way the discourses of the market place are colonizing ever greater areas of the public sphere (Habermas, 1984).

6.6 Sponsorship

One of the more recent developments in corporate communications is the introduction of different kinds of sponsorship as a way of projecting a positive image of the business to the public at large, and to particular groups of stakeholders.

Sponsorship has been defined as 'an investment, in cash or kind, in an activity, in return for access to the exploitable commercial potential associated with this activity' (Meenaghan, 1991, p. 238). Sponsorship is therefore not just philanthropy, but a form of giving which brings returns for the giver. This is not to say that companies do not undertake some activities that might be classed as pure philanthropy – but if they do, these are not understood as sponsorship. In the words of Erdogan and Kitchen (1998, p. 370), sponsorship entails 'promoting a company's interests and its brands by tying them with a specific and meaningfully related event, organization or charitable cause'. Sponsorship is therefore closer to public relations than to marketing, but is related to both.

In general terms, sponsorship functions by creating a connection between the company or brand and an organization, activity or event that target consumers are likely to value. The positive association that is generated is supposed to help to improve the company or brand image and enhance the corporate reputation. The sponsoring company thus commits itself to an external cause, and fosters good will through its benevolent actions, or strengthens its own image through association with particular attributes of the sponsored activity. These links may be intrinsic to the action or event, but that is not to say that they are self-evident. In reality, advertising and other public relations activities are needed to bring out the intended association between the sponsored action and the company's own characteristics, and to ensure that the sponsorship activity projects the intended set of values. In fact, considerable efforts are usually made to forge discursive bonds between the sponsored action and the company or its attributes. Let us look in more depth at how this is done.

We know that it is important to build associations between the company and the action or event. Thus the type of event or action that is sponsored is a crucial factor in the type of meaning that can be made. Every sponsored activity offers certain possibilities, in accordance with the way it is perceived in the public eye, in terms of values and qualities. These features have been described as 'image values' (Meenaghan and Shipley, 1998, p. 342). Thus a sponsored sport event is potentially associated with values such as health, youth, energy, speed, and in some cases even masculinity. On the other hand, an activity or event related to social causes generates feelings of admiration, gives the impression that the company is responsible, caring and concerned. When a company plans to undertake sponsorship activities, it chooses actions or events that are compatible with its desired corporate image and communications strategy, and considers the target audience, which may consist of potential customers, or may be more widely focused.

Once the choice has been made, a considerable communications activity is set in motion, to highlight the desired connections and ensure that a positive association is created and maintained. This desirable effect of sponsorship has been described as ensuring that the values of the activity itself are 'drained' onto the sponsoring brand (Garzone, 2010, p. 55). Most sponsorship activities are accompanied by press releases, advertising posters, merchandising and so on, in which discursive resources are used to direct the audience's attention towards the features of the sponsor company that the event is supposed to highlight.

One of the more straightforward types of event at which sponsorship has become commonplace is the sports event. Evangelisti Allori (2010) analyses sponsorship at the Winter Olympics in Turin in 2006. On the most basic level, the companies that sponsored the event included the Olympic logo on their webpages or as part of a special logo for the year, to build a visual connection between the company and the event, and thereby to share in its positive associations. Since their logo also appears on Olympic material, they simply become more visible, appearing before a world audience, in itself a worthwhile objective. However, other companies brought out the philanthropic aspect of their patronage, through special slogans such as 'helping make Olympic dreams come true', and repeated use of verbs within the semantic range of 'help', 'provide' and 'support' (Evangelisti Allori, 2010, p. 89). Companies whose sponsorship was of a more focused nature also made this explicit in order to underline positive attributes of their own.

On striking example of the exploitation of sponsorship activities can be found in the Annual Report for 2010 published by Aberdeen Asset Management plc.

The entire front cover of the Report is a birds-eye view of a female rowing team against a background of black water. Inside, we find the following explanation, alongside a miniature version of the photograph and the logotype of the Dad Vail Regatta:

23. Aberdeen signed a four year agreement this year which saw it become the title sponsor of Dad Vail Regatta, the largest collegiate regatta in the United States. The event is rowed on the Schuylkill River in Philadelphia during the week end of the second Saturday in May, with hundreds of North American colleges and universities taking part.

This in itself might merely be a generous act. However, against the black water background of the front cover, above the name of the company and in a larger font size, we find the striking motto 'Global strength local knowledge'. Inside, on the first main page, the company defines itself as championing 'close-knit teams' and 'interdependence'. Interestingly enough, on the inside back cover, the motif of the rowing team is shown again, with a different caption:

24. The Dad Vail Regatta is the largest intercollegiate regatta in the United States. It has a long history in Philadelphia and Aberdeen's three year sponsorship of the event ensures that it remains in this historic US city.

So the global–local balance is again emphasized, and a further connection between the company's values and the rowing image is created in an allusive manner. The commitment to the 'local', which is a leitmotif established on the front cover and hammered home through the corporate values statements and company self-presentation, is illustrated by the company's sponsorship activity which 'ensures' that the event remains where it should be.

Sponsorship is thought to be a useful tool for companies whose reputation has been tarnished, or who wish to bring about a thorough 'rebranding' and change of image. Garzone (2010) describes the discursive strategies applied by the accountancy firm Accenture after its association with various financial scandals. She shows how Accenture concentrated its sponsorship efforts on the areas of sports and the up-market end of the arts, in order to project values associated with health, youth, energy, speed and masculinity, on the one hand, and sophistication, elite membership, seriousness and discernment, on the other. Sponsorship centred on elite precision sports such as golf and formula one, and on world-class art exhibitions and classical concerts. All of these activities were grouped together discursively under a single slogan: 'High performance. Delivered'. Garzone points out that the transfer of values is always realized through the 'high performance' theme, which is a constant throughout the advertising and press releases for the campaign. The Accenture website proclaims, with regard to its sponsorship of golf (quoted in Garzone, 2010, p. 62).

25. The Accenture Match Play Championship has generated many
    dramatic and captivating moments in golf. Learn more about these key
    high-performance moments in the tournament's history.

With regard to formula one, the publicity material states (Garzone, 2010, p. 70):

26. Accenture has helped the team achieve high performance and has brought
    rigorous precision to the function of the whole organization.

Even the arts are brought under this heading, as in the case of the Rheingau Musik Festival, which is held up as 'another example of how Accenture collaborates with individuals and organizations to help them achieve high-performance results' (p. 71). Thus the attributes naturally associated with the activities themselves are framed in a particular way, and above all, the (less obvious) link with the company is accentuated. In this way, the values of accuracy, precision, rigour and elite membership intrinsic to the sponsored activities are intended to reflect back onto the company and enhance its image.

In a sense, in all of this, we can see that sponsorship is advertising carried one stage further. An advertisement can show an image of a yacht or a racing car, and build a mental association between it and a watch, say. In the case of sponsorship, the association is not built between a picture and a product, but between something real – a sports event, a yachting race – and a product. The difference is, perhaps, not so great, except in terms of the social and cultural impact of sponsorship activities. Sponsorship is conceptually framed as a live advertisement.

7

Interpreting Corporate Discourse

This final chapter will draw together the different threads that run through the rest of the book, and offer some ideas about how these threads can be woven together into a coherent pattern. Starting from an overview of the findings set out in the previous chapters, I will go on to propose some explanations concerning the ways that discourse functions in corporate contexts, showing how these discourses differ fundamentally from those found in other areas of life, such as academia, the sciences or education. Finally, I shall analyse these ideas in the light of some critical perspectives on corporate discourse, in order to explain the ideological dimensions of corporate discourse and its importance in our understanding of the contemporary world.

7.1 Discourses and discourse

When we consider the various manifestations of corporate discourse that are analysed in the earlier chapters of this book, we can see that certain characteristic ways of communicating appear to traverse most of the areas examined. We can observe that there is something we might call 'corporate discourse' that runs through many different genres. Thus although a webpage is different from a job advertisement or an Annual Report, there are aspects of a common 'voice', a common 'language', a common way of understanding and thinking about the things that are important, that we could describe as corporate discourse. However, we should note that there are also genres in which the discourse differs. The greatest exception to the general rule is the language of advertising, which is as broad and varied as, say, the language of poetry. Although the linguistic and semiotic resources used in advertising may overlap with those that are deployed in what we have called 'corporate discourse', the scope of what is possible is immeasurably wider.

So what can we say about the kind of 'corporate discourse' that pervades genres like the Annual Report and review, the job advertisement, the employee website and the general website? Reading texts of these kinds, we soon become aware that at least two major purposes shape the way they were written: to provide the type and amount of information that the company deems appropriate, and to enhance the company's image in the eyes of stakeholders. Moreover, although each of the genres we have examined, with the possible exception of the general company website, has a specific target audience in mind, in each genre there is evidence that other audiences or readers are also being addressed, as companies become increasingly aware of the general need for 'impression management' in all the company's public actions. Thus even genres as seemingly straightforward and transactional as the job advertisement are increasingly being coopted into the company's general public relations activities.

An extensive examination of the research carried out on these fields within the professional perspective shows that 'impression management' is indeed in the writers' minds when they work on material of this kind. The 'promotional turn' that is increasingly encountered in discourses far away from the commercial field is now all-pervasive in the business world. Even ostensibly transactional genres (letters, job advertisements) or those which were formerly understood as mainly informational (Annual Reports) are now seen as a vehicle for managing the kind of impression that the company makes on the people who encounter it. This also extends to relationships between the company and its employees, which are now seen as requiring conscious, active management through internal 'public relations' exercises, as employees are increasingly encouraged to 'buy in' to the corporate mission and ideology. Further, it is now understood that all of the company's relationships, with clients or customers, government or state, competitors, investors, stakeholders in general and, of course, the media, can and should be managed through discourse. Discourse is one of the corporation's most powerful tools in the current configuration of society.

7.2 Corporate discourse in a wider perspective

One way of understanding what corporate discourse is would be to begin by considering what corporate discourse is not. If we look at the general map of literacy practices that most people encounter in the course of their education and experience, we will find a large number of discourses that contrast dramatically with the discourses of the corporate enterprise. Taking the example of academic discourses, for example, we will see that these are primarily concerned with constructing and evaluating knowledge. Academic writers strive to find a voice that is appropriate to the academic community to which they aim to belong, and which positions them with regard to other members of that community. Academic discourses both reflect and reproduce the epistemology and social practices of particular disciplines. The individual writer must learn how to operate within this code or key, and how to promote his/her own status within the discursive community. As Hyland says (2009, p. 18), academic discourses are 'part and parcel of institutional and community practices: they are situated activities which regulate meaning-making in complex ways and represent particular social relations and ways of seeing the world'.

We could summarize this by saying that academic discourse is concerned with meaning-making within a community of practice that centres on academic research, and is produced by individuals or groups of individuals who seek to position themselves towards other members of this community and towards their objects of study. Corporate discourse obviously contrasts with this in a number of ways. First, corporate discourse is evidently a collective, rather than an individual, enterprise. The texts considered in these books – Annual Reports, advertisements, websites – are almost all texts that have no single, identifiable author. The few supposed exceptions to this – the 'letter to shareholders', for example – have been examined in detail because of their exceptional nature. The net effect of this 'collective' writing activity is to generate a voice that is the 'corporate' voice, a voice that may differ in some respects from sector to sector, but which is surprisingly homogeneous. Although academic writers acquire a 'disciplinary voice' (Hyland, 1999), they still write under their own responsibility (as individuals or as research teams), individually take credit for their achievements and individually bear the blame for their failures.

A second way in which corporate discourse differs from academic discourse is that it is largely concerned with promotion of the corporate entity. Although in academic discourse subtle strategies are often used to promote the writer and the discipline, this is ostensibly never the primary function of the academic text. Corporate discourse operates through entire genres that are mainly promotional, such as the website or advertisement, and others that have a high overt promotional content, like the annual review. Moreover, it also differs in the type of promotional strategy that is used. Corporate discourse projects a specific set of values that contrast sharply with those upheld in academic language: it extols values such as profitability, cost-effectiveness or expansion, which are accepted as good by general consensus. There is no need for corporate texts to explain why these are good, or to justify the measures used to establish how they have been achieved, since the underlying utilitarian worldview is tacitly accepted. Compared with academic discourse, corporate discourse takes many aspects for granted, apparently feeling little need to justify many of its claims in terms of either method or epistemology.

Thirdly, corporate discourse has a very different social function from most academic discourse. Although academic life is partly structured around groups and 'schools', these are loose configurations of independent scholars or scientists who choose to construct meaning in a particular way. To some extent, the 'worlds of discourse' they build may be influenced or underpinned by external power structures, to the extent that some experts have even criticized particular groups for practising a form of academic 'branding' (Billig, 2002). However, the academic world admits considerable plurality of thought, and few would deny that freedom of expression is a fundamental right. Although the epistemological bases of academic work vary greatly, at least in the empirical disciplines the researcher is committed to methodological rigour and accurate reporting of results. The scientist who fakes results or makes a major error of method or interpretation is likely to lose his/her professional credibility, not to mention his/her funding and chances of promotion. Corporate discourse, on the other hand, is not concerned with self-expression, or, by and large, with the world of ideas. Although some genres are subject to stringent external controls – the 'auditor's statement' in the Annual Report is a case in point – others, like advertising, have enormous scope for creativity. The purpose of corporate discourse is to present the company to its multiple stakeholders in such a way that they will continue to work for it, invest in it or generally support it. This purpose fundamentally constrains the extent to which it is likely to tell the unvarnished truth or even acknowledge the existence of ideas that are not aligned with its own interests.

7.3 The promotional turn

So what can we say about this 'corporate discourse'? First of all, we might notice the overwhelming effort that is made throughout the genres we have analysed to 'promote' the company itself, and to present all its activities in a glowing light. To do this, a large amount of information is provided. Yet the presentation of this information is not carefully hedged, as it might be in a scientific paper where the writer's own credibility as a reputable scientist is at stake, and he/she is thus unwilling to overstate his/her case or take unnecessary risks by questioning established truths. The information provided in corporate genres is always presented in the most positive terms possible, in such a way that some critics have found it to be 'misleading' to the layperson (Bhatia, 2004).

Celebration and persuasion

Corporate discourse is overwhelmingly promotional in tone, to the extent that it might strike us as monotonous and uninteresting. Explanations of discourse in this area sometimes stay on the level of 'they would say that, wouldn't they': companies are expected to present themselves in the most positive light, and that is precisely what they do. Analysis can shed light on the techniques they use to do this, or on the extent to which they tell the truth, but the phenomenon itself might seem quite banal and hardly worthy of comment.

A more penetrating analysis, however, would suggest that corporate self-promotion is rather more interesting than that. This phenomenon fits into a long tradition of self-aggrandizing and self-exaltatory discourses that extends back across the centuries. From the perspective of classical rhetoric, we might say that the rhetoric of the corporate body tends mainly to belong to the category of the epideictic (Perelman and Olbrechts-Tyteca, 1969; Aristotle, 1991). Unlike the other two principal types of rhetoric, namely political and legal rhetoric, epideictic rhetoric is not immediately designed to make its hearers come to a decision about an issue at trial or a course of action to be followed. According to Aristotle, an orator sets different goals according to the type of speech he is making: in political or deliberative oratory, the aim is to advise listeners on the most appropriate solution; in legal oratory, to establish what is just; and in epideictic oratory, to recognize values and to praise them. In the subsequent development of rhetorical theory across the centuries, the first two types were appropriated by philosophy and dialectics, whereas epideictic rhetoric came to be thought of as a kind of degenerate eloquence, designed merely to please the audience and enhance facts that everyone already agreed on. Perhaps for this reason, the concept of epideictic rhetoric was discarded by later theoreticians, and the ideas associated with it later came to be studied under the heading of 'literature', or were revisited in the context of religious edification (Perelman and Olbrechts-Tyteca, 1969, pp. 48–50). None the less, some authors have rescued the notion of epideictic rhetoric for use in modern contexts, most particularly when interpreting the language used in the field of public relations and business in general (Elwood, 1995).

The importance of epideictic rhetoric therefore lies in its function in securing and strengthening the adherence of an audience to the ideas that are presented. The intensity of this adherence is not only important from an intellectual point of view (that is, in making people believe that something is right in a theoretical sense), but is also highly significant in terms of creating a sense of unity among the audience and preparing the ground for a future call to action. In the words of Perelman and Olbrechts-Tyteca (1969, p. 50), this is where the true importance of epideictic rhetoric lies: 'it strengthens the disposition toward action by increasing adherence to the values it lauds'. Moreover, these authors also make another point which is relevant here: the fundamentally optimistic character of much epideictic discourse (Perelman and Olbrechts-Tyteca, 1969, p. 51). This type of oratory, they comment, is 'more reminiscent of a procession than a struggle', and tends to be practised by those who defend the traditional, accepted values of a society, certainly not those which stir up controversy or foment revolution. Epideictic discourse has no fear of contradiction, and tends to elevate general assumptions, or ideas that have achieved a certain social acceptance, onto the level of established values, if not eternal truths. We may associate epideictic rhetoric with the praise poems that celebrate the feats of rulers in the ancient world. Yet this type of rhetoric also exists in present-day society in many forms. We need think only of national ceremonies to commemorate historical events, eulogies at funerals, prize-giving ceremonies and many similar speech events with an important social status. Such discourse invites no discussion, opens no dialogue. In a Bakhtinian sense, it is fundamentally monologic (Bakhtin, 1981), because although in principle any rhetorical device is permissible, the aim is ultimately to promote the communion of the audience and the consolidation of established values. Alternative views may be entertained, but only in the sense of straw men that are held up to be knocked down. In a sense, there are no surprises, because we already know everything that we are told. Yet this very predictability presents a greater challenge to the speaker/writer, because it is necessary to hold people's attention even though they know what is going to be said. Many of the manifestations of corporate discourse that we have seen in this book – reports, job advertisements, websites – bear the unmistakable hallmarks of epideictic rhetoric.

However, if we examine the phenomenon of the epideictic in more depth, we will perceive that the increased adherence and solidarity between speaker and audience that it foments is particularly important in ideological terms:

it strengthens bonds and increases people's willingness to act. As Crable and Vibbert point out (1995, p. 31), 'even people who disagree with a message can be motivated to act on agreed-upon beliefs'. This kind of value-reinforcement has a significant role, in that it sets out explicitly, and fortifies, the shared ideas that form the basis for persuasion, be it in the political arena, or in the context of ethics or law. Such rhetoric is sometimes blended with premise-building arguments, that is, proposals that establish a novel point, which may often be slipped in as 'common sense' alongside a selection of non-polemical statements expressing shared values (Toulmin, 1969). The type of public relations activity carried out by lobbying groups is often of this premise-establishing kind, and is backed up with epideictic rhetoric celebrating values that are uncontroversial.

The discourse of many corporate genres belongs mainly to the category of the epideictic. It is intended to celebrate what is unconditionally accepted as 'good' within the corporate world, embracing the values of utilitarianism, building confidence in the corporation, its members and its activities and creating a sense of community among its stakeholders. By stressing values such as efficiency and cost-effectiveness, or emphasizing the importance of family life, the community and the environment, companies tell us nothing that we do not already know. Yet by emphasizing that they subscribe to these generally accepted values, they are forging rhetorical links of solidarity with their audience. The more this audience (customers, workers, investors, the public) identify with these ideas, the more likely they will be to accept the company's actions and, where necessary, to support them.

Establishing credibility, building ethos

In another perspective, we can see that this type of discourse and the corporate 'self' that it projects play a major role in establishing the credibility of the organization, that is, building the corporate 'ethos'. 'Ethos' is defined classically as 'the impression which the speaker, by means of his words, gives of himself' (Perelman and Olbrechts-Tyteca, 1969, p. 319). Speakers need to have a credible 'ethos' if they are to convince their audience, or ensure their continued attention. This appears to be simple, but in normal circumstances it is actually somewhat risky for any speaker to indulge in large amounts of self-praise. As a response to this inherent difficulty, different strategies have been developed in different areas that make it possible for writers or speakers to praise themselves without overly offending their readers or hearers. In academic writing, the issue of how writers project a credible discoursal self in different disciplines has been the subject of considerable analysis (Ivanic, 1998; Hyland, 2001). In journalism, columnists and leader writers use a slightly different range of techniques to construct an authoritative authorial voice (López Pan, 2010). In other areas, such as autobiography, the projection of self is a major concern, and all the techniques of creative literature can be brought into play to this end.

In corporate discourse, the construction of ethos relies on a combination of strategies. First, there is an almost overwhelming insistence on collective identity: the corporate 'we', which reports achievements in positive terms, and is used variously to include 'we the employees', 'we the management', 'we the company and its investors' and 'we the general public'. Self-praise is risky when one individual indulges in it in front of others, not least because it may imply a loss of face to the others. However, self-praise is socially admissible if the entity being praised is a collective 'us' that potentially involves the reader/listener. Secondly, by piling up information and building up the company's achievements in terms of numbers, years, size, turnover and so on, the reader/listener is presented with an entity that is quasi-objectively made to seem extremely significant and worthy of respect. 'Loci of quantity' are a classic means by which a rhetor can intensify his arguments. Negative results or less-than-favourable data are downplayed, and the discourse is overwhelmingly positive, serving to boost the corporate ethos in a seemingly objective manner. Thirdly, an increasing emphasis on quality and on external 'validations' and 'audits' serves to complement the traditional emphasis on quantity by emphasizing 'loci of quality', an aspect that is arguably increasingly important in times of economic recession when positive figures are harder to achieve, and when heightened awareness of issues such as social justice and environmental protection leads to a greater need for companies to account for their actions. Finally, the multimodal presentation of corporate information, with its attractive design, high-quality presentation and carefully branded image, is also conducive to presenting a corporate image that is as positive and trustworthy as possible. We could also add that even the apparently more 'personal' aspects of corporate publications, such as the 'letter to shareholders' or the 'testimony' provided by satisfied workers or customers, are merely another way of boosting the corporate ethos: by projecting the same positively framed discourse in the first person, these texts give a 'personal touch', show the 'human face' of the company. Yet the message is fundamentally the same: these first-person texts exist to boost the corporate image and strengthen the collective ethos.

However, the story does not end here. We should not forget that these corporate genres have very concrete purposes of a commercial nature.

Advertising is intended to make people buy the product. Annual Reports are at least partly shaped by the desire to reassure investors and encourage them to maintain their shares in the company. Company websites are designed to present a positive image that will attract new customers, strengthen relations with existing customers, show the markets in general what the company has to offer, head off competition and so on. The purpose of the corporation is fundamentally a commercial one. And yet, in order to operate commercially, the company has to present itself as making a positive contribution to society. This aspect of the corporate ethos varies from sector to sector. As we have seen, in some sectors (tobacco companies are perhaps the most obvious example), companies sense an urgent need to justify their activities to the world at large. In others, such as mining or oil production, companies place a heavy emphasis in many of their corporate communications on safety measures and protection of the environment. Many companies now include a 'corporate social responsibility' or 'sustainability' section in their reports or publish a special report containing information of this kind. In addition to this, certain types of company have a specifically 'ethical' corporate image, and place their environmental or other commitments in the foreground of their self-representation. Since these facets are part of their specific corporate mission and identity, they constitute an important aspect of their brand image.

Although these activities are fundamental to the reinforcement of the company's ethos, they are in some sense not just epideictic and 'self-celebratory', but also merge into the realm of the political, in the classical sense. We could say that they help to clear the decks for action. Corporate self-enhancement messages not only celebrate 'established' or 'accepted' values: they actively anticipate criticisms that are probably being levelled against the companies, setting the scene to conduct a vigorous self-defence. The oil company that congratulates itself on reducing the number of casualties or investing in environmental protection is attempting to ward off criticism directed against this sector because of its track record of dangerous practices or environmental disasters. Corporate discourse thus contains a consistent tendency to pre-empt and defuse criticism on concrete issues. This function is carried out without explicit discussion of the different arguments, as we might find in scientific discussions or media reports on the issues in question. Instead of setting out the different facts and opinions, the company puts forward its side of the case, emphasizing facts that support it and largely ignoring those that do not. Occasionally, in the wake of a major disaster, the company has the need to look these issues in the face, but even then, the full extent of the situation is not relayed to the reader. The most typical strategy for narrating disasters and failures in corporate discourse is to represent them as external events which 'happened' to the company, and to portray the company as a brave survivor which is valiantly combating adversity.

7.4 Critical interpretations

From the angle of critical discourse analysis, both of the aspects of corporate discourse that we have seen to be most characteristic – the epideictic/celebratory and the political/persuasive – can be analysed in greater depth as part of the ideological mechanisms which create and perpetuate the state of affairs in the world that permits corporations to act as they do. Since critical discourse analysis provides a more developed account, let us examine these phenomena in the light of two concepts in particular: general notions about the ideological underpinning of the current socio-economic system, and specific issues related to the role of discourse.

Despite the vast differences and disagreements between theorists on almost every particular, there is a general consensus that our world system is undergoing a profound shift that involves a dramatic acceleration of time-space distantiation, thorough-going changes in economic relations, a reconfiguration of social relations and a crisis in traditional value systems (Habermas, 1979; Giddens, 1991; Featherstone, 1995). Simplifying greatly, we could say that in the past, people made personal, moral and existential choices that were informed by the thought-systems (religion, morality, social expectations and so on) current in the particular culture in which they grew up. Institutions like companies were embedded in social systems that provided a firm structure within which people could live their lives, and the parameters within which such institutions had to operate were well defined. Consumption and employment existed, of course, but were subordinated to other values and structures.

In the age of globalization, there is now an unprecedented degree of interpenetration between the global and the local, the personal and the systemic (Habermas, 1979). As the sociocultural systems of the world are weakened and subordinated to late-capitalist economic values and procedures, people are losing their sense of worth, and coming to believe that *having* is more important than *being* in a 'reversal of the hierarchy of values' (John Paul II, 1987). Many theorists feel that a 'post-traditional' or 'postmodern' society is emerging in which inherited values no longer shape social life in unquestionable ways. People now have to make choices about aspects of their lives that were previously regarded as self-evident (Giddens, 1991). Although this might initially seem to offer a welcome expansion of human freedom, the consequences may often lead to confusion or even despair. Even human relationships are now shaped less by traditional norms, more by a kind of affective 'cost-benefit ratio' that individuals calculate on an ongoing basis (Giddens, 1991). In such a view, a void is left by the erosion of time-honoured cultural systems, which means that life is increasingly threatened by meaninglessness.

To fill this glaring absence, people increasingly grasp at new structures, searching for ideas and values around which they can build a meaningful life. It is evident that two of these new structures are the type of 'identity' and 'community' offered by the brand, in terms of consumption, and the corporation, in terms of employment. Through advertising and publicity, people are persuaded to construct their identity by what they consume, and to assume commonality with those who identify with the same brand. Through socialization into the company, workers also construct an identity at another level, taking on some of the values and attributes that are expected of them in their role. Of course, both these forms of identification are likely to be partial, since human beings are complex entities with multiple social, affective and intellectual needs. Moreover, it is arguable that the consumer culture, in particular, generates insecurity and 'radical dissatisfaction' at the same rate as it provides material satisfaction (Beabout and Echeverria, 2002, p. 350). Yet structures like this go some way to filling the gap left by other structures, other forms of community, which shaped people's lives in the past. Moreover, the fact that such a gap has to be filled places enormous potential in the hands of those know how to fill it.

On the other hand, the question as to how to live in the globalized world has also led to the emergence in the public sphere of a 'new' morality based on environmentalism, a 'healthy lifestyle' and a rather tenuous concept of global citizenship, to mention just a few of its salient features. All of these elements have filtered through into the value system that underpins corporate communication, and are represented in its discourses. As in the case of consumption and employment, these concepts match with a particular sensibility that is the result of global economic and social trends. However, arguably the power balance here is different. Whereas the companies lead the way in promoting consumption and employee socialization, because it is in their interest to try to shape consumers and employees discursively in this way (Foucault, 1972), it is probably fair to say that they have taken environmental and social causes on board in response to external pressures. This is at least partly an exercise in legitimation, essentially designed to create an ideological space within which the institution can continue to operate, enjoying sufficient social acceptance to pursue its activities freely (van Dijk, 1998). By expressing commitment to certain ideas that are highly valued in public opinion, the company hopes to generate a positive evaluation and public image. The discourses it uses to proclaim its commitment combine classic epideictic elements (self-praise, promotion of socially shared values) with aspects of explanation and self-defence. It thus hopes to sway public opinion in order to avoid being discredited, and thereby to preserve its own freedom of action.

There is thus a circulation of influence in which companies both exert pressure and receive it. However, it should be noted that although there is a degree of give and take, the corporate world still wields enormous economic power. Unless there is a political will to demand accountability, there will be a limit to the efforts companies are prepared to make to put socially approved values into practice, even though their sustainability reports will feature all the discourses of environmental conservation. Large public relations operations are cheaper and easier to put into motion than, say, a thorough rehaul of the company's environmentally threatening activities.

The role of discourse in this process cannot be underestimated. Although legal and economic constraints are important, it is largely through discourse – public discourse, media discourse, advertising and so on – that these ideas and pressures are transmitted in both directions. Companies use discourse to construct roles for employees and consumers, but discourse also shapes companies. Sociologists talk of the formative role of language in the process of 'structuration' (Giddens, 1984), whereby discourse shapes and changes social realities; while discourse analysts are in no doubt that discourse plays a major role in the construction and reproduction of social roles and structures (Chouliaraki and Fairclough, 1999). Yet in the changing scenario sketched out above, discourses themselves are also undergoing some transformations. The radical unsettling of the boundaries of social life is also reflected in discursive practices (Habermas, 1979). On the one hand, new discourses are gaining prominence: we have seen how new discourses of sustainability and of quality standards run in parallel with familiar neo-liberal discourses of efficiency and profitability. On the other, the nature of the discourses themselves is changing, as the boundaries between genres and functions are being blurred. Texts with neatly assigned reader roles (investor, customer, employee) have given way to texts that mainly offer consumer subject positions, or that address general stakeholders who may take on any of these roles at a given moment. The trend towards conscious 'impression management' at all levels of the corporate communications enterprise contributes to this effect, since it often seems to shape its messages for a general consumer/client addressee. Theorists like Habermas (1979) and Giddens (1991, 1994) have commented on the erosion of worker/family/citizen roles and the increasing prominence of consumer and client roles in people's changing relationship to the state. In corporate discourse, too, there seems to be a preference for subsuming all the possible stakeholder roles into one consumer/client role which can be offered, with some nuances, to employees, shareholders and customers alike. More extreme critical voices like Baudrillard (1998) have drawn attention to the ideological role of the discourses of advertising and promotion in the system of social control and regulation which integrates people into ways of behaving and thinking. In their view, the corporate discourse system meshes with other orders of discourse to configure and perpetuate the hegemonic social order (Foucault, 1972). Individuals are offered roles as consumers and producers, and are thereby constructed as compliant members of society, cooperating willingly in their own manipulation and subjugation, and fulfilling the utilitarian understanding that people and things are all replaceable, marketable commodities.

At the same time, our exploration of corporate discourse has also revealed a destabilization of discursive forms, a trend towards discursive hybridity, as genres blend together, mimic each other and interact with each other in online media. Advertising simulates journalism, reviews usurp the position of reports, information appears with a pop-up or video-game format. One way of understanding this phenomenon is to say that some discourses that are particularly powerful in the current system, such as promotional discourses, are infiltrating into areas where other discourses used to predominate, and 'colonizing' these areas, as is indeed also the case in other areas of life (Fairclough, 1995a; Bhatia, 2004). It is arguable that the implications of this are different, depending on the area. In advertising, almost any form of genre-play is to be expected. This is an area that often seems to be closer to poetics and the creative arts, even though it is fundamentally commercial in its underlying motivation. There seems to be socially accepted licence for advertisers to treat other genres however they choose, precisely because audiences are generally aware that the advertisement is an advertisement, and so this is a legitimate move in the game. However, advertising also sometimes oversteps its limits, for example when companies sponsor films about themselves, or present advertorials in increasingly sophisticated disguises. In other circumstances, genre-bending may be quite intentionally manipulative, as in the case of the 'letter to shareholders', when a misleading promotional message is expressed through an ostensibly objective informational genre.

7.5 Concluding thoughts

The discourse of large corporations is the discourse of extremely powerful organizations that often have not been held accountable for their actions. It is important to understand the tendencies at work in this discourse, and to develop a critical awareness of the ways in which these organizations attempt to shape our world and our lives. Just as corporations increasingly make efforts to produce such discourses, the citizens of the world need to learn how to read them, how to contrast them with their own values and beliefs, and where necessary, how to reject them. In all of this, education has a fundamental role to play: not just school education, but the more profound education in values that is transmitted through family, cultural heritage and religion. In a world increasingly structured by the consumer paradigm, it might be easy to lose sight of some basic values in human life that cannot be bought or sold, and should not merely be consumed. Utilitarianism offers a civilization of production and use, a civilization of things, not people, in which people count only as subjects and objects of consumption. The consumer society operates in a spirit of reductionist materialism, reducing the human being to the economic sphere, where having is more than being. Likewise, concerning employment, we need to remember that workers are more than production machines, more than the sum of the parts envisaged by the corporate socialization system. People need to understand the far-reaching significance of work for integral personal fulfilment: work enhances our dignity and creativity, linking us to others in a progressively expanding network of solidarity. Finally, it is also important for the professionals of the future to have a sound basis in moral and ethical values that will enable them to challenge corporate practices where necessary. Only then will they be able to contribute to the restructuring of the economy in such a way that human beings and their natural and cultural environment are placed at its centre.

Bibliography

Abrahamson, E. and Amir, E. (1996), 'The information content of the president's letter to shareholders'. *Journal of Business Finance and Accounting*, 23, (8), 1157–82.

Accounting Standards Board. (1993), *Operating and Financial Review*. London: Author.

Afros, E. and Schryer, C. (2009), 'Promotional (meta) discourse in research articles in language and literary studies'. *English for Specific Purposes*, 28, (1), 58–68.

Ambler, T. and Barrow, S. (1996), 'The employer brand'. *The Journal of Brand Management*, 4, 185–206.

Anderson, B. (1991), *Imagined Communities* (2nd edn). London: Verso.

Angus, S. (2000), 'Advertorials: an unholy marriage'. *Editor and Publisher*, 133, (31), 46.

Aristotle. (1991), *On Rhetoric* (tr. G. A. Kennedy). Oxford: Oxford University Press.

Ashforth, B. and Mael, F. (1989), 'Social identity theory and the organization'. *Academy of Management Review*, 14, 20–39.

Ashforth, B. and Saks, A. (1996), 'Socialization tactics: longitudinal effects on newcomer adjustment'. *Academy of Management Journal*, 39, 149–78.

Aslam, M. (2006), 'Are you selling the right colour? A cross-cultural review of colour as a marketing cue'. *Journal of Marketing Communication*, 12, (1), 15–30.

Bakan, J. (2004), *The Corporation: The Pathological Pursuit of Profit and Power*. London: Free Press.

Bakhtin, M. (1981), *The Dialogic Imagination*. Austin: University of Texas Press.

Balasubramanian, S. K. (1994), 'Beyond advertising and publicity: hybrid messages and public policy issues'. *Journal of Advertising*, 23, (4), 29–46.

Baldry, A. and Thibault, P. J. (2006), *Multimodal Transcription and Text Analysis. A Multimedia Toolkit and Coursebook*. London: Equinox.

Balmer, J. (1998), 'Corporate identity and the advent of corporate marketing'. *Journal of Marketing Management*, 14, (8), 963–96.

Baron, R. and Byrne, D. (2000), *Social Psychology* (9th edn). Boston: Allyn and Bacon.

Barthes, R. (1977), *Image-Music-Text*. London: Fontana.

Bartlett, S. and Jones, M. J. (1997), 'Annual reporting disclosures 1970–90: an exemplification'. *Accounting, Business and Financial History*, 7, 61–80.

Baudrillard, J. (1998), *The Consumer Society*. London: Sage.

Bazerman, C. (1988), *Shaping Written Knowledge*. Madison: University of Wisconsin Press.

— (1994), 'Systems of genres and the enactment of social intentions', in A. Freedman and P. Medway (eds), *Genre and the New Rhetoric*. London: Taylor and Francis, pp. 79–101.

Beabout, G. R. and Echeverria, E. J. (2002), 'The culture of consumerism: a Catholic and personalist critique'. *Journal of Markets and Morality*, 5, (2), 339–83.

Beattie, V. and Jones, M. (2008), 'Corporate reporting using graphs: a review and synthesis'. *Journal of Accounting Literature*, 27, 71–110.

Bennett, R. (2002), 'Employers' demands for personal transferable skills in graduates: a content analysis of 1000 job advertisements and an associated empirical study'. *Journal of Vocational Education and Training*, 54, (4), 457–76.

Berger, A. (2004), *Ads, Fads and Consumer Culture: Advertising's Impact on American Character and Society*. Lanham: Rowman and Littlefield.

Bhabha, H. (1990), *Nation and Narration*. London: Routledge.

Bhatia, V. K. (2004), *Worlds of Written Discourse: A Genre-Based View*. London: Continuum.

Bhatia, V. K. and Lung, J. (2006), 'Corporate identity and generic integrity in business discourse', in J. C. Palmer-Silveira, M. F. Ruiz-Garrido and I. Fortanet Gómez (eds), *Intercultural and International Business Communication*. Bern: Peter Lang, pp. 265–85.

Biber, D. (2006), *University Language: A Corpus-Based Study of Spoken and Written Registers*. Amsterdam and Philadelphia: John Benjamins.

Billig, M. (1995), *Banal Nationalism*. London: Sage.

— (2002), 'Critical discourse analysis and the rhetoric of critique', in G. Weiss and R. Wodak (eds), *Critical Discourse Analysis: Theory and Interdisciplinarity*. London: Palgrave Macmillan, pp. 35–46.

Birkner, K. and Kern, F. (2004), 'Impression management in East and West German job interviews', in H. Spencer-Oatey (ed.), *Culturally Speaking – Managing Rapport through Talk across Cultures*. London: Continuum, pp. 255–71.

Blumer, H. (1969), *Symbolic Interactionism: Perspective and Method*. New Jersey: Prentice-Hall.

Boeker, W. (1992), 'Power and managerial dismissal: scapegoating at the top'. *Administrative Science Quarterly*, 37, (3), 400–21.

Boorstin, D. J. (1974), *The Americans: The Democratic Experience*. New York: Vintage.

Breeze, R. (2011a), 'Hybridity and genre-bending in company reports and reviews', in I. Elorza, O. Carbonell, R. Albarrán, B. García Riaza and M. Pérez Veneros (eds), *Empirical and Analytical Tools for 21st Century Applied Linguistics*. Salamanca: Ediciones Universidad de Salamanca, pp. 319–26.

— (2011b), 'Pragmatic aspects of job interviews', presented at *First International Conference on English for International and Intercultural Communication*, Zaragoza, June 2011.

— (2011c), 'Critical discourse analysis and its critics', *Pragmatics*, 21, (4), 493–525.

— (2012), 'Legitimation in corporate discourse: oil corporations after Deepwater Horizon'. *Discourse and Society*, 23, (1), 3–18.

Brummett, B. (1995), 'Scandalous rhetorics', in W. Elwood (ed.), *Public Relations Enquiry as Rhetorical Criticism. Case Studies of Corporate Discourse and Social Influence*. Westport: Praeger, pp. 13–24.

Brundtland Commission (1987), *Our Common Future*. Oxford: Oxford
University Press. Accessed 21 March 2013 on: http://conspect.nl/pdf/
Our_Common_Future-Brundtland_Report_1987.pdf

Bunting, M. (2004), *Willing Slaves: How the Overwork Culture is Ruining our Lives*.
London: HarperCollins.

Burke, K. (1950), *A Rhetoric of Motives*. Berkeley, CA: University of California Press.

— (1969), *A Grammar of Motives*. Berkeley: University of California Press.

Callan, S. and Thomas, J. (2009), 'Corporate financial performance and corporate social
performance: an update and reinvestigation'. *Corporate Social Responsibility and
Environmental Management*, 16, 61–78.

Cameron, G. (1994), 'Does publicity outperform advertising? An experimental test of
the third-party endorsement'. *Journal of Public Relations Research*, 6, (3), 185–207.

Cameron, G. and Ju-Pak, K. (2000), 'Information pollution? Labelling and format of
advertorials'. *Newspaper Research Journal*, 21, (1), 65–76.

Capriotti, A. and Moreno, P. (2007), 'Corporate citizenship and public relations: the
importance and interactivity of social responsibility issues on corporate websites'.
Public Relations Review, 33, 84–91.

Catenaccio, P. (2011), 'Social and environmental reports: a short-term diachronic
perspective on an emerging genre', in G. Garzone and M. Gotti (eds), *Discourse,
Communication and the Enterprise. Genres and Trends*. Bern: Peter Lang, pp. 169–91.

Cerin, P. (2002), 'Communication in corporate environmental reports'. *Corporate Social
Responsibility and Environmental Management*, 9, 46–66.

Cha, S. and Edmondson, A. (2006), 'How values backfire: leadership, attribution and
disenchantment in a values-driven organisation'. *Leadership Quarterly*, 17, (1), 57–78.

Cheney, G. (1983), 'The rhetoric of identification and the study of organizational
communication'. *Quarterly Journal of Speech*, 69, 143–58.

Cheney, G. and Vibbert, S. L. (1987), 'Corporate discourse: public relations and issue
management', in F. M. Jablin, L. L. Putnam, K. H. Roberts and L. W. Porter (eds),
Hand Book of Organizational Communication. Beverley Hills: Sage Publications,
pp. 165–94.

Chilton, P. (2004), *Analysing Political Discourse*. London: Routledge.

Choo, C. W. (2006), *The Knowing Organization: How Organizations Use Information to
Construct Meaning*. New York: Oxford University Press.

Chouliaraki, L. and Fairclough, N. (1999), *Discourse in Late Modernity. Rethinking
Critical Discourse Analysis*. Edinburgh: Edinburgh University Press.

Christensen, L. (2002), 'Corporate communication: the challenge of transparency'.
Corporate Communications: An International Journal, 7, (3), 162–8.

Christie, F. and Martin, J. (1997), *Genre and Institutions. Social Processes in the
Workplace and School*. London: Cassell.

Coe, R. (2002), 'The new rhetoric of genre: writing political briefs', in A. M. Johns
(ed.), *Genre in the Classroom: Multiple Perspectives*. Mahwah: Lawrence Erlbaum,
pp. 197–207.

Companies Act (2006), Accessed 2 May 2012 on: www.legislation.gov.uk/ukpga/2006/46/contents

Cook, G. (1992), *The Discourse of Advertising*. London: Routledge.

Cooke, H. (2006), 'Seagull management and the control of nursing work'. *Work, Employment and Society*, 20, (2), 223–43.

Corvellec, H. (2001), 'Talks on tracks – debating urban infrastructure projects'. *Studies in Cultures, Organizations and Societies*, 7, 25–53.

— (2007), 'Arguing for a licence to operate: the case of the Swedish wind power industry'. *Corporate Communications*, 12, (2), 129–44.

Coseriu, E. (1980), *Textlinguistik: eine Einführung*. Tübingen: Narr.

Courtis, J. K. (1997), 'Corporate annual report graphical communication in Hong Kong: effective or misleading?' *Journal of Business Communication*, 34, 269–88.

Crable, R. and Vibbert, S. (1995), 'Mobil's epideictic advocacy. "Observations" of Prometheus bound', in W. Elwood (ed.), *Public Relations Enquiry as Rhetorical Criticism. Case Studies of Corporate Discourse and Social Influence*. Westport: Praeger, pp. 27–46.

Czarniawska, B. (2004), *Narratives in Social Science Research*. London: Sage.

Czarniawska, B. and Gagliardi, P. (2003), *Narratives We Organise By*. Philadelphia: John Benjamins.

Dahl, S. (2000), 'Cultural values in beer advertising in the UK, the Netherlands and Germany'. Paper presented at Intercultural Discourse Research Day, Luton, accessed 2 June 2012 on: www.stephweb.com/capstone/

Daskalaki, M. (2000), 'Induction programmes in the age of "corporate culture": the "sophisticated subject"'. *Business and Professional Ethics Journal*, 19, (3–4), 199–231.

David, C. (2001), 'Mythmaking in annual reports'. *Journal of Business and Technical Communication*, 15, 195–222.

Degano, C. (2010), 'Linguistic perspectives on image construction and moral identity. The case of banks', in P. Evangelisti Allori and G. Garzone (eds), *Discourse, Identities and Genres in Corporate Communication*. Bern: Peter Lang, pp. 235–62.

DeGenaro, W. (2009), 'Legitimating corporate education: two-year college mission statements'. *International Journal of Critical Pedagogy*, 2, (1), 100–18.

De Mooij, M. (2010), *Global Marketing and Advertising: Understanding Cultural Paradoxes*. London: Sage.

Dentchev, N. (2004), 'Corporate social performance as a business strategy'. *Journal of Business Ethics*, 55, 397–412.

Devitt, A. (2004), *Writing Genres*. Carbondale: Southern Illinois University Press.

Dholakia, R., Zhao, M., Dholakia, N. and Fortin, D. (2000), *Interactivity and Revisits to Websites: A Theoretical Framework*. Accessed 27 March, 2002, on: http://ritim.cba.uri.edu/wp2001/wpdone3/Interactivity.PDF

Ditlevsen, M. (2012), 'Telling the story of Danisco's annual reports (1935 through 2007–8) from a communicative perspective'. *Journal of Business and Technical Communication*, 26, (1), 92–115.

Djonov, E. (2007), 'Website hierarchy and the interaction between content organisation, webpage and navigation design: a systemic functional hypermedia discourse analysis perspective'. *Information Design Journal*, 15, (2), 144–62.

Dolphin, R. (1999), *The Fundamentals of Corporate Communication*. Oxford: Butterworth Heinemann.

— (2004), 'The strategic role of investor relations'. *Corporate Communication: An International Journal*, 9, (1), 25–42.

Douglis, P. (2000), 'Photojournalism: telling it like it is'. *Communication World*, 17, 44–7.

Dowling, G. (2001), *Creating Corporate Reputations*. Oxford: Oxford University Press.

Droge, C., Germain, R. and Halstead, D. (1990), 'A note on marketing and the corporate annual report: 1930–1950'. *Journal of the Academy of Marketing Science*, 18, (4), 355–64.

Ducrot, O. (1980), *Les Échelles Argumentatives*. Paris: Les Editions de Minuit.

Du Gay, P. (1996), *Consumption and Identity at Work*. London: Sage.

Eckman, A. and Lindlof, T. R. (2003), 'Negotiating the gray lines: an ethnographic case study of organizational conflict between advertorials and news'. *Journalism Studies*, 4, (1), 65–77.

Edwards, M. R. (2005), 'Employer and employee branding: HR or PR?', in S. Bach (ed.), *Managing Human Resources: Personnel Management in Transition*. Oxford: Blackwell, pp. 266–86.

Ellsworth, R. (2002), *Leading with Purpose: The New Corporate Realities*. Stanford: Stanford University Press.

Elwood, W. (1995), *Public Relations Enquiry as Rhetorical Criticism. Case Studies of Corporate Discourse and Social Influence*. Westport: Praeger.

Engberg, J. and Heller, D. (2008), 'Vagueness and indeterminacy in law', in V. K. Bhatia, C. N. Candlin and J. Engberg (eds), *Legal Discourse across Cultures and Systems*. Hong Kong: Hong Kong University Press, pp. 145–68.

Erdogan, Z. B. and Kitchen, P. J. (1998), 'Managerial mindsets and the symbiotic relationship between sponsorship and advertising'. *Marketing Intelligence and Planning*, 16, (6), 369–74.

Evangelisti Allori, P. (2010), 'Corporate identity and image promotion through sponsoring international sports events. A view from the web', in P. Evangelisti Allori and G. Garzone (eds), *Discourse, Identities and Genres in Corporate Communication*. Bern: Peter Lang, pp. 75–98.

Evangelisti Allori, P. and Garzone, G. (eds) (2010), *Discourse, Identities and Genres in Corporate Communication*. Bern: Peter Lang.

Fairclough, N. (1985), 'Critical and descriptive goals in discourse analysis'. *Journal of Pragmatics*, 9, 739–63.

— (1989), *Language and Power*. London: Longman.

— (1992a), *Discourse and Social Change*. Cambridge: Polity.

— (1992b), 'Discourse and text: linguistic and intertextual analysis within discourse analysis'. *Discourse and Society*, 3, (2), 193–217.

— (1993), 'Critical Discourse Analysis and the marketisation of public discourse: the universities'. *Discourse and Society*, 4, (2), 133–68.

— (1995a), *Critical Discourse Analysis*. London: Longman.

— (1995b), 'Critical discourse analysis and the marketisation of public discourse in the universities', in N. Fairclough (ed.), *Critical Discourse Analysis: The Critical Study of Language*. London: Longman, pp. 130–66.

— (1996), 'A reply to Henry Widdowson's "Discourse analysis: a critical view"'. *Language and Literature*, 5, (1), 49–56.

— (2000), *New Labour, New Language?* London: Routledge.

Fairclough, N. and Wodak, R. (1997), 'Critical discourse analysis', in T. van Dijk (ed.), *Discourse as Social Interaction*. London: Sage, pp. 258–84.

Featherstone, M. (1995), *Undoing Culture. Globalisation, Post-modernism and Identity*. London: Sage.

Ferstel, J. W. (1989), 'Annual reports, brochures, and newsletters', in C. Sides (ed.), *Technical and Business Communication: Bibliographic Essays for Teachers and Corporate Trainers*. Urbana: NCTE, pp. 223–40.

Flanders, A. (1970), *Management and Unions*. London: Faber and Faber.

Flowerdew, J. and Wan, A. (2010), 'The linguistic and the contextual in applied genre analysis: the case of the company audit report'. *English for Specific Purposes*, 29, (2), 78–93.

Foley, J. P. (1998), 'Ethics in advertising. A look at the report by the Pontifical Council for Social Communications'. *Journal of Public Policy and Marketing*, 17, (2), 313–15.

Fontana Dictionary of Modern Thought (1988). Accessed on: 18 February 2013 http://readon.sg/det_9433460.aspx

Foucault, M. (1969), *The Archaeology of Knowledge*. London: Routledge.

— (1972), *The Order of Things*. London: Tavistock.

— (1981), 'The order of discourse', in R. Young (ed.), *Untying the Text: A Post-Structural Anthology*. Boston: Routledge & Kegan Paul, pp. 48–78.

Fowler, R. (1993), 'Hysterical style in the press', in D. Graddol and O. Boyd-Barrett (eds), *Media Texts: Authors and Readers*. Clevedon: Multilingual Matters, pp. 90–9.

Fox, R. and Fox, J. (2004), *Organizational Discourse: A Language-Ideology-Power Perspective*. Westport: Praeger.

Freedman, A. (1993), 'Show and tell? The role of explicit teaching in the learning of new genres'. *Research in the Teaching of English*, 27, 222–51.

— (1999), 'Beyond the text: towards understanding the teaching and learning of genres'. *TESOL Quarterly*, 33, (4), 764–7.

Freedman, A. and Medway, P. (1994), *Genre and the New Rhetoric*. London: Taylor and Francis.

Frenkel, S., Korczynski, M., Donohue, L. and Shire, K. (1995), 'Re-constituting work: trends towards knowledge work and info-normative control'. *Work, Employment and Society*, 9, (4), 773–96.

Frowfelter-Lohrke, C. and Fulkerson, C. L. (2001), 'The incidence and quality of graphics in annual reports: an international comparison'. *Journal of Business Communication*, 38, 337–58.

Galliot, M. (1955), *La publicité à travers les âges*. Paris: Éditions Hommes et Techniques.

Gamble, G., Hsu, K., Jackson, C. and Tollerson, C. (1996), 'Environmental disclosures in annual reports: an international perspective'. *International Journal of Accounting*, 31, (3), 293–331.

Garcés-Conejo Blitvich, P. (2010), 'Who "we" are: the construction of American corporate identity in the corporate values statement', in M. Ruiz-Garrido, J. C. Palmer-Silveira and I. Fortanet-Gomez (eds), *English for Professional and Academic Purposes*. Amsterdam: Rodopi, pp. 121–39.

Garzone, G. (2005), 'Letters to shareholders and chairman's statements: textual variability and generic integrity', in P. Gillaerts and M. Gotti (eds), *Genre Variation in Business Letters*. Bern: Peter Lang, pp. 179–204.

— (2010), 'Multiple sponsorships and advertising in the discursive construction of corporate identity', in P. Evangelisti Allori and G. Garzone (eds), *Discourse, Identities and Genres in Corporate Communication*. Bern: Peter Lang. pp. 51–74.

Gee, J. (1996), *Social Linguistics and Literacies: Ideology in Discourses*. London: Taylor and Francis.

Geertz, C. (1973), *The Interpretation of Cultures*. New York: Basic Books.

Gergen, K. J. (1999), 'Toward relational selves', in K. J. Gergen (ed.), *An Invitation to Social Construction*. London: Sage, pp. 115–41.

Giddens, A. (1979), *Central Problems in Social Theory: Action, Structure, and Contradiction in Social Analysis*. Los Angeles: University of California Press.

— (1984), *The Constitution of Society: Outline of the Theory of Structuration*. Cambridge: Polity Press.

— (1991), *Modernity and Self-Identity*. Cambridge: Polity Press.

— (1994), 'Living in a post-traditional society', in U. Beck, A. Giddens and S. Lash (eds), *Reflexive Modernization. Politics, Tradition and Aesthetics in the Modern Social Order*. Cambridge: Polity Press, pp. 54–109.

Gillaerts, P. and van de Velde, F. (2011), 'Metadiscourse on the move. The CEO's letter revisited', in G. Garzone and M. Gotti (eds), *Discourse, Communication and the Enterprise. Genres and Trends*. Bern: Peter Lang, pp. 151–68.

Glaser, B. (1992), *Basics of Grounded Theory Analysis*. Mill Valley: Sociology Press.

Goffman, E. (1979), *Gender Advertisements*. London: Macmillan.

Goletiani, L. (2011), 'Gazprom's environmental report: peculiarities of an emerging genre', in G. Garzone and M. Gotti (eds), *Discourse, Communication and the Enterprise. Genres and Trends*. Bern: Peter Lang, pp. 255–77.

Gollin, S. (1999), 'Why? I thought we'd talked about it before: collaborative writing in a professional workplace setting', in C. Candlin and K. Hyland (eds), *Writing: Texts, Processes and Practices*. London: Longman, pp. 267–90.

Goodacre, H. (2010), 'Limited liability and the wealth of "uncivilised nations": Adam Smith and the limits to the European Enlightenment'. *Cambridge Journal of Economics*, 34, 857–67.

Goodman, M. (2000), 'Corporate communication: the American picture'. *Corporate Communications: An International Journal*, 5, (2), 69–74.

Gotti, M. (2011), 'Discursive changes in corporate and institutional communication', in G. Garzone and M. Gotti (eds), *Discourse, Communication and the Enterprise. Genres and Trends*. Bern: Peter Lang, pp. 29–48.

Grice, H. P. (1989), *Studies in the Way of Words*. Harvard: Harvard University Press.

Gush, J. (1996), 'Assessing the role of education and training in meeting the needs of the retail sector'. *Education + Training*, 38, (9), 5–13.

Gustavsen, P. and Tilley, E. (2003), 'Public relations communication through corporate websites: towards an understanding of the role of interactivity'. *Prism*, 1, 1–14. http://praxis.massey.ac.nz/fileadmin/Praxis/Files/Journal_Files/issue1/refereed_articles_paper5.pdf

Habermas, J. (1967), *Erkenntnis und Interesse*. Frankfurt am Main: Suhrkamp.

— (1979), *Communication and the Evolution of Society*. Boston: Beacon Press.

— (1984), *Theory of Communicative Action. Vol. 1: Reason and the Rationalization of Society* (tr. T. McCarthy). Cambridge: Polity Press.

Hall, S. (1996), 'The question of cultural identity', in S. Hall, D. Held, D. Hubert and K. Thompson (eds), *Modernity: An Introduction to Modern Societies*. Oxford: Blackwell, pp. 596–634.

Halliday, M. A. K. (1978), *Language as Social Semiotic: The Social Interpretation of Language and Meaning*. London: Edward Arnold.

— (1994), *Introduction to Functional Grammar*. London: Arnold.

Halliday, M. and Hasan, R. (1976), *Cohesion in English*. London: Longman.

Halliday, M. and Matthiesen, C. (2004), *An Introduction to Functional Grammar*. London: Arnold.

Hatch, M. and Schultz, M. (1997), 'Relations between organizational culture, identity and image'. *European Journal of Marketing*, 32, (5–6), 356–65.

Heeter, C. (2000), 'Interactivity in the context of designed experiences'. *Journal of Interactive Advertising*, 1, (1). Available at: http://jiad.org/vol1/no1/heeter

Heinze, N. and Hu, Q. (2006), 'The evolution of corporate web presence: a longitudinal study of large American companies'. *International Journal of Information Management*, 26, 313–25.

Hickson, C. R. and Turner, J. D. (2005), 'Corporation or limited liability company', in J. McCusker, S. Engerman, L. Fischer, D. Hancock and K. Pomeranz (eds), *Encyclopaedia of World Trade since 1450*. New York: Macmillan.

Hildebrandt, H. and Snyder, R. (1981), 'The Pollyanna hypothesis in business writing: initial results, suggestions for research'. *Journal of Business Communication*, 18, 5–15.

Hochschild, A. R. (1983), *The Managed Heart: Commercialisation of Human Feeling*. Berkeley: University of California Press.

Hofstede, G. (2001), *Culture's Consequences: Comparing Values, Behaviors, Institutions, and Organizations across Nations.* Thousand Oaks: Sage.

Hoshino, K. (1987), 'Semiotic marketing and product conceptualisation', in J. Umiker-Sebeok (ed.), *Marketing and Semiotics.* Amsterdam: Mouton de Gruyter, pp. 41–55.

Hultman, K. (2005), 'Evaluating organizational values'. *Organizational Development Journal*, 23, (4), 32–44.

Hyland, K. (1998), 'Exploring corporate rhetoric: metadiscourse in the CEO's letter'. *Journal of Business Communication*, 35, 224–45.

— (1999), 'Disciplinary discourses: writer stance in research articles', in C. Candlin and K. Hyland (eds), *Writing: Texts, Processes and Practices.* London: Longman, pp. 99–121.

— (2000), *Disciplinary Discourses: Social Interactions in Academic Writing.* London: Longman.

— (2001), 'Humble servants of the discipline? Self-mention in research articles'. *English for Specific Purposes*, 20, (3), 207–26.

— (2004), 'Disciplinary interactions: metadiscourse in L2 postgraduate writing'. *Journal of Second Language Writing*, 13, 133–51.

— (2005), 'Stance and engagement: a model of interaction in academic discourse'. *Discourse Studies*, 6, (2), 173–92.

— (2009), *Academic Discourse.* London: Continuum.

Hynes, G. and Janson, M. (2007), 'Global imagery in online advertisements'. *Business Communication Quarterly*, 70, (4), 487–92.

Ivanic, R. (1998), *Writing and Identity: The Discoursal Construction of Identity in Academic Writing.* Amsterdam and Philadelphia: John Benjamins.

Izquierdo Alegría, D. (2010a), '¿Publi como acortamiento de público? Evolución del tipo de texto publirreportaje y aprovechamiento (per)suasivo de esta vinculación'. *Anuario de Estudios Filológicos*, xxxiii, 129–45.

— (2010b), 'El nombre de un tipo de texto como estrategia (per)suasiva: el caso del publirreportaje'. *Español Actual*, xcii, 125–52.

Jablin, F. M. (1987), 'Organizational entry, assimilation and exit', in F. M. Jablin, L. L. Putnam, K. H. Roberts and L. W. Porter (eds), *Handbook of Organizational Communication.* Beverley Hills: Sage, pp. 679–740.

Jameson, D. A. (2000), 'Telling the investment story: a narrative analysis of shareholder reports'. *Journal of Business Communication*, 37, 7–38.

John Paul II. (1987), *Sollicitudo Rei Socialis.* Vatican City: Libreria Editrice Vaticana.

Kempin, F. G. (1990), *A Historical Introduction to Anglo-American Law.* St Paul: West Publishers.

Kilgarriff, A., Rychly, P., Smrz, P. and Tugwell, D. (2004), 'The sketch engine', in G. Williams and S. Vessier (eds), *Proceedings of 11th EURALEX International Conference*, 105–16.

Kohut, G. and Segars, A. (1992), 'The president's letter to stockholders: an examination of corporate communication strategy'. *Journal of Business Communication*, 29, (1), 7–21.

Kraimer, M. L. (1997), 'Organization goals and values: a socialization model'. *Human Resource Management Review*, 7, (4), 425–48.

Kress, G. and van Leeuwen, T. (1996), *Reading Images: The Grammar of Visual Design*. London: Routledge.

— (2001), *Multimodal Discourse. The Modes and Media of Contemporary Communication*. London: Arnold.

Kunda, G. and Ailon-Souday, G. (2006), 'Managers, markets and ideologies: design and devotion revisited', in S. Ackroyd, R. Batt, P. Thompson and P. Tolbert (eds), *The Oxford Handbook of Work and Organization*. Oxford: Oxford University Press, pp. 200–19.

Kyoto Protocol (1997), Accessed 21 March 2013 on: http://unfccc.int/kyoto_protocol/items/2830.php

Lagace, M. (2006), 'Corporate values and employee cynicism'. *Harvard Business School Working Knowledge*, 27 August.

Lanham, R. (1974), *Style: An Anti Textbook*. New Haven: Yale University Press.

Lave, J. and Wenger, E. (1999), 'Legitimate peripheral participation', in P. Murphy (ed.), *Learners, Learning and Assessment*. London: Sage, pp. 83–9.

LDP (London Development Partnership) (2000), *A Skills Strategy for all London's People: Strategy and Three Year Action Plan*. London: Publications Office, Greater London Authority.

Lee, T. (1994), 'The changing form of the corporate annual report'. *The Accounting Historians Journal*, 21, (1), 215–32.

Leech, G. N. (1983), *Principles of Pragmatics*. London: Longman.

Levitt, T. (1983), 'The globalization of markets'. *Harvard Business Review*, 61, (3), 69–81.

Lin, D. (1998), 'Automatic retrieval; and clustering of similar words'. *Proceedings of COLING-ACL Montreal*, 768–74.

Lipovsky, C. (2010), *Negotiating Solidarity: A Social-Linguistic Approach to Job Interviews*. Newcastle: Cambridge Scholars Publishing.

Lischinsky, A. (2011), 'In times of crisis: a corpus approach to the construction of the global financial crisis in annual reports'. *Critical Discourse Studies*, 8, (3), 153–68.

Livesey, S. (2001), 'Eco-identity as discursive struggle: Royal Dutch Shell, Brent Spar and Nigeria'. *Journal of Business Communication*, 38, 58–91.

— (2002a), 'The discourse of the middle ground: Citizen Shell commits to sustainable development'. *Management Communication Quarterly*, 15, 313–49.

— (2002b), 'Global warming wars: rhetorical and discourse analytic approaches to ExxonMobil's corporate public discourse'. *Journal of Business Communication*, 39, 117–48.

López Pan, F. (2010), 'La oralidad fingida y la construcción de columnista como personaje. Dos estrategias para la construcción del ethos del columnista', in C. Martínez Pasamar (ed.), *Estrategias Argumentativas en el Discurso Periodístico*. Frankfurt am Main: Peter Lang, pp. 193–220.

Lord, H. L. (2002), 'Annual reports: a literature review (1989–2001)'. *Journal of Technical Writing and Communication*, 32, 367–89.

Lyons, L. (2011), '"I'd like my life back". Corporate personhood and the BP oil disaster'. *Biography*, 34 (1), 96–108.

Maat, H. (2007), 'How promotional language in press releases is dealt with by journalists: genre mixing or genre conflict?' *Journal of Business Communication*, 44, 59–95.

Malavasi, D. (2006a), 'Banks' annual reports: an analysis of the linguistic means used to express evaluation'. Accessed on 2 May 2012: www.businesscommunication.org/conventions/Proceedings/2005/ABCEurope2005Proceedings.html

— (2006b), 'Banks' annual reports: an analysis of lexical evaluation across some sections', in M. Bondi and J. Bamford (eds), *Managing Interaction in Professional Discourse: Intercultural and Interdiscoursal Perspectives*. Rome: Officina Edizioni, pp. 147–58.

— (2010), 'The multifaceted nature of banks' annual reports as informative, promotional and corporate communication practices', in P. Evangelisti Allori and G. Garzone (eds), *Discourse, Identities and Genres in Corporate Communication*. Bern: Peter Lang, pp. 211–33.

— (2011), '"Doing well by doing good": a comparative analysis of Nokia's and Ericsson's corporate social responsibility reports', in G. Garzone and M. Gotti (eds), *Discourse, Communication and the Enterprise. Genres and Trends*. Bern: Peter Lang, pp. 193–212.

Malinowski, B. (1923 / 1969), 'The problem of meaning in primitive languages', in C. K. Ogden and I. A. Richards (eds), *The Meaning of Meaning: A Study of the Influence upon Thought and of the Science of Symbolism*. London: Routledge & Kegan Paul, pp. 296–336.

Martin, J. (1992), *English Text: System and Structure*. Amsterdam: John Benjamins.

— (1997), 'Analysing genre: functional parameters', in F. Christie and J. Martin (eds), *Genre and Institutions: Social Processes in the Workplace and School*. London and Washington: Cassell, pp. 3–39.

Martin, J. and White, P. (2004), *The Language of Evaluation: Appraisal in English*. Basingstoke: Palgrave Macmillan.

Mazza, C. (1999), *Claim, Intent and Persuasion. Organizational Legitimacy and the Rhetoric of Corporate Mission Statements*. Norwell: Kluwer.

McAlexander, J., Schouten, J. and Koenig, H. (2002), 'Building brand community'. *Journal of Marketing*, 66, (1), 38–54.

McDonald, P. and Gandz, J. (1992), 'Getting value from shared values'. *Organizational Dynamics*, 20, (3), 64–77.

McKinney, M. S. (1995), 'The rhetoric of indoctrination', in W. Elwood (ed.), *Public Relations Inquiry as Rhetorical Criticism*. Westport: Praeger, pp. 175–90.

McKinstry, S. (1996), 'Designing the annual reports of Burton PLC from 1930 to 1994'. *Accounting, Organizations and Society*, 21, (1), 89–111.

McLuhan, M. (1964), 'Keeping upset with the Joneses', in M. McLuhan (ed.), *Understanding Media*. London: Routledge, pp. 226–33.

Meenaghan, J. (1991), 'The role of sponsorship in the marketing communication mix'. *International Journal of Advertising*, 10, (1), 35–47.

Meenaghan, T. and Shipley, D. (1999), 'Media effect in commercial sponsorship'. *European Journal of Marketing*, 33, (3–4), 328–47.

Melewar, T. and Karaosmanoglu, E. (2006), 'Seven dimensions of corporate identity. A categorisation from the practitioners' perspectives'. *European Journal of Marketing*, 40, (7–8), 846–69.

Milliman, J., Czaplewski, A. and Ferguson, J. (2003), 'Workplace spirituality and employee work attitudes'. *Journal of Organizational Change Management*, 16, (4), 426–47.

Nake, F. and Grabowski, S. (2001), 'Human-computer interaction viewed as pseudo-communication'. *Knowledge-based Systems*, 14, (8), 441–7.

Nelson, M. (2000), The business English lexis site. Accessed 8 May 2012 from: http://users.utu.fi/micnel/business_english_lexis_site.htm

Nguyen, N. and Leblanc, G. (2001), 'Corporate image and corporate reputation in customers' retention decisions in services'. *Journal of Retailing and Consumer Services*, 8, (4), 227–36.

Owen, D. and O'Dwyer, B. (2008), 'Corporate social responsibility: the reporting and assurance dimensions', in A. Crane, A. McWilliams, D. Matten, J. Moon and D. Siegel (eds), *The Oxford Handbook of Corporate Social Responsibility*. Oxford: Oxford University Press, pp. 384–412.

Paine, L. (2003), *Value Shift: Why Companies Must Merge Social and Financial Imperatives to Achieve Superior Performance*. London: McGraw-Hill.

Pan, P. L. and Xu, J. (2009), 'Online strategic communication: a cross-cultural analysis of US and Chinese corporate websites'. *Public Relations Review*, 35, 251–3.

Penrose, J. M. (2008), 'Annual report graphic use'. *Journal of Business Communication*, 45, 158–80.

Perelman, C. and Olbrechts-Tyteca, M. (1969), *The New Rhetoric: A Treatise on Argumentation*. Notre Dame: University of Notre Dame Press.

Pollach, I. (2005), 'Corporate self-presentation on the WWW: strategies for enhancing usability, credibility and utility'. *Corporate Communications: An International Journal*, 10, (4), 285–301.

Poncini, G. and Hiris, L. (2006), 'When (un)ethical behaviour is an issue for the industry: an examination of CEO letters of securities brokerage firms', in G. Garzone and S. Sarangi (eds), *Discourse, Ideology and Specialized Communication*. Bern: Peter Lang, pp. 207–332.

Pontifical Council for Social Communications (1997), *Ethics in Advertising*. Vatican City: Vatican Documents.

Ponzio, A. (2006), 'Indexicality theory', in J. Mey and K. Brown (eds), *Concise Encyclopaedia of Pragmatics*. Oxford: Elsevier, pp. 379–85.

Poppi, F. (2011), 'Companies' websites as vehicles for expressing corporate identity: a case study on the case of English as a lingua franca', in G. Garzone and M. Gotti (eds), *Discourse, Communication and the Enterprise. Genres and Trends*. Bern: Peter Lang, pp. 131–48.

Potter, J. (1996), *Representing Reality: Discourse, Rhetoric and Social Construction*. London: Sage.

Preston, A., Wright, C. and Young, J. (1996), 'Imag(in)ing annual reports'. *Accounting, Organizations and Society*, 21, (1), 113–37.

Rafaeli, S. (1988), 'Interactivity: from new media to communication', in R. Hawkins, J. Wiemann and S. Pingree (eds), *Sage Annual Review of Communication Research: Advancing Communication Science*. Beverly Hills: Sage, pp. 110–34.

Rathbun, G. (2007), 'Silenced by a mission statement: an organization's cloak of ambiguity'. *Human Communication*, 10, (4), 547–56.

Rodríguez, R. and Mora, K. (2002), *Frankenstein y el Cirujano Plástico*. Alicante: Publicaciones de la Universidad de Alicante.

Rokeach, M. (1973), *The Nature of Human Values*. New York: Free Press.

Rothery, J. (1996), 'Making changes: developing an educational linguistics', in R. Hasan and G. Williams (eds), *Literacy in Society*. London: Longman, pp. 86–123.

Rousseau, D. (1998), 'Why workers still identify with organizations'. *Journal of Organizational Behavior*, 19, 217–33.

Russell-Loretz, T. (1995), 'Janus in the looking-glass: the management of organizational identity in corporate recruitment videos', in W. Elwood (ed.), *Public Relations Inquiry as Rhetorical Criticism*. Westport: Praeger, pp. 156–72.

Rutherford, B. (2005), 'Genre analysis of corporate annual report narratives: a corpus linguistics-based approach'. *Journal of Business Communication*, 41, 349–78.

Salsnik, E. (2010), 'Advertorials in the Italian press: the impact of corporate identity strategies on linguistic features', in P. Evangelisti Allori and G. Garzone (eds), *Discourse, Identities and Genres in Corporate Communication*. Bern: Peter Lang, pp. 185–208.

Sancho Guinda, C. (2001), 'The pragmatic candidate: towards a new face value', in J. C. Palmer, S. Postseguillo and I. Fortanet (eds), *Discourse Analysis and Terminology in Languages for Specific Purposes*. Castellón: Publicacions de la Universitat Jaume I, pp. 225–37.

Sartain, L. and Finney, M. (2003), *HR from the Heart: Inspiring Stories and Strategies for Building the People Side of a Great Business*. New York: AMACOM.

Schein, E. (1964), 'How to break in the college graduate'. *Harvard Business Review*, 42, 68–76.

Scheuer, J. (2001), 'Recontextualisation and communicative styles in job interviews'. *Discourse Studies*, 3, (2), 223–48.

Scollon, R. and Scollon, S. (2001), *Intercultural Communication*. Oxford: Blackwell.

Scott, M. (2007), *WordSmith Tools 5.0*. Oxford: Oxford University Press.

Securities and Exchange Commission (SEC) (2002), Accessed 2 May 2012 on: www.sec.
    gov/answers/annrep.htm http://www.sec.gov

Silverman, D. (1993), *Interpreting Qualitative Data: Methods for Analysing Talk, Text
    and Interaction.* Englewood Cliffs: Prentice Hall.

Simpson, L. (2000), 'The annual report: an exercise in ignorance?' *Accounting Forum*,
    24, 231–47.

Slapper, G. (2012), 'Moral balance sheet'. *Open Minds*, 29.

Smith, A. (1776), *An Enquiry into the Nature and Causes of the Wealth of Nations.*
    London: Clarendon.

— (1991), *National Identity.* Harmondsworth: Penguin.

Smith, M. and Taffler, R. (2000), 'The chairman's statement – a content analysis of
    discretionary narrative'. *Accounting, Auditing and Accountability Journal*, 13, (5),
    624–47.

Smith, R. (1999), 'Images of language in advertising in Scotland'. *Scottish Language*, 18,
    52–68.

— (2004), 'Languages other than English in the Scottish press', in J. Derrick McClure
    (ed.), *Doonsin' Emerauds: New Studies in Scots and Gaelic.* Belfast: Queen's
    University Belfast, pp. 103–14.

Solin, A. (2011), 'Genre', in J. Zienkowski, J. O. Östman and J. Verschueren (eds),
    Discursive Pragmatics. Amsterdam: John Benjamins, pp. 119–34.

Solomon, M., Bamossy, G., Askegaard, S. and Hogg, M. K. (2006), *Consumer Behaviour:
    A European Perspective.* Harlow: Pearson.

Spang, K. (2005), *Persuasión: fundamentos de retórica.* Pamplona: EUNSA.

Spencer-Oatey, H. and Franklin, P. (2009), *Intercultural Interaction. A Multidisciplinary
    Approach to Intercultural Communication.* London: Palgrave Macmillan.

Stanton, P. and Stanton, J. (2002), 'Corporate annual reports: research perspectives
    used'. *Accounting, Auditing & Accountability Journal*, 15, 478–500.

Stöckl, H. (2004), *Die Sprache im Bild – Das Bild in der Sprache. Zur Verknüpfung von
    Sprache und Bild im massenmedialen Text. Konzepte, Theorien, Analysemethoden.*
    Berlin: de Gruyter.

— (2010), 'Sprache-Bild-Texte lesen. Bausteine zur Methodik einer Grundkompetenz',
    in H. Diekmannshenke, M. Klemm and H. Stöckl (eds), *Bildlinguistik.* Berlin: Erich
    Schmidt, pp. 43–70.

Stokes, G. and Hallett, S. (1992), 'The role of advertising and the car'. *Transport Reviews*,
    12, (2), 171–83.

Suntrust Interactive Job Interview. Accessed 29 August 2012 on: www2.suntrust.com/
    careers/

Swales, J. (1981), *Aspects of Article Introductions.* ESP Monograph No. 1. Aston:
    University of Aston.

— (1990), *Genre Analysis: English in Academic and Research Settings.* Cambridge:
    Cambridge University Press.

Swales, J. and Rogers, P. (1995), 'Discourse and the projection of corporate culture: the
    mission statement'. *Discourse and Society*, 6, (2), 223–42.

Sydney Morning Herald. (2012), 'McDonalds finds another channel to take its story to the market'. 31 March 2012.

Thibault, P. (2001), 'Multimodality and the school science textbook', in C. T. Torsello, G. Brunetti and N. Penello (eds), *Corpora Testuali per Ricerca, Traduzione e Apprendimento Linguistico.* Padova: Unipress, pp. 293–335.

Thomas, J. (1997), 'Discourse in the marketplace: the making of meaning in annual reports'. *Journal of Business Communication*, 34, (1), 47–66.

Thompson, G. (2001), 'Interaction in academic writing: learning to argue with the reader'. *Applied Linguistics*, 22, (1), 58–78.

Thompson, P. and van den Broek, D. (2010), 'Managerial control and workplace regimes: an introduction'. *Work, Employment and Society*, 24, (3), 1–12.

Tonnies, F. (1971), *Fernando Tonnies on Sociology: Pure, Applied and Empirical: Selected Writings.* Chicago: University of Chicago Press.

Topalian, A. (2003), 'Executive perspective: 1. Experienced reality. The development of corporate identity in the digital era'. *European Journal of Marketing*, 37, (7–8), 1119–32.

Tosun, N. (2004), 'Financial value and public relations'. *Corporate Communications: An International Journal*, 9, (3), 202–8.

Toulmin, S. (1969), *The Uses of Argument* (2nd edn). Cambridge: Cambridge University Press.

Twitchell, J. B. (1996), *Adcult USA. The Triumph of Advertising in American Culture.* New York: Columbia University Press.

Ungerer, F. (2003), 'Muted metaphors and the activation of metonymys in advertising', in A. Barcelona (ed.), *Metaphor and Metonymy at the Crossroads: A Cognitive Perspective.* Berlin: Walter De Gruyter, pp. 321–40.

Van de Mieroop (2007), 'The complementarity of two identities and two approaches: quantitative and qualitative analysis of institutional and professional identity'. *Journal of Pragmatics*, 39, (6), 1120–42.

van Dijk, T. (1991), *Racism and the Press.* London: Routledge.

— (1993), *Elite Discourse and Racism.* Newbury Park: Sage.

— (1998), *Ideology: A Multidisciplinary Approach.* London: Sage.

— (1999), 'Critical Discourse Analysis and conversation analysis'. *Discourse and Society*, 10, (4), 459–60.

— (2008), *Discourse and Context: A Socio-Cognitive Approach.* Cambridge: Cambridge University Press.

Van Lee, R., Fabish, L. and McGaw, N. (2005), 'The value of corporate values'. *Strategy and Business*, 39, 1–14.

Van Leeuwen, T. (2005), *Introducing Social Semiotics.* London: Routledge.

van Riel, C. and Balmer, J. (1997), 'Corporate identity: the concept, its measurement and management'. *European Journal of Marketing*, 31, 5/6, 340–55.

Vázquez Orta, I. and Foz Gil, C. (1995), 'The persuasive function of lexical cohesion in English: a pragmatic approach to the study of chairman's statements'. *Estudios Ingleses de la Universidad Complutense*, 3, 87–100.

Verschueren, J. (2012), *Ideology in Language Use*. Cambridge: Cambridge University Press.

Warren, R. (1999), 'Against paternalism in human resource management'. *Business Ethics: A European Review*, 8, (1), 50–9.

Weber, M. (1978), *Economy and Society*. Berkeley: University of California Press.

Whetstone, J. T. (2003), 'The language of managerial excellence: virtues as understood and applied'. *Journal of Business Ethics*, 44, (4), 353–7.

Widdowson, H. (1998a), 'The theory and practice of critical discourse analysis'. *Applied Linguistics*, 19, (1), 136–51.

— (1998b), 'Communication and community: the pragmatics of ESP'. *English for Specific Purposes*, 17, (1), 3–14.

Winter, S. J., Saunders, C. and Hart, P. (2003), 'Electronic window dressing: impression management with websites'. *European Journal of Information Systems*, 12, 309–22.

Wodak, R. (2011), 'Critical linguistics and critical discourse analysis', in J. Zienkowski, J. O. Östman and J. Verschueren (eds), *Discursive Pragmatics*. Amsterdam: John Benjamins, pp. 50–70.

World Climate Programme (1979). Accessed 21 March 2013 on: www.wmo.int/pages/prog/wcp/index_En.html

World Meteorological Organization (1979), *Proceedings of The World Climate Conference*, Report No. 537. Geneva: WMO.

Yoshida, M. (2008), 'Interactivity, interpassivity and possibilities beyond dichotomy', in F. Eckardt (ed.), *Situations, Practices, Encounters*. Leipzig: Frank and Timme, pp. 57–80.

Zahrly, J. and Tosi, H. (1989), 'The differential effect of organizational induction process on early work role adjustment'. *Journal of Organizational Behavior*, 10, (1), 59–74.

Advertisements

Citroën TV commercial
    www.youtube.com/watch?v=GMQnPWjK5pE
Miss Dior advertisements
    www.mimifroufrou.com/scentedsalamander/Miss-Dior-Cherie-EDP-Ad.jpg
    www.fragrantica.es/perfume/Dior/Miss-Dior-Cherie-L-Eau-5722.html
Renault Kangoo advertisement
    www.autospectator.com/cars/renault/0037734-new-2008-renault-kangoo-advertising-campaign-featuring-039-simpsons-039

Index

Lightning Source UK Ltd.
Milton Keynes UK
UKOW07f1132200215

246602UK00002B/103/P